Praise for *Arabia Incognita*

"Sheila Carapico and MERIP reports have been central voices in informing the public about the realities of the Middle East, beyond the glib talking points of politicians and pundits. Yemen is surely the most strategically important country to be so studiedly ignored in the West, and this volume gathering up incisive essays on its contemporary history and politics is essential reading."

—JUAN COLE
Richard P. Mitchell Collegiate Professor of History,
University of Michigan

"Sheila Carapico's masterful compilation of selected Middle East Research and Information Project reports is required reading for anyone seeking to understand the Yemen catastrophe and its Middle East-wide implications. Many are responsible for the disaster, first and foremost Yemen's political elites whose promising national dialogue failed. At the same time, abject failures of analysis keep the United States and Saudi Arabia from looking beyond their respective preoccupations with killing terrorists and confronting Iran. Until they do, 'Arabia' will remain 'Incognita' at unacceptable human and strategic cost for all concerned."

—CHARLES DUNBAR
US Ambassador to Yemen, 1988–91

"This richly varied compendium of articles by foremost scholars of Yemen and the Arabian Peninsula brings together some of the most incisive, thoughtful, cant-free, and trenchant analysis of this misunderstood region. Perfect for understanding the political economy, geopolitics and social relations of the region, these scholars cut through ideology and myth to provide a lucid picture of how Arabian Peninsula works."

—LALEH KHALILI
Professor of Middle East Politics, Department of Politics
and International Studies at SOAS, University of London

"Unfortunately, Yemen remains deeply undercovered and misunderstood, despite the gravity of its recent crises and the deep regional and global implications of its slide into civil war. Thus, a volume like this—composed of a diverse array of takes on key issues by some of the most respected experts on the country—represents a deeply valuable addition to the literature available on Yemen. It is a must read to understand the larger picture of what's happening in Yemen."

—FAREA AL-MUSLIMI
Chairman of the Sana'a Center for Strategic Studies

"Sheila Carapico's *Arabia Incognita* is essential reading—it explores the sinews of power and paranoia that emanate from Saudi Arabia, ensnaring the smaller emirates and creating mayhem in Yemen, the poorest country in the Middle East. Thoughtful and well-informed scholars write with compassion about the Arabian Peninsula, which is well-known only as cliché but not considered as a real place, where real people live."

—VIJAY PRASHAD
Author of *The Death of the Nation and the Future of the Arab Revolution* (2016)

"An indispensable guide for students, *Arabia Incognita* combines a thoughtful introduction, well-chosen excerpts from former *Middle East Report* articles and other relevant sources, as well as incisive cartoons from local newspapers to illuminate how the oil-producing absolute monarchies of the Gulf have sought to control, and now pacify through direct war, the restive, poorer inhabitants of the more populous, politically vibrant southwest corner of the Peninsula. Attending to cold war dynamics, the ongoing effects of US imperialism, and competing regional forms of solidarity, *Arabia Incognita* is a valuable contribution about a world of which most Americans know little, despite its centrality to US and North Atlantic security interests."

—LISA WEDEEN
Mary R. Morton Professor of Political Science and co-director of the Chicago Center for Contemporary Theory at the University of Chicago

ARABIA
INCOGNITA

Just World Books
Timely Books for Changing Times

Just World Books exists to expand the discourse in the United States and worldwide on issues of vital international concern. We are committed to building a more just, equitable, and peaceable world. We uphold the equality of all human persons. We aim for our books to contribute to increasing understanding across national, religious, ethnic, and racial lines; to share more broadly the reflections, analyses, and policy prescriptions of pathbreaking activists for peace; and to help to prevent war.

To learn about our existing and upcoming titles or to buy our books, visit our website:

www.JustWorldBooks.com

Also, follow us on Facebook, Twitter, and Instagram!

Our recent titles include:

- *America's Continuing Misadventures in the Middle East,* by Chas W. Freeman
- *War Is a Lie*, by David Swanson
- *The General's Son, Second Edition*, by Miko Peled
- *Survival and Conscience: From the Shadows of Nazi Germany to the Jewish Boat to Gaza*, by Lillian Rosengarten
- *The People Make the Peace: Lessons from the Vietnam Antiwar Movement,* edited by Karín Aguilar-San Juan and Frank Joyce
- *Gaza Unsilenced*, edited by Refaat Alareer and Laila El-Haddad
- *Baddawi*, by Leila Abdelrazaq
- *Chaos and Counterrevolution: After the Arab Spring*, by Richard Falk
- *Palestine: The Legitimacy of Hope*, by Richard Falk
- *Chief Complaint: A Country Doctor's Tales of Life in Galilee,* by Hatim Kanaaneh
- *Gaza Writes Back: Short Stories from Young Writers in Gaza, Palestine,* edited by Refaat Alareer
- *The Gaza Kitchen: A Palestinian Culinary Journey,* by Laila El-Haddad and Maggie Schmitt

DISPATCHES FROM YEMEN AND THE GULF

ARABIA
INCOGNITA

SHEILA CARAPICO, EDITOR

Just World Books
Charlottesville, Virginia

Published in association with the Middle East Research and Information Project (MERIP)

Just World Books
Timely Books for Changing Times

Just World Books is an imprint of Just World Publishing, LLC.

Cover design and typesetting by Diana Ghazzawi for Just World Publishing, LLC.

Publisher's Cataloging in Publication
(Provided by Quality Books, Inc.)

Arabia incognita (2016)
    Arabia incognita : dispatches from Yemen and the Gulf
  / Sheila Carapico, editor.
    pages cm
    Includes bibliographical references.
    LCCN 2015953892
    ISBN 978-1-68257-003-6
    ISBN 978-1-935982-92-0 (EPUB)
    ISBN 978-1-935982-93-7 (Mobi)
    ISBN 978-1-935982-94-4 (PDF)

    1. Middle East--History.   I. Carapico, Sheila,
editor. II. Title.

DS62.4.A69 2016   956
                QBI15-600239

Contents

Maps

Table

Political Cartoons by Samer Mohammed Al-Shameeri

Editor's Note

Helena Cobban of Just World Books invited me to "curate" a collection of my articles about Yemen and the Arabian Peninsula from the archives of *Middle East Report*. Her proposal came in May 2014, amidst veritable chaos in southwest Arabia, soon after the start of the Saudi-led military campaign. Along with *Middle East Report* editor Chris Toensing, we decided to include a cross-section of authors and a longitudinal perspective beginning with the early days of Middle East Report and Information Project (MERIP), as well as include blog posts that stand the test of time and *Middle East Report Online* (*MERO*) entries. They are presented for readers who follow current events but are not conversant with the politics of the Peninsula. Indeed, even avid news junkies and prominent pundits would not be conversant in the internal dynamics of what has remained Arabia Incognita.

The articles in this volume come from the annals of the Middle East Report and Information Project (MERIP) about the Arabian Peninsula, including both articles for the print magazine and online materials. From the rich, robust archive collection of dispatches, those republished here most directly explain the social, economic, political and military background to the convulsions in the Peninsula during 2015/16. Most selections are abridged or excerpted from more detailed accounts, and some are short vignettes from longer pieces (which you'll find set apart in gray boxes throughout the book). Note that copious end notes from magazine articles and scrupulous links from web publications are deleted.

Therefore, academic researchers or others seeking further detail and documentation are strongly encouraged to consult the original print or electronic versions.

The montage of articles, excerpts, vignettes, and visuals presented here capture memorable moments from contemporary Arabian history in approximately chronological order. While most readers would logically start reading "at the beginning," which is roughly the middle of the 20th century, I must say that readers struggling to make sense of headlines but quite unfamiliar with the politics, cultures and economies of the Peninsula might prefer to begin with the readings in the last part of the book, about the Saudi-led intervention in Yemen, and then back to the "Arab Spring," earlier aspects of the (Anglo-) American relationship with Gulf oil monarchies before, during, and after the Cold War, and social dynamics in a sub-region of the globe that is paradoxically both pivotal and peripheral.

The book features two kinds of original illustrations graciously donated by colleagues. First, Director of Spatial Analysis Lab at the University of Richmond Kimberley Brown, GIS Technician Taylor Holden, and interns Marissa Parker, Olivia Mobayed, and Andrew Talbot created a series of custom maps for this volume. Secondly, the Sana'a-based political cartoonist Samer Mohammed al-Shameeri generously granted permission to reproduce several of his many satirical portrayals of Yemeni politics and the Saudi-led intervention (note that the originals are in color). Al-Shameeri, a graduate of the media studies program at Sana`a University, has won awards from the International Yemen Cartoon and Caricature Contest and the 11th International Cartoon Contest in Syria, and was nominated for the Arab journalism award.

My thanks go out to Helena Cobban, Kim MacVaugh, Diana Ghazzawi and Brian Baughan for their help in producing this book

Introduction

This book is titled *Arabia Incognita* because I believe that the large, strategically crucial landmass known as the Arabian Peninsula is far too little known and even less understood: This book attempts to remedy that situation.

This landmass has long been central to US and North Atlantic security interests and energy policies. However, even for many generally well-informed citizens elsewhere, the realities and dynamics of this crucial part of the Middle East still remain largely a *terra incognita*. This book presents a treasure trove of materials that were originally published between 1980 and 2015 in the resolutely independent periodical *Middle East Report* (*MER*), through the editorial collective, the Middle East Research and Information Project (MERIP), of which I am honored to have served for more than 20 years, and its online versions *Middle East Report Online* (*MERO*) and the MERIP Blog. As someone who has studied the politics of Yemen and the Gulf since the 1970s, I have pulled these articles together into this anthology in an attempt to help readers around the world understand the societies, politics and geopolitics of the countries of the Arabian Peninsula more richly than they have before.

The Arabian Peninsula is a distinct landmass, surrounded on three of its four sides by strategically significant bodies of water: the Red Sea, the Indian Ocean, and the Persian Gulf. It is home to, broadly speaking, three very different kinds of natural and human environments: the arid, sparely populated but oil-rich expanses of deserts of the interior, most of which are in present-day Saudi Arabia; the string of former trading posts along the Persian Gulf coast, many of which, also being hydrocarbon-rich, have been transformed into extremely wealthy city-states in the past forty years; and Yemen, a mountainous and heavily populated country that sprawls north and east from the southwest corner of the peninsula and has been plagued by civil conflict and instability since 2012 (and subjected to harsh military assaults from a Saudi-led coalition since March 2015).

The co-location of very different kinds of society on the Arabian Peninsula has tied their destinies together for eons. Of the three kinds of societies found in the Arabian Peninsula, the one with which most outsiders may have the most familiarity is the string of super-rich city-states along the sinuous coast of the Persian Gulf. First-class globe-trotters may have passed through the upscale airport in Dubai (which is one of seven tiny princedoms that make up the United Arab Emirates, UAE), or may have flown on Emirates Airlines. American or European students and tourists may have spent time in the state-of-the-art branch campuses of western universities established in Qatar or the UAE, or in the museums and shopping malls that now dot much of the UAE. Over the past fifty years millions of contract workers—pursuing a range of occupations, from hotel managers, to construction workers, to teachers—have flocked to the Gulf city-states from Asia, the Arab world, and Eastern Africa. Some have remained there for decades (generally, under tight surveillance); others, once their contracts have finished or if they have raised their voices seeking better working conditions or greater freedoms, have been summarily returned to their original homes. Al-Jazeera, the global news network based in the Qatari capital Doha, is now a familiar brand-name worldwide. Doha and several other twenty-first-century Persian Gulf cities glimmer with high-modernist architecture financed from petrochemicals, built by South Asian migrant laborers, and made livable only by relentless air-conditioning.

Since 1981, Saudi Arabia and the five other Arab states along the Gulf have worked together in a joint defense organization called the Gulf Cooperation Council (GCC), which has been strongly supported by the United States and its NATO allies and provides a massive market for Western arms manufacturers. Tens of thousands of American armed service personnel have spent time in the Gulf protecting the oil-rich monarchies against threats from the Soviet Union, Iraq and Iran.

The second broad environment in the Peninsula is the vast desert interior, most of which lies within Saudi Arabia. While millions of Muslims journey to Mecca for the annual *hajj* pilgrimage, relatively few Christians or Jews—apart from oil executives and military contractors—have been permitted to visit the ultra-secretive Kingdom of Saudi Arabia. (Only in Saudi Arabia and Oman are citizen-subjects the majority of residents.) Saudi Arabia is the only state in the world to be named for its founding family, the descendants of whom still hold tightly to the reins of government there today. From its very beginning, in the eighteenth century of the common era, the "Saudi" political system was based on the maintenance of tight alliance between the "al-Saud" (the Saud family) and the descendants and followers of a puritanical and highly intolerant religious leader called Muhammad ibn 'Abd al-Wahhab. The Wahhabis, as these religio-sectarian activists are known, continue to play an important role in the kingdom's internal governance—and in many aspects of its foreign policy—to this day.

Yemen's mountainous, relatively fertile and heavily populated environment provides a strong contrast to the natural and human geography of most of Saudi Arabia. In the days of the British Empire, the Yemeni city of Aden, perched at the corner where the Red Sea joins the Indian Ocean, was a vital coaling station for British ships traveling to India or points further east. The present-day Republic of Yemen stretches up along the Red Sea a little, and out along the Indian Ocean coast to join with Oman. Its many mountain fastnesses contain a diverse array of micro-cultures, many of them with long and distinguished urban traditions—and a correspondingly great array of political movements, some regional, some religious, some ideological, and some more interest-based.

In this book, you will find more writings about Yemen than about any of the other countries of the Arabian Peninsula. The reason for this is simple. Contributors to *Middle East Report* are overwhelmingly social scientists, along with a smattering of journalists. And the kind of field research that social scientists do, or the kind of free-ranging, on-the-ground reporting that good journalists seek to do, is extremely hard to do in Saudi Arabia or any of the other monarchies of the Arabian Peninsula. Nearly all those monarchies have truly terrible human rights records and afford no protection whatever for the freedom of most forms of information-gathering, association or expression. Saudi Arabia, where in May 2014 blogger Raif Badawi was sentenced to ten years in prison and 1,000 public lashings with a whip, purely for what he had published on his blog, may have the very worst record in this regard. But the other GCC members are not far behind when it comes to stifling free inquiry and free expression. Until the exigencies of war overtook it in early 2015,

Yemen provided a much more fertile and welcoming environment for the kinds of inquiry that MER contributors like to pursue. Nonetheless, both in MER in general and in the compilation of this anthology, we have worked hard to include well-informed dispatches from other countries in the Peninsula.

In 2011, news consumers worldwide became somewhat familiar with the exciting news coming out of Yemen, which was the only place in the Peninsula apart from the city-state of Bahrain where the kinds of popular mobilization typical of the "Arab Spring" gained any real foothold. Yemeni pro-democracy organizer Tawakkul Karman was even awarded the Nobel Peace Prize for her role in helping lead the Yemeni movement. But in Bahrain, the king, with considerable military help from Saudi Arabia, was able to beat back the democracy movement. And in Yemen, in March 2015, amid the deep political turmoil into which the country had fallen, Saudi Arabia's newly installed King Salman and his defense minister (and son), Mohammed bin Salman, ordered air strikes to try to reverse military gains by a Yemeni militia known as the Houthi movement

King Salman's colossal military operation in Yemen was joined by the UAE and some other regional coalition partners, deploying advanced weapons and surveillance technology sold by the United States, the United Kingdom, France and Canada. As Yemen's ports, utilities and other infrastructure were pounded by many long months of aerial bombardment and a naval blockade, humanitarian catastrophe ensued for an already impoverished population of nearly 27 million Yemenis. United Nations relief agencies, human rights observers and historic conservationists drew some attention to this crisis, though de-escalation and ceasefire still seemed far away.

King Salman may have hoped for a speedy victory; but such was not to be. Though the Saudi-led coalition succeeded in pushing back the Houthis from Aden and some other areas of south Yemen, they made little headway in restoring any legitimate, functioning government anywhere in the country. And while the battles between the Saudi-led coalition and the Houthis continued in many of the western and central parts of the country and broad swathes of the east, al-Qaeda of the Arabian Peninsula (AQAP, long a target of American drone strikes) and even the so-called Islamic State in Iraq and Syria (ISIS, newly arrived in Yemen) were often gaining ground.

•••••

The nine chapters in *Arabia Incognita* are arranged in a broadly chronological way, and allow the reader a number of different entry points into
the "story" of the Arabian Peninsula in modern times. Chapter One starts
with an excerpt from a magisterial 1980 survey by the (now sadly deceased) London-based writer Fred Halliday of the history of the Persian/
Arabian Gulf region between 1958—which saw anti-monarchist revolutions in two major Arab countries, Iraq and Egypt—and 1979, which saw
one in neighboring Iran. Needless to say, all those developments had a
strong impact on the countries of the Arabian Peninsula. Chapter One
also includes a good account of a little-remembered but crucial event that
occurred in Saudi Arabia in November 1979, and a survey of Gulf affairs
that Joe Stork wrote in 1985, updating Halliday's earlier record.

In Chapter Two, "Cold War and Unification in Two Yemens," we take
a first dive into the complex history and politics of Yemen. Until May
1990, the country now known as Yemen was two countries. The Yemen
Arab Republic, also known as North Yemen, had been independent from
the Ottoman empire since 1918, while the southern areas of the country
continued to be ruled by Britain until 1967, when London ceded power to
national liberation fighters who soon consolidated their rule under a socialist leadership as the People's Democratic Republic of Yemen. When the
two states united, they chose the former capital of North Yemen, Sana'a, to
continue as the capital of the united state. In Chapter Two, Fred Halliday
sets the scene by recounting the main points in the history of the two
Yemens. The chapter then moves to social science, with an ethnographic study of two families' lives in North Yemen that I wrote with Cynthia
Myntti in 1991 and a study of the economic dimension of Yemeni unity
that I wrote in 1993.

Chapter Three takes us through some of the tumultuous developments Yemen witnessed soon after unification. Just three months after
that historic milestone, Iraqi dictator Saddam Hussein sent the entire
Middle East into turmoil when he invaded Kuwait. Yemen had for many
decades been a large-scale exporter of migrant labor to the rich Gulf countries; when the rulers of Kuwait and their allies in Saudi Arabia and other
GCC countries judged that Yemen's newly united government was insuf-
ficiently supportive of their stand against Saddam, they summarily expelled more than a million Yemeni workers back to their homes. The first
two pieces in Chapter Three cover some of those developments. The next
two pieces cover the notable, well-organized set of parliamentary elections
held throughout the country in April 1993. Sadly, the promising prospect

raised by those elections did not last long. The final piece in the chapter is an essay I wrote in 1994 titled "From Ballot Box to Battlefield."

Most of the "story" as told to this point has been one of secular politics and social science. In Chapter Four we (re-)encounter another strong strand in the history of the Arabian Peninsula by presenting seven pieces that explore different parts of the story of (often competing) political Islams in the region, written between 1997 and 2009. This chapter starts with an excerpt from a powerful, late-2001 description by Khaled Abou El Fadl of the Wahhabi doctrine that has semi-official status in Saudi Arabia. It also includes a first (fall 2004) introduction for readers to the ideology and thinking of the Houthis, who would later emerge as such powerful actors in Yemen.

Chapter Five takes the reader back into social science, presenting some very informative studies of the issues of water, oil, and migrant labor that have always played a strong role in the development and politics of the countries of the Arabian Peninsula—and certainly, in the relations among them.

With Chapter Six, "The Roots and Course of the 2011 Uprisings," many readers will start to encounter more materials about events that they remember from recent news reports. The chapter starts with a prescient piece from 2006, "Foreboding about the Future in Yemen," by Sarah Phillips. In the next piece, Susanne Dahlgren reminds us that the "Southern Cause" was still a live issue in Yemen in 2010. Then, as noted earlier, Yemen was one of the numerous Arab countries that saw an eruption of the "Arab Spring" in early 2011. Chapter Six contains three pieces about Yemen published on our blog between February and October of 2011. It then zigzags between Kuwait, Yemen and Qatar with updates on post–Arab Spring developments through the end of 2013. (The vignette from Kuwait was by the powerful, recently deceased analyst Mary Ann Tétreault.) Of the Arabian Peninsula countries, Bahrain was the other main one, in addition to Yemen, that saw notable popular mobilizations at the time of the Arab Spring. The dolorous developments in Bahrain are addressed in another article, Toby Jones's "Embracing Crisis in the Gulf," that is included in Chapter Seven.

The theme of Chapter Seven is the deep, continuing and mainly military engagement of the United States in the affairs of the Arabian Peninsula. The ten pieces here span the period from the FBI's very controversial (in Yemen) investigation of the October 2000 bombing of the USS *Cole*, in Aden's harbor, through the growing disquiet in some circles in the

United States over the drone-bombing by both the CIA and the US military of numerous locations and targets in southern and eastern Yemen. Along the way, this chapter deals in some depth with aspects of the "arms for oil" deal that lies at the heart of the relationship that Washington (and to a lesser extent its Western allies) has with the despotic and retrograde kingdom of Saudi Arabia. In a March 2014 piece included here, Toby Jones presciently notes that the Saudi rulers harbored a particular fear that any easing of the United States' longstanding conflict with Iran might cause Washington to reconfigure or downgrade its relationship with Riyadh.

Chapter Eight returns the book's focus strongly to Yemen, where it picks up the story of the post–Arab Spring deterioration by charting the political "implosions" in the country in the course of 2014. Despite this generally pessimistic narrative, however, the chapter opens with a very lively description by Katherine Hennessey of a 13-play theater festival held in Sanaʻa, March through May 2014. Hennessey notes in her account that no fewer than four of the 13 plays presented featured suicide bombings as a subject. Her piece nevertheless reminds us that in Yemen as in other areas plagued by terrible civil conflict, many aspects of daily—even cultural—life continue, a powerful testimony to the strength of the human spirit. It is also worth noting that in no other country in the Arabian Peninsula can one find the kind of indigenous cultural resources that would allow nationals of the country to put on a theater festival on anything like this scale.

Chapter Eight ends with an article I wrote with Stacey Philbrick Yadav in late 2014, detailing the breakdown of a peace initiative that the GCC had formulated for Yemen. It thus provides an appropriate segue into Chapter Nine, which charts the first six months of the military attack that Saudi Arabia launched against the Yemeni Houthis in March 2015. In this chapter we see the strong interaction of the sometimes extremely "local" internal politics of Yemen with the "global" geopolitics of the relationship between Saudi Arabia and the United States, in which the Saudi rulers' wariness of Iran and Washington's continued pursuit of its (often frighteningly ill-focused) "global war on terror" both remained strong factors.

Many Gulf royals and their friends have tried to portray recent developments in Yemen—as throughout the rest of the Middle East—as a winner-takes-all contest between unreconcilable Sunni Muslim and Shi'a Muslim forces, or as an attempt by the Saudis and their allies to halt and roll back an insidious expansion of (Shi'a) Iranian power and influence. Such depictions fail to provide much analytical purchase.

Eschewing such simple dichotomies, the selections in this anthology instead trace the roots of the complex conflict in Yemen back to the popular struggles of the 1960s, taking the story through the 2011 uprisings and beyond. Cumulatively they explain both how Yemen fell apart and the circumstances and background of the Gulf monarchies' intervention. Reporting at the time and mostly from on the spot, these dispatches feature local events in the former South and North Yemen, moments of "unity," parallel disharmonies in the seemingly placid Gulf petro-kingdoms, wider pan-Arab movements and active American security engagement. Although our main focus is on the Peninsula, rivalries between the Gulf kingdoms and the Islamic Republic of Iran during and since the Iran-Iraq war, the monarchies' panic after Iraq's invasion of Kuwait, and two American wars in Iraq form the essential backdrop to the drama in Yemen. The majority of texts presented here document Yemen's gritty, tumultuous and colorful instability; but stories from Saudi Arabia and other Arab Gulf states illuminate socioeconomic connections, power configurations and ideological trends connecting the Peninsula as a whole. I hope that after reading this book, you will find this part of Arabia to be a lot less *Incognita*.

—Sheila Carapico
Richmond, Va.
December 20, 2015

1 The Arabian Peninsula, 1958–85

The year 1979 was a tectonic one for the politics of the Arabian Peninsula. The area's two largest immediate neighbors, Iran and Iraq, both saw notable political developments: In Iran, this was the Islamic Revolution, which toppled the strongly pro-American rule of the Shah, while in Iraq, it was Saddam Hussein's seizure of power in a coup. Further afield, the Soviet Union invaded Afghanistan, and Egypt signed a peace treaty with Israel. At the end of 1979, Saudi Arabia had its biggest internal shock ever, when hundreds of Salafi/Wahhabi extremists took over the Grand Mosque complex in Mecca, announced the birth of a new, non-monarchist fundamentalist order in the region and managed to keep control of the mosque for several days. (This latter event, little remembered today in the West, would have long-lasting consequences. It led Saudi Arabia's eponymous ruling family, al-Saud, to enact a new policy of trying to export domestic supporters of Wahhabism to pursue their zealous callings anywhere else but in the Kingdom. Many of those Saudi nationals who were encouraged to leave went speedily to Afghanistan where they joined the anti-Soviet struggle and laid the basis for what would later become al-Qaeda.)

It is fitting that this anthology starts with a broad survey of the political history of the Gulf/Peninsula area that was written in early 1980 by Fred Halliday. His piece surveys the political currents that criss-crossed the area in the 21 years between 1958, when anti-monarchist revolutions rocked both Egypt and Iraq, and 1979. It provides considerable useful background that can help readers understand the dynamics of the Peninsula today.

The next selection is a description that long-time MERIP Executive Director Jim Paul pulled together in 1980, using many non-English sources, of the seizure of the Grand Mosque and how it was finally ended. Paul's piece stood for many years as the best account of the mosque takeover published anywhere in English. It underscores the fragile nature of the compact that the al-Saud political rulers have always had—indeed, continue to have—with the Wahhabi networks that form a seemingly essential, though often uneasy, pillar of their rule.

The year 1980 also was momentous for the Peninsula, for in September that year Saddam Hussein launched a large-scale invasion of Iran with the aim of toppling the Islamic Republic. He may have thought that with his large army, copious financial support from Saudi Arabia and other Gulf states and the implicit support of Washington for his venture, he could speedily succeed. But in 1985, *Middle East Report*'s long-time editor, Joe Stork, wrote the survey of recent developments in the Gulf region that is the third of our selections here, Saddam's army was still badly bogged down in Iran. (It was not until August 1988 that the two states finally ended the war.) With great prescience, Stork's piece also tracks some new steps the US military was taking to establish a presence in the Gulf—a follow-on to the British Royal Navy, which had left its last bases there in 1971.

The editors of *Middle East Report* wrote in early 1985:

> The contemporary opposition movements in the Arabian Peninsula have their origins in two processes of radicalization in Middle Eastern politics. The first was the rise of radical nationalists, Nasserists and Baathists, and of communist parties in the 1950s and 1960s, and the second is the spread of the radical Islamic groups in the latter part of the 1970s. The political organizations now engaged in opposition politics in the peninsula spring essentially from these two competing trends.

Since 1985, the supporters of radical political Islam have come increasingly to outnumber those of the radical (secular) nationalism. These three articles from *Middle East Report* help us understand how this came about.

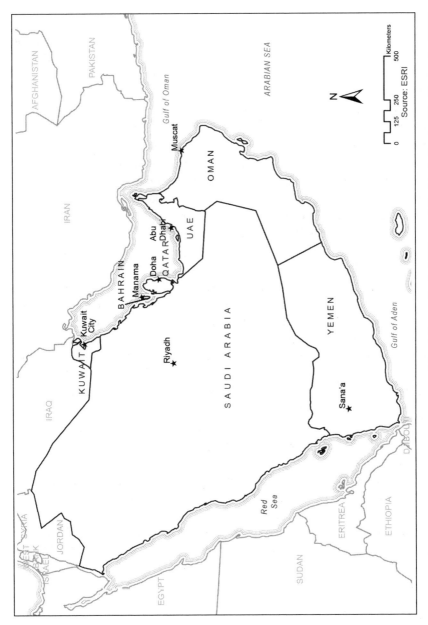

Map 1: States, Capital Cities, and Borders in the Arabian Peninsula. (2015) Produced by the Spatial Analysis Lab, University of Richmond

The Gulf between Two Revolutions, 1958–79

Fred Halliday • *MERIP Reports* 85, Feb. 1980

The political situation in the region surrounding the Gulf appears to be re-entering a period of considerable turmoil. The most evident manifestations are the revolution in Iran, the break between Egypt and the majority of Arab states in the Gulf following Camp David, and the outbreak of anti-government violence in Saudi Arabia. There are other developments of a more local character which spring from causes specific to the countries in question—the uncertain "stop-go" policies of the rulers of Kuwait and Bahrain toward elected parliaments, the persistent divisions within the UAE, the reemergence of unrest in north Oman, conflicts within the Saudi ruling family. The old focus of Peninsula politics, North Yemen, has once more become a center of regional conflict. On the margins of the region, developments in Ethiopia and in Afghanistan have confirmed the sense of many of the Gulf's rulers that hostile forces are gaining strength just over the horizon.

Separate from these events is a more diffuse set of issues relating to the pattern of social and economic development in the oil-producing states and the related problem of the links between the Gulf and the oil-importing industrialized countries. While oil revenues continue to rise, the post-1973 boom in the Gulf has slowed down. New social tensions, created by the oil-based changes and by the shortsightedness of the Gulf rulers themselves, are becoming more prominent inside these states at the very moment that the international economic environment on which the Gulf relies is becoming even less favorable. The major oil-importing countries are going through a protracted recession: Stagnation and inflation have eroded the terms of trade of the Organization of Petroleum Exporting Countries (OPEC) countries and cut back the attractiveness for the oil states of investment in the industrialized world.

[...] This nexus of strategic and local socioeconomic problems underlies and reinforces the more immediate, more strictly political tensions evident in the states surrounding the Gulf.

[...]

Simultaneous Formation, Separate Development

The relative separation of the Gulf from events in Egypt and the Mashreq [the Arab east] throughout most of this century occurred in spite of the fact that both areas shared a common moment of historical formation. The collapse in World War I of two of the three main regional powers—Russia and Turkey—led to the establishment of the contemporary state system. In the Ottoman territories of the Mashreq new state entities appeared through colonial delimitation—Palestine, Jordan, Syria and Lebanon. Egypt had already been occupied by Britain in 1882, yet here too the war had a decisive political impact, leading to the emergence of the first nationalist movement of a mass character....

In the Gulf and Peninsula, the war had equally important consequences. In Iraq the British installed the Hashemite monarch Feisal [I] in 1920. In North Yemen a new independent and unified state emerged under the control of the Hamid ad-Din imams. In Arabia in the aftermath of the war the Saudi family unified the Arabian deserts into a single state for the first time in centuries. In Iran, World War I swept away the remnants of the Qajar dynasty, providing the vacuum in which Reza Khan seized power in 1921. In 1926 he established the new Pahlavi dynasty.

Within eight years of the end of World War I, therefore, new royal families had come into power in the four most populous states of the region: Between them the Saudi, Hamid ad-Din, Hashemite and Pahlavi regimes formed the basis for a stable and conservative regional system, running from Khorasan in the northeast to Bab al-Mandab in the southwest. Britain, the dominant military power in the Gulf, held formal colonial power only in the small coastal sheikhdoms of the Peninsula, and in Iraq up to 1932. The new regimes, backed by imperialist power, bore the main burdens of political consolidation.

[...]

In the Arab Gulf region there was, through the 1950s, no decolonization struggle or sustained political opposition. The Palestine issue did not play as significant a role here as elsewhere. There were nationalist demonstrations in favor of Egypt in 1956 in Aden, Kuwait and Bahrain, and failed uprisings in North Yemen (1948) and Oman (1957–59), but these oppositions were contained. The regimes under strong British influence were in no position to wage a challenge, even Iraq, which had been formally independent since 1932. Moreover, Arab oil represented a far smaller percentage of world output then, and the oil that was blocked from reaching Europe by the closure of the Suez Canal in 1956–57 was easily compensated for by increased Venezuelan output. The regimes themselves were alarmed by the nationalism advocated by [Egyptian president] Nasser; opposition political groups favoring one or another brand of Arab nationalism had only begun to develop. Compared to either the Mashreq or the Maghreb, the Gulf was politically isolated, anesthetized to the effects of the Palestine question and the rise of Arab nationalism. Here the dissolution of the post-1918 system was to come later. Yet when it did come it happened in a remarkably synchronic form, as can be seen by studying six key components of the regional system.

Iraq: 1958–75

The breakdown in the Gulf region began in the late 1950s, leading to a decade and a half of turmoil that ended in the mid-1970s when a new Gulf order emerged. It is possible to chart how the early isolation of the Gulf from the rest of Arab politics was gradually broken down, and how the new order that structured the Gulf's role in the Middle East generally was being built out of the dissolution of the old.

The first major breach in the Gulf's stability came with the July 1958 revolution in Iraq. This initiated a period of protracted governmental instability in Baghdad, with four successive military regimes and several other coup attempts. Baghdad antagonized the major oil companies by nationalizing 99 percent of the Iraq Petroleum Company's concession area in 1961. The dispute with the Kurds erupted militarily from 1961 to 1970 and again in 1974–75. Finally, relations between Iraq and its neighbors worsened to the point that throughout the 1960s Iraq presented itself as, and was seen as being, a threat to Western interests in the Gulf.

[...]

The Yemens and Oman: 1962–75

The second major breach of the region's isolation was the North Yemeni revolution of September 1962. In the eight-year civil war which followed, Egypt and Saudi Arabia backed the two opposing sides. It contributed to the start of a guerrilla movement in British-ruled South Yemen in 1963 and, in 1967, the establishment of the People's Democratic Republic of Yemen (PDRY). After making gains in South Yemen, the guerrilla movement spread to the Dhofar province of the Sultanate of Oman in 1965. The war in North Yemen, fought by Saudi Arabia and Egypt at one remove, polarized Arab politics. Through the Egyptian intervention in North Yemen, Arab nationalism had a major impact on the Arabian Peninsula for the first time. Yet it was here that the conservative leadership in the Gulf was able to fight back and use the Egyptian failure in North Yemen to build the future Cairo-Riyadh alliance. After the Israeli defeat of Egypt in 1967, King Feisal [of Saudi Arabia] forced Egypt to pull out of North Yemen in return for financial aid that Egypt so desperately required. Egypt henceforth ceased to support opposition movements in the Arabian Peninsula, and from Nasser's death in 1970 until 1978 the Cairo-Riyadh axis was the most influential in the Arab world.

The consequences of 1967 were equally important in the Peninsula itself, in differing ways. In North Yemen the war dragged on for another three years, until a conservative coalition involving representatives of both sides was established in 1970. Although an independent republic in name, the newly formed Yemen Arab Republic was from then on effectively under the political and economic domination of Saudi Arabia. In South Yemen the guerrillas of the National Liberation Front were provoked by 1967 to turn against Egypt and began, amid immense economic problems, the most consistent socialist transformation of any country in the Arab world.

The counterrevolutionary character of the Gulf has been most evident in Oman. Many agree that 1973 was the watershed year. In the aftermath of the rise in oil prices, Iran dispatched several thousand counterinsurgency troops to attack the guerrilla-held areas of Dhofar. The People's Front for the Liberation of Oman fought bravely against the thousands of well-armed troops sent to crush them, but it was compelled by the end of 1975 to abandon the liberated territories it had held since the late 1960s. It was forced to resort to underground political work; the few military forces remaining in the mountains posed no serious threat to the establishment of counterrevolutionary control. The occupation of the Dhofari mountains by the combined Omani and Iranian forces in 1975 put an end at least temporarily to the 13 years of armed conflict between revolutionary and conservative forces that had begun in North Yemen in 1962.

Saudi Arabia: 1962–75

The year 1975 marked a watershed in Saudi Arabia when in March King Feisal was assassinated, and when the effects of the increased oil revenues were manifested in the Five-Year Plan commenced that year. Feisal himself came to power under the uncertain conditions of the early 1960s, when the republican coups in Baghdad and Sana'a had removed two of the Saudi family's fellow monarchies in the area. Under pressures from the US and from concerned members of the dynasty, the incumbent King Saud was displaced and Feisal installed. Under his guidance, Saudi Arabia underwent a number of changes designed to consolidate the existing political system: Slavery was formally abolished, a more modern army was built up, education was cautiously expanded, a budget was instituted, and some of the more conspicuously wasteful royal family expenditure was cut.

Feisal was in some respects a transitional character. Domestically he was loath to share power with other than a very few members of his family. In foreign policy it was Islam rather than any supposed "Arab dimension" that dominated his thinking. [...] Regionally, Feisal maintained a stubborn and hostile attitude toward several neighbors for outmoded dynastic reasons, such as refusing to recognize the UAE when it was formalized in 1971.

Feisal's death at a time of more general change put an end to the transitional period represented by his reign. A new, more decentralized family team came to power, under the joint leadership of King Khalid and Prince Fahd. The new development plan, ten times larger than the previous one, introduced far more widespread economic changes, and in foreign policy the anomalies of Feisal's period were soon removed. Within a year of his death, working diplomatic relations were established with the UAE and the PDRY. The Islamic emphasis of Saudi pronouncements was toned down in favor of a more specifically "Arab" orientation.

[...]

British Decolonization: 1961–75

Iran was closely involved in bringing to an end another process that had begun in the early 1960s and came to an end around 1975: British decolonization. The first colony in the region which Britain left in this period was Kuwait, in 1961. South Yemen followed in 1967, and in 1971 Britain gave up its last formal colonies in the Gulf, handing independence to Bahrain, Qatar and the seven sheikhdoms of the UAE. Yet Britain remained apparently as strong as ever in Oman, never an official colony. No flags were lowered and raised, but Britain in effect ceased to be the dominant power in the Sultanate in 1975. There was an increase in Omani participation in government and trade following the accession of Sultan Qaboos to power in 1970. Iran, rather than Britain, was now the most powerful outside military influence. Britain retained military bases in the area up to March 1977 and after that provided military assistance, as it did to the other states in the Gulf it had once ruled.

Oman exemplifies two aspects of this decolonization process that affected the character of the overall change in the Gulf. While the British maintained close ties with these independent states, other states came in part to play Britain's regional role. The US acquired a stronger military and political position than it previously had, while at an intermediate level it fostered the "twin pillar" policy of promoting Iran and Saudi Arabia to responsibility for security in the area. Saudi Arabia, whose armed forces were insignificant, had the main financial power, which it used in the Gulf and the region generally. Iran had little money to spare but had the military resources to patrol the waters of the Gulf, to send troops to Oman, and to guarantee the Kuwaitis in the event of any Iraqi menace.

[...]

The system that evolved to replace the colonial one goes a considerable way to explaining the curious history of the Gulf Security Pact. Advocated by the Shah in the mid-1970s, this project was given varying degrees of support by the other Gulf states, Iraq excepted. The justification that it was needed to unite the region against "outside interference" was rather mysterious, since there seemed to be no obvious threat against which the Gulf had to unite and there was already a massive US presence there to the tune of thousands of military personnel and many tens of billions of dollars' worth of military hardware. It was also unclear why the other states could not have signed a pact over Baghdad's objections. In fact, the rhetoric about "outside" (i.e., Soviet) influence was designed to divert attention from the reality of this US military deployment, and from the fact that the main threats were internal, from the populations of these countries themselves, or came from regional powers, as evidenced by Iran's seizure of the Gulf islands in 1971.

[...]

Oil and OPEC: 1960–75

In the corporate board rooms, government cabinet meetings, and academic seminars of the Western world, the formation of OPEC in 1960 was considered something of a joke, and certainly not important, for almost a decade. OPEC was intended to protect oil producers' revenues, yet the price of oil did not rise until 1970–71, when the oil states were able to redress the balance of power that had prevailed up to that time. The quintupling of prices between 1970 and 1974 and the rise in OPEC revenues from $5.2 billion to $75 billion in those years was a momentous and generally unanticipated revenge for the inertia of the previous decade. It provoked alarm in the advanced capitalist countries and naive hopes in the developing world. In 1974 there was speculation about a US military invasion of the Middle East, about a collapse of the world financial system and about a rapid and successful economic transformation of the Middle East.

[…]

The problems surrounding oil after the 1973 events involved not so much dramatic changes in the existing structure or multiplications of the price for oil, but issues such as industrialization and agricultural development, direct access by the producers to the markets of the advanced capitalist countries, thereby bypassing the major oil companies, and problems of unity within OPEC as the conflicts between those with surplus revenues (Saudi Arabia) and those with revenue shortages (Iran and Algeria) became sharper. The prominence which these issues acquired indicated that a new chapter in the politics of oil had begun, that the conflicts of the future would reflect but not repeat the changes of the 1971–73 period.

[…]

The capacity of Iran and the Arab Gulf states to play a larger role in the region was not merely a function of their relative economic strength or the needs of the confrontation states. It rested upon the re-stabilization of the Gulf itself in the mid-1970s and the support of the US. Because the Saudi, Iraqi and Iranian regimes had been able to consolidate themselves and quell their opponents nearer home, they were in a position to pursue an active foreign policy. The price of the intervention by Iran and the conservative Arab states outside the Gulf was paid by the local opposition forces, particularly by those in Oman and North Yemen.

The relationship with the US, the other essential precondition of this new regional influence, involved a political-military alliance and a broader coincidence of interests in promoting capitalist relations in the region. Although the US had privileged relations with both Saudi Arabia and Iran since the mid-1940s, it acquired a new significance in the 1970s as a result of both the British withdrawal and the purchase of US military equipment with increased oil revenues. Beyond the much publicized military dimension, this growth in US influence also involved the construction of a new system at the political and economic levels, one particularly evident in the US role in Saudi development projects.

[...]

The New Instability

The present set of problems has affected the Gulf states in their relations with the Western world, in their relations with other Arab states and in their internal political situations. In the case of each country, one can discern both the maturing of problems from the earlier reorganization and boom, and the much greater interrelatedness between events in the Gulf and events elsewhere in the Middle East.

The Iranian revolution was in the long run a product of the policies pursued by the Shah's regime over the previous 25 years, and of the manner in which the country's oil revenues were being spent. Among the immediate causes can be counted the Shah's policies that increased the level of active political opposition, as well as dealing the exiled Ayatollah Khomeini back in the game: Anti-inflation measures angered the bazaar merchants, and the more strident official political tone indicated a new element of uncertainty at the top. The Iranian revolution involved a very marked nationalist rejection of Iran's foreign policy alignment, of the way in which Western culture was being introduced into Iran, and of the Shah's links with countries such as Israel. But it also received a certain impulsion from the downturn in the Iranian economy which occurred in 1977, brought about in part by the recession in world markets.

The political situation within the Arab states themselves has also been noticeably unsettled. Kuwait lost military protection against possible Iraqi annexation and faces new Shi'a dissent and pressures for a return to elections. In Bahrain, where some of the Shi'a population has evinced sympathy for Khomeini, the al-Khalifa family must be wondering if they too will be cast as Yazids (devils) in the manner of the Shah. In the Emirates the fall of the Shah has upset the previous balance between Dubai and Abu Dhabi by depriving the former's ruler, Sheikh Rashid, of his Iranian patron. In Oman the removal of Iranian troops, and even more so of Iranian military guarantees in the event of substantial conflict in the future, have deprived the Sultan of his main prop at a time when some dissent is becoming evident as a result of his wasteful spending policies.

[...]

The situation in both parts of Yemen has escaped from the controls which, in the mid-1970s, Saudi policies seemed to have imposed. The Saudi attempt to entice South Yemen with financial aid after the establishment of diplomatic relations in March 1976 did not succeed: Relations between the two countries deteriorated in late 1977 under the double impact of events in the Horn of Africa and the assassination of North Yemeni president Ibrahim al-Hamdi by people believed to have been sympathetic to Saudi Arabia. Although the South Yemenis paid a price for the cessation of Saudi aid, the focus of conflict was in North Yemen, where the killing of al-Hamdi initiated a new round of unrest within the army and some parts of the countryside. This led to the June 1978 crisis in which the presidents of both parts of Yemen were killed, and to the February 1979 war between the Yemen Arab Republic (YAR) and the People's Democratic Republic of Yemen (PDRY). The March 1979 unity agreement between the two states is, like its 1972 predecessor, little more than an agreement not to wage war against each other. There is no indication that the instability in North Yemen has ceased. Once again the conflict in North Yemen, the most populous state in the Peninsula and one with probably greater influence on Saudi Arabia than any other, has become an active component in the politics of the Arabian Peninsula.

[...]

Ironically, by creating rather brittle political systems, these rulers may be storing up greater dangers for themselves in the future. The Shah has already paid the price. In Oman the Sultan has for a time fought off the rebels in Dhofar, but in the nine years since coming to power his economic record has been lamentable, and the indications are that political opposition is growing in the north of Oman, distinct from that in Dhofar. The Emirates have, after eight years of independence, failed to establish a central army or a central bank, and the wasteful competition on prestige projects such as multiple airports in close proximity makes a mockery of regional development. In Bahrain and Kuwait the limited experiences of elected assemblies were terminated under Saudi pressure in the mid-1970s, and despite their show of outward calm, it is known that the Saudi rulers, like their associates in the smaller Gulf states, are more than disturbed by events in Iran and by the possibility of continuing political turmoil there.

The uncertainty of the Gulf rulers is related to the new round of difficulties encountered in their relations with the major industrialized countries, which are undergoing a recession not caused by the oil price hikes but conveniently blamed on OPEC. Faced with the recession, and with growing public disagreement among themselves, the industrialized countries are bound to be less tolerant of the actions of the OPEC states than was previously the case, especially if Saudi Arabia and the Gulf producers oppose US policy in the sphere of Arab-Israeli relations. In the end, the Saudis and the other Gulf rulers, dependent for military and economic support on the US, will allow their fear of "communism" to prevail over their distaste for Israel.

[...]

Insurrection at Mecca

Jim Paul • *MERIP Reports* 91, Oct. 1980

On November 20, 1979, the first day of Islam's fifteenth century, 50,000 pilgrims in the Great Mosque of Mecca had just finished the first prayer as dawn was breaking. The blare of a loudspeaker jarred the stillness, as a voice began reciting the Qur'an. Soon the same voice began to denounce the Saudi regime, and announced the arrival of a Mahdi (savior) to cleanse a corrupt Arabia.

The faithful sat thunderstruck. Hundreds, perhaps a thousand of the Mahdi's followers, including some women and children, emerged from the midst of the crowd to take charge. Equipped with walkie-talkies, machine guns and automatic rifles, they bolted shut the main doors and took up positions of defense. Some stood guard on the seven minarets. Others positioned themselves along the parapets and upper windows of the huge structure.

When the Saudi authorities became aware of what was happening, they rushed army units as well as police and National Guard to the scene. By mid-morning, the mosque was surrounded. The troops tried to advance, but could make little headway against fierce fire from the insurgents within.

The extent of the insurrection was threatening. News came from Medina of an attempt to seize the Prophet's Mosque there, and there were reports of disturbances elsewhere in the Kingdom. The ruling family was ill-prepared. Crown Prince Fahd was in Tunis for an Arab summit meeting. Prince Abdallah, head of the National Guard responsible for protecting the royal family and the oil fields, was in Morocco. Ailing King Khalid ordered his brothers Prince Sultan and Prince Nayef, the ministers of defense and interior, to take charge. They hurried from Riyadh to Mecca to direct the military operations.

Uncertain about the extent or the source of the insurrection, the princes immediately contacted key foreign allies, ordered Mecca sealed off, and cut all communications within the Kingdom. In all the main cities, troops cleared and patrolled the streets.

The princes faced several dilemmas. The Great Mosque, a special responsibility of the Saud family, should not be damaged. It was still filled with pilgrims—some perhaps from important families—who should not be harmed. It is a privileged sanctuary under the laws of Islam, in principle beyond the reach of Saudi state security forces. King Khalid called upon the leading interpreters of Islamic law in the Kingdom, the council of the *ulama* [religious scholars]. After some deliberation, the *ulama* sanctioned state intervention and the use of violence to protect the holy place.

The Great Mosque proved a difficult target. Because of the sanctity of the building and the pilgrims inside, heavy weapons could not be used in a frontal attack. Yet against light arms the structure was uniquely defensible. Its maze of pilloried galleries, tiny rooms, porticoes, windows, staircases and grilled stonework provided ideal cover for the insurgents, who continued to hold high vantage points atop the seven towering minarets.

When the forces of the regime tried to come in with helicopters they were driven off by machine-gun fire from the ground. During the morning of November 21, gunfire crackled around the mosque as Saudi army troops tried to work their way inside. Additional troops and armor were airlifted into Mecca. The mosque was surrounded by thousands of troops, a fleet of armored personnel carriers, armored cars and other assault forces. But in spite of growing troop strength, the besiegers were unable to advance. Saudi troops were poorly coordinated. Officers argued over tactics and who was to blame. The soldiers and guardsmen fought with little of the commitment of their adversaries.

Although some Saudi forces were now able to enter the mosque, fire from the insurgents kept them pinned down. Casualties on both sides were heavy as the fighting continued. On November 22, Prince Abdallah returned from Morocco to join in coordinating the siege. The armed forces advanced very slowly. The insurgents still controlled much of the mosque from behind barricades on the ground floor and from positions on the terraces and minarets.

On November 23, a five-man French anti-terrorist squad arrived with a planeload of special explosives and gas. Battles that day dislodged the insurgents from the upper stories of the mosque and drove them to the ground floor. After another two days of fighting, the remaining insurgents retreated into the basement, a labyrinth of more than 200 rooms and passages, where the battle raged on. As the fighting continued, word came on November 29 of violent Shi'i demonstrations in the oil-producing province. Twenty-thousand National Guard troops were used to quell those disturbances, while preparations were made for the final assault on the mosque insurgents.

The final attack was launched on the night of December 3, after nearly two weeks of fighting. Although the insurgents' military leader had been captured and the proclaimed Mahdi himself killed, the battle lasted all night. More than 100 on both sides were killed and many more wounded. Of the original force of insurgents, only 170 survived.

The Significance of the Takeover

A month later, in early January 1980, the chief of staff of the Saudi armed forces, the air force and land forces commanders, and the governor of Mecca (a brother of the king) were replaced in an extensive military and administrative shakeup. Sixty-three of the insurgents were publicly executed on January 6 in the central squares of several Saudi cities. The insurrection was over, but many questions remained. Who were the rebels? Where had they secured their arms and military training? What was the political significance of their daring, if suicidal, act?

The chief organizer and military leader of the group was Juhaiman ibn Saif al-Otaiba, a former member of the National Guard who had received some US military training. The Otaiba tribe had many grievances against the Saudi ruling family, and Juhaiman was able to bring a number of his kinspeople into the insurrection. His brother-in-law, Mohammad bin Abdullah al-Quraishi, a theological student at the Islamic University in Mecca, was the proclaimed Mahdi.

The main path of recruitment, however, was not tribal but religious. Religiously oriented youth, mainly theology students disoriented and enraged by the social changes taking place in the Kingdom, joined up. A few were foreigners of like persuasion. The regime has hinted that the insurgents were supported from the outside—Democratic [South] Yemen, Israel, Egypt, the Soviet Union, even the US. But they apparently got their support from within Saudi Arabia, from dissidents in the military and the religious hierarchy, and even perhaps from some members of the royal family.

Like the Shah, the Saudi rulers prepared the way for a religious opposition by systematically eliminating all modern, secular opposition forces. But unlike the Shah, who laid claim to a modernist, secular ideology, the Saudi regime claims to base itself on Islamic fundamentalism. The character of the opposition is therefore ironic, especially at a time when Saudi-financed fundamentalist groups have become increasingly active throughout the Muslim world, threatening regimes and political movements opposed by the Saudis.

But the Saudi regime has always contended with the uncertain allegiance of Islamic fundamentalists. In the late 1920s, Ibn Saud had to wipe out his own fanatical shock troops, the Ikhwan, with the help of British air power. As the modern, oil-based transformation has proceeded, the contradiction between the regime and its ideological base has grown steadily more acute. The *ulama* and tribal leaders, the major guardians of fundamentalism, are opposed to the centralization of power by the ruling family and the state. Their social position is further weakened by the growing influence of the bourgeoisie, the technocrats and the foreign advisers. They have become logical leaders of opposition movements that can draw support from the mass of displaced Bedouins and small peasants. The insurgents, in their pamphlets, show the rage and confusion of this backward-looking alliance. Identifying themselves as students of the *shari'a* (Islamic law), they speak of their disgust to see their professors "bought by a corrupt regime with money and promises of promotion." One of their tracts claims that the Grand Mufti himself was sympathetic to their cause, reproaching them only for "concentrating their attacks on the Saudi regime when all Islamic regimes are corrupt." Their pamphlets also confirm the existence of several other fundamentalist groups, including the Muslim Brotherhood, who they criticize for being "led by foreigners, Indians or Pakistanis."

"Where are we?" asks Juhaiman in one of his writings. He answers:

They slander us from all quarters and tell lies about us.... We are Muslims who wanted to learn the Law and quickly understood that it couldn't be done in these schools, colleges, and universities...where no one dares say a bad word about the government.... We have broken with the opportunists and other bureaucrats who serve the government.... We know that one day we will be strong enough to name among us a Mahdi, to take refuge at his command in the Great Mosque of Mecca, where we will proclaim the beginning of a new Islamic state.

Juhaiman and his group did not seize the Great Mosque in the manner of a modern insurrectionary movement but with a fantastic dream of restoring a purified order to Arabia. They even apparently thought that the earth would open to engulf the army of unbelievers come to dislodge them. As such, their rebellion was bound to fail. But it has left its political mark nonetheless. It has reminded both the shaken regime and its worried allies that the House of Saud has less and less room for maneuver between disaffected traditionalist elements and the emerging modern forces.

Author's Note: This article is based on a careful review of the many and varied accounts of the Mecca events in major US and European newspapers and journals. Our assessment of the significance of these events is indebted to our correspondence with Ghassan Salameh.

Prospects for the Gulf

Joe Stork • *MER* 132, May/Jun. 1985

All of the small Arab states of the Persian Gulf are now well into their second decade as independent political entities. Bahrain, Qatar and the seven principalities making up the UAE became independent in 1971. Kuwait's independence goes back another decade. Oman, though never a colony, traces its present regime to the British-induced palace coup of 1970. Whether because of or in spite of the startling explosion of wealth in the 1970s, because of or in spite of the fall of the Shah and the war between Iran and Iraq, they have survived as states and their regimes have displayed unanticipated continuity. The turbulence of the 1970s roared around them, as around the eye of a storm. The UAE stayed united while Pahlavi Iran, the "guardian of the Gulf," collapsed in a revolutionary paroxysm. None of the smaller states have experienced as serious a political tremor as Saudi Arabia did in November 1979, with the takeover of Mecca's Grand Mosque. But neither were the small states insulated from the turmoil. Sabotage and demonstrations in Kuwait and Bahrain, ruling circle paralysis in the UAE and deportations of tens of thousands of "alien" workers up and down the Gulf have been regular features of the new age. It is not clear that survival of these states has been accompanied by any substantial degree of internal political consolidation, and the new strains and stresses of economic uncertainty, coupled with the emergence of social forces nurtured in the profligate environment of the 1970s, leave the political future of the Gulf surrounded by question marks.

The circumstances of the Gulf states in the mid-1980s are different in several respects from the preceding era. In the first place, they are operating in a phase of economic contraction. One thing not achieved in the wash of petrodollars was much diversification of their economic base, and today these economies are more tied than ever to the fortunes of the international oil market. From 1980 to 1983, the members of the Gulf Cooperation Council (the smaller states plus Saudi Arabia) saw their oil revenues drop by half, from $145 billion to $72 billion. Along with the constraints on trade and political uncertainties imposed by the Gulf war [Iran-Iraq War], this has helped to "shake out" some of the more speculative accumulation ventures. Numerous firms have gone bankrupt or simply disappeared. Recent months have seen a series of mergers among banks and investment houses in Kuwait, Abu Dhabi and Dubai as a result of "non-performing" loans and bad investments, consolidations that involve substantial government bailouts. The collapse of the unofficial stock market nearly three years ago still reverberates in Kuwait today. This incident may have cost the Kuwaiti treasury the equivalent of a year's oil revenues. Share values on the official Kuwaiti stock market and real estate values—two prominent investment havens—have dropped by half over the last couple of years, and many Kuwaiti experts feel they have not yet descended to levels representing true values. In Bahrain, commercial rents have dropped from over $26 per square foot to $8 or $9, and business people there are counting, perhaps unrealistically, on the soon-to-be completed causeway with Saudi Arabia to produce a new real estate boom. Throughout the Gulf, it seems, the money machines are not working like they used to.

Secondly, political chills have accompanied the cooling off of the economy. The Iranian revolution and the subsequent war with Iraq have further eroded the relative insulation of the Gulf states from the political currents traversing the region. Initially all the Gulf states quietly but unambiguously supported Iraq in the military conflict. They diverted tens of billions of dollars in "loans" to Saddam Hussein's war treasury. Kuwait was Iraq's chief port for shipments of war materiel, foodstuffs and other critical imports. Bahrain and Oman rashly offered their territories as staging points for Iraqi warplanes before Iranian threats and Saudi and American intercession dissuaded them. Iranian recovery on the battlefield, especially in 1982, prompted a panicky, barely disguised neutrality. Kuwait and the UAE in particular drew back from closer alignment with Iraq under Gulf Cooperation Council auspices. Kuwait, the most populous of the small Gulf states and the one with the most sophisticated economy, was also the most vulnerable geographically to both combatants. The UAE, and Dubai in particular, has important trading ties with Iran that proved useful to Tehran as well and encouraged the UAE to see itself as a potential mediator in the conflict. Bahrain, with its oppressed Shi'i majority, was particularly susceptible among the Gulf states to the revolutionary appeal of the Islamic Republic, and there was frequent agitation and street clashes in the 1979–81 period, culminating in the December 1981 arrest of some 73 young militants, on charges of plotting the violent overthrow of the Khalifa regime.

The Gulf Cooperation Council

A third feature of the present period is the emergence of a new regional political system centered on the Gulf Cooperation Council. The formation of the GCC was motivated both by economic and security concerns. The member states of the GCC share traditional family regimes, based on tribal affiliations later cemented under British colonial domain, and have no history of sustained decolonization struggles. They have a combined population today of approximately 13 million, of whom 5 million are immigrant workers. This unique demographic structure is even more startling if Saudi Arabia is left out of the calculations: The small Gulf states have a population of 4.1 million, of whom 59 percent are foreign laborers. The largest numbers of these are Palestinian, Egyptian, Pakistani and Indian.

The growth of these immigrant communities may have peaked as the construction boom in the Gulf has leveled off, but their numbers and proportion are not likely to diminish appreciably, as the need for workers in every other sector continues. The governments have used the GCC framework to coordinate policies on immigration and to establish a common passport and naturalization system. They have built up their police and security apparatuses and exploited the vulnerability of the foreign workers to deportation. The last few years have been characterized by periodic purges of foreign workers. In June 1982, for instance, the UAE arrested and deported 2,000 persons without proper papers, and Kuwait expelled more than 25,000 that November. Kuwait has expelled thousands more in the two years since, especially after a series of Iranian-inspired bombings in December 1983. The last several years have been ones of great insecurity for foreigners.

The idea of a Gulf collectivity had been haphazardly advanced by Iran, Iraq and Saudi Arabia ever since the period of British withdrawal (1968–71). But there was no enthusiasm among the smaller states for any

framework whose main effect would be to advance Iranian or Iraqi hegemony in the Gulf. In 1975, Saudi Arabia, Kuwait, the UAE and Qatar set
up the Arab Industries Organization, a joint effort to establish Arab-run
armaments factories in Egypt, but this project was canceled in reaction
to Camp David. Saudi Arabia continued to promote a political framework in which it would play the dominant role. Gulf tours by Saudi King
Khalid in March 1976 and Interior Minister Prince Nayif in October 1976
led to a very low-profile agreement to share intelligence and internal security information. In the economic domain, the Gulf Organization for
Industrial Consultancy was formed, with Iraq as a member, in November
1976, and the idea of a Gulf common market was proposed a year later.
The military and security aspects of cooperation took on greater urgency
following the Iranian revolution, and Iraq began to participate in the
intelligence-sharing process. Saudi Arabia took the lead in establishing
bilateral security pacts with the small Gulf states, and set up security
committees with Pakistan and Jordan, two states whose troops play key
advisory and mercenary roles in the armed forces of all the Gulf states.
The GCC was formally inaugurated at a first summit meeting on May
26, 1981. A "mini-common market" agreement went into effect in March
1983. Politically, the GCC has emerged as a bloc within OPEC and within
the Arab League. It has superseded the Organization of Arab Petroleum
Exporting Countries (OAPEC) in trade negotiations with the European
Common Market, for instance.

Military Foothold

A fourth feature of the Gulf in the 1980s is that the US has completed the
process of replacing Britain as the paramount outside power. The fall of the
Shah removed Iran as the chosen instrument for this transition. Working
now through Saudi Arabia and Oman, the US military presence in the
region is more pronounced and visible than in the 1970s. In both Saudi
Arabia and Oman, the US has mapped out and supervised the construction of an enormous military infrastructure of bases, weapons systems,
intelligence networks and joint commands. Secretary of Defense Caspar
Weinberger, in a February 1982 visit to Riyadh, urged Saudi Arabia to assume an even more visible security coordination and assistance role in the
GCC. Washington's rationale is that GCC responsibility for internal security functions, and the bilateral agreements for joint intervention among
the GCC member states, should minimize the need for direct US military
intervention in the event of a coup or insurgency while at the same time

maximizing the facilities and weapons inventories available for such intervention should it be required.

A key element here is the sale of American-made Airborne Warning and Control System (AWACS) surveillance planes to Saudi Arabia. This huge arms deal gave the Saudis the necessary military weight vis-à-vis Iran and Iraq to make credible its military linkages with the smaller states, while it avoided the issues of sovereignty and patriotic credibility that would be attached to any formal US basing structure in the Peninsula. The Saudis have subsequently pushed the other Gulf states to contract for air defense systems that could be tied into the AWACS net. These involve an increased US military advisory role in those states. One of the problems in coordinating the military forces of the Gulf states is the variety of different weapons systems even within individual services, with little compatibility. The AWACS deal is one step toward an increased level of standardization, at least in this area of air defense.

Washington has made a virtue of the political constraints that prevent Saudi Arabia from granting formal US basing rights in its territory, but it has cultivated a more unrestricted relationship with Oman. Following a June 1980 agreement with Sultan Qaboos, the US has spent at least a quarter of a million dollars modernizing bases at Masirah Island, Sib, Thumrait and Khasab and has held a series of joint military exercises—Bright Star, Jade Tiger and Beacon Flash. Sultan Qaboos, increasingly reclusive and autocratic by most accounts, has delegated most important decision-making to a handful of American, British and Arab advisers linked to their respective intelligence services. The role of these foreign advisers, and the perception of widespread corruption within the Sultan's regime, has even some American officials worried about the longevity of this relationship, but for the present it has provided the US with its most secure military foothold in the Gulf region.

The US also has a formal military presence in Bahrain. Ever since World War II, the US has had a small destroyer-led naval force, called MIDEASTFOR, based at the port of Jufayr. When the British withdrew, the US renegotiated this access with the Khalifa regime. The regime announced immediately after the October War of 1973 that it would terminate the agreement, but a new, more remunerative agreement was concluded in July 1975. More restrictions on the US presence were negotiated in June 1977. Most recently, the US Central Command set up its "forward headquarters element" on the Bahrain-based fleet. According to Lt. Gen. Robert Kingston, head of Central Command, "This element serves as my liaison with our embassies and the nations of the region. It also aids in planning and coordinating joint exercises and performs other duties that benefit my command." The US also apparently has temporary emergency landing rights at Bahrain's main airport and similar use of the big Jabal 'Ali port outside Dubai.

The Threat Within

Under the cover of a multilateral indigenous solution to potential external threats, the US has managed to extend its own military arm over the entire Arab side of the Gulf, and the rhetoric of "outside threats" has provided the necessary pretense for that military presence.

But the real threats are internal. The articles in this issue [of *Middle East Report*] examine structural problems facing Bahrain and Kuwait, the two Gulf states whose economic and political institutions are the most developed and sophisticated, and whose social forces are most advanced. These two states, uniquely in the Gulf, share the experience of limited parliamentary politics. The ruling families in both instances abolished even these very restricted exercises in democracy—Bahrain in 1975, Kuwait in 1976. At least in the Bahraini case, Saudi pressure was a major factor. Kuwait reinstated its parliament in 1981 in an even more restricted format, but the elections in February 1985 and the assertiveness of the nationalist deputies has already astounded political circles in the region. The Kuwaiti minister of justice, a member of the ruling family, was forced to resign on May 5 when the parliament censured him for the laws compensating investors in the unofficial stock market crash: The minister's 12-year-old son received $3.4 million as an injured "small investor." The oil and industry minister, another ruling family scion, is now confronting sharp questions concerning the Kuwait Petroleum Company's acquisition of the US minerals firm Santa Fe International.

Bahrain's ruling family shows no signs of following its Kuwaiti counterpart in allowing the resumption of open politics. The Bahraini response to popular discontent has been to use Saudi financial contributions to strengthen the state's repressive apparatus on the one hand and to increase the government payroll on the other. Bahrain's ruling circles continue to stress Bahrain's future as a "service station" satellite to the Saudi economy. With the expected completion of the causeway between the island and Saudi Arabia this fall, Saudi military access to and political influence in Bahrain will be even greater.

In the UAE, certain unresolved questions of how this consensual federation can move beyond mere political maintenance may soon come to the fore. Differences between the component princedoms, especially Abu Dhabi and Dubai, had been suppressed in the face of the dangers emanating from Iran and the Gulf war. Now Dubai's Sheikh Rashid, prime minister of the UAE, is on his deathbed. None of his sons are politically competent to take his place. There are still some dozen border disputes among the emirates, and while no one feud threatens to destroy the union, the cumulative impact of the disputes may leave the ruling families with little leeway to undertake necessary reforms.

With the very partial exception of Kuwait, there has been no maturation of political institutions in the Gulf consonant with the enormous social and economic changes that have occurred over the last two decades. Military and security forces have been lavished with equipment and mercenary troops, but each regime in the GCC has felt compelled to guard against potential coups by minimizing the means of coordination between, for instance, its own air force and land forces. "The most important military balance in most Gulf nations," Anthony Cordesman observes, "is often the one that prevents their own military forces from seizing power."

At its fifth and most recent summit, in Kuwait in late November 1984, the GCC announced the formation of a "joint force," capable of intervening in any threat against a member state. The many conditions and qualifications attached to this "joint force," after two years of debate and feasibility studies, testified to the still rudimentary state of cooperation among the Gulf regimes. Joint military maneuvers in Saudi Arabia just before the summit were described by diplomats as "haphazard and chaotic." Under the new plan, there is a small headquarters staff in Saudi Arabia, and each country will designate certain units (totaling, by different estimates, anywhere from 3,000 to 13,000 men) for collective intervention. GCC Secretary-General 'Abdallah Bishara described its "significance" as "more political and symbolic than military." Since the bulk of these designated forces are Saudi, the agreement may serve more as a license for Saudi intervention in the smaller states than any real joint effort. Kuwait has taken great pains to argue that this force cannot be used to counter "internal subversion," when in fact this is its only conceivable utility.

To this point, the ruling clans of the Gulf have preserved their borders and their trappings of sovereignty. They have maneuvered through a number of nasty situations, but none have faced the sort of external or internal challenge that would certify their legitimacy and longevity. Their working classes are disenfranchised, isolated and vulnerable. Privilege and differential access to rentier wealth have moderated potential discontent among their citizenry. Nevertheless, it would be rash to assume that the dangerous combination of war and revolution has exhausted yet its potential on the Arab side of the Gulf.

2 Cold War and Unification in Two Yemens

The following selections are about the two Yemens during the 1970s and '80s, a period defined internationally by the Cold War and within the Peninsula by the great wealth that accrued to the monarchies during the "oil boom."

Historically labeled on European maps as "Arabia Felix" (Happy Arabia) for its verdant farmlands, by the middle of the twentieth century Yemen was anything but. It remained by far the most populous and densely populated part of the Peninsula, and Aden was still its most important seaport, drawing traders and immigrants from the Indian Ocean and beyond. Yet, or therefore, it was also the most unstable. Moreover, in a terrain of striking ecological variation, there were strong local and regional identities, with stark contrasts between towering highlands and the coasts, areas washed by monsoons and semi-arid regions, the colony and the hinterland.

The 1960s were a decade of rapid, profound changes. Secular officers unseated a 1000-year-old Zaydi Imamate in the North in 1962; in 1967 South Yemen declared its independence after over a century of British imperial rule. The upheavals left the southwest quadrant of Arabia as a Cold War fault line, and simultaneously as the increasingly impoverished corner of an otherwise prosperous Peninsula.

Between roughly 1969 and 1989, two unstable regimes each failed to establish viable states. The following selections offer some vivid glimpses into lived experiences in different cities, villages and social classes as well as analysis of the differences, similarities and convoluted interactions between the governments based in Sana'a and Aden, respectively. Between the effects of the oil boom in neighboring counties, the geo-strategic reverberations of the Cold War and bad domestic governance, Arabia Felix became the conflict-ridden periphery of the GCC.

We first meet President ʿAli ʿAbdallah Salih, whose long rule prompted the 2011 uprising, in Fred Halliday's account of his observations and interviews in 1984 in Sanaʿa and Taʿiz in 1984. The second piece is Halliday's reaction to the implosion of the Aden regime in 1986. A couple of years later Cynthia Myntti and I compared my notes on family life from the old city of Sanaʿa with hers from a farming village between Taʿiz and Aden. Note, in light of the sectarian rhetoric and violence in 2015, that none of us thought to mention that Sanaʿa was predominantly Zaydi whereas both Taʿiz and the people in the southern regions were Shafiʿi. We noted piety but not denominational differences, which seemed utterly irrelevant; we analyzed hard power and economic forces buffeting both politics and everyday life. The South was called Socialist, although my analysis in the final selection notes more similarities than differences between the "socialism" of the People's Democratic Republic and the "no doors" policies of the Sanaʿa regime: Both underdeveloped economies were dependent on the vicissitudes of foreign aid and workers' remittances. Halliday and I each indicate negotiations over unification, which happened years later, just as the Cold War ended.

The ethnographic observations, economic factors and regional variations in the years leading up to the unity agreement of 1990 also help explain the 1994 civil war and provide geographic perspective and political antecedents to the events of 2011–15.

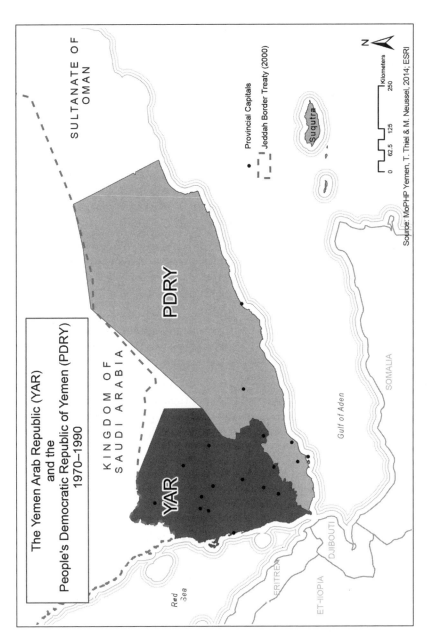

Map 2: The Yemen Arab Republic and the People's Democratic Republic of Yemen. (1970–90)
Produced by the Spatial Analysis Lab, University of Richmond

North Yemen Today

Fred Halliday • *MER* 130, Jan./Feb. 1985

The streets of Sana'a, the North Yemeni capital, appear to condense some of the most divergent elements of Third World economic change and political upheaval. Perhaps nowhere else in the Middle East, or indeed elsewhere in the Third World, do the antinomies of combined and un-even development come so dramatically to the surface. The city is full of consumer goods brought in on the emigrants' remittances and foreign aid that make up nearly all of the country's foreign exchange earnings. Filipino workers in hardhats are digging up the roads to install sewerage systems. Aid agencies of many stripes are plying their wares and plans. Most men of commerce are indigenous to North Yemen, but their ranks are swollen by thousands of compatriots who have come from the People's Democratic Republic in the south to escape state control, or from sections of the Yemeni diaspora in Ethiopia, Kenya, Vietnam or Britain. They push their goods onto the streets and sit on the floor inside their shops, chewing qat [a mildly narcotic leaf].

Commercial capitalism is alive and well, at least as long as the monies from abroad pour in. For a country whose exports come to only 1 percent of its imports, the Yemen Arab Republic (YAR) is doing well indeed. The politics of the city are also vigorously displayed. Much in Sana'a is reminiscent of the period when Gamal Abdel Nasser dispatched Egyptian forces in the 1960s to save the new republic from the Saudi- and British-backed royalist rebels. The policemen direct traffic in Egyptian-style white uniforms. The slogans on the banners across the streets proclaim the YAR's loyalty to Arab unity in tones of Nasserist enthusiasm now unheard in their country of origin. The majority of the 23,000 schoolteachers in the country are from Egypt, and these *gallabiyya*-clad men are numerous in the markets and squares of Sana'a and other cities.

Ta'iz, the southern city, has a more drab, nondescript character, and its idiom is littered with the traces of Adeni vocabulary derived from the days of British rule. Sana'a, by contrast, retains much of its historic character: The old city remains as it was many hundreds of years ago, a spectacularly beautiful collection of stone houses with white lime wash patterns, little walled gardens, narrow streets and white minarets. It is probably the most architecturally alluring and unified city of the whole Islamic world. Most men wear the *fouta*, or kilt. In the afternoon, the whole city slows down considerably for the chewing of qat: This practice is limited to Thursday afternoons and Fridays in the PDRY, but no constraints apply in the more riotous north. Here, as in the south, the stimulations of alcohol have now been added.

Sanaʻa is not North Yemen. The contrast between city and country-side, one that lay at the heart of the civil war in the 1960s, and which Sanaʻa experienced dramatically during the siege of 1967–68, when it was saved only by a massive Soviet airlift, is still there. The majority of the country remains rural, and farming still accounts for some 85 percent of the labor force. The peasantry is dominated by tribal loyalties and is deep-ly suspicious of any government at the center. Adult illiteracy is extremely high—over 80 percent—and less than 40 percent of children are in school. Rural health schemes are slight. Many warn visitors against traveling out-side the cities at night.

On the Chinese-built road north of Sanaʻa that runs to the spectacular mountain fortress town of Hajjah, where the imam kept his opponents in dungeons, it does not take long to run into roadside vendors selling fruit, smuggled in from Saudi Arabia to circumvent a ban imposed in October 1983 to cut foreign exchange loss. On the road south from Sanaʻa, past a landscape of water towers (*nuba*) and hillside terraces, there were eight *marakiz al-taftish* (roadblocks [or checkpoints]), designed both to find smugglers and their wares and to check vehicles for arms belonging to the underground National Democratic Front. (One's bags and books are also carefully scrutinized at the airport.) The war of the 1960s and the influx of emigrants' monies in the 1970s have not decisively weakened tribal loy-alties in the countryside: They have, rather, provided new ways in which people can amass local power, bending and adapting the traditional forms of control to take advantage of the new, plentiful supplies of guns and money. For a little while now, the government has banned tribesmen from bringing arms into the largest cities. But outside Sanaʻa and Taʻiz most men carry them, and the government's ability to control these areas di-rectly remains limited. Such control as exists is mediated by tribal chiefs. The Saudis still give subsidies to the northern tribes, an estimated $60 to $80 million each year.

The city to which Sanaʻa bears greatest resemblance is Kabul. There is the same smell of eucalyptus trees, the same sense of altitude and dust, of harsh sunlight on the sharp bare mountains around the town, of hooting cars, of an atypical, often beleaguered urban setting threatened by a counterrevolutionary, tribal world beyond. There are times in North Yemen when one wonders how the republic ever survived the onslaughts of the 1960s. Nor does the comparison with Kabul end there, for in the main square of the city, the Midan al-Tahrir, named after its Egyptian counterpart and stretching away from the former palace of the imams, there stands, as in Kabul, a Soviet-built T-34 tank, on a pedestal, with a little garden and an "eternal flame." The tank in Kabul reportedly had burst into what was the palace of President Daud in April 1978, beginning the Great Saur Revolution; the one in Sana'a was used to attack the imam's palace on the night of September 26, 1962.

The Revolution and the State

Despite all its conservatism and social confusion, the YAR remains a country that has gone through a revolution. The old political order was destroyed: The imam lives in exile in Kent, England, and his many relatives are in Saudi Arabia. The old ruling caste of *sada* [the plural of *sayyid*], who controlled much of the state and judicial processes in the pre-1962 period, and who presented themselves as direct descendants of the Prophet Muhammad, no longer hold power as a social group. Some, as individuals, are influential in the affairs of state, and others can be seen still walking the streets, with their *jambiyas* (daggers) in the *sayyid* position—in the middle, instead of on one side of their belts. But the monarchy and its associated caste have been destroyed. With this, North Yemen was wrenched into the capitalist market over the past two decades with a vengeance.

The legitimacy of the revolution is important in the regime of President 'Ali 'Abdallah Salih. The slogans around Sana'a proclaim his loyalty to the "glorious September 26 revolution." Television programs for children show the old days of the imam's tyranny, and then picture the coming of the revolution, the expansion of education and establishment of justice. The imam's palaces, where Imam Yahya, under the influence of morphine, would play with his imported toys and a slave would crank up the lift with a winch, are now museums of the revolution or hotels. The main street in Sana'a is named after one of the organizers of the 1962 revolution, a man who died in the first days, 'Abd al-Mughni. The three main streets in Ta'iz are called September 26, Gamal Abdel Nasser and Liberation.

This proclamation of a revolutionary ideology has recently taken a new twist in the process of collaboration and rivalry with the South. Just as in the PDRY, where President 'Ali Nasir Muhammad has three titles, dutifully repeated after every mention of his name (secretary-general of the party, chairman of the council of ministers, president of the Supreme People's Council), so in the YAR, 'Ali 'Abdallah Salih has acquired his ritual triplet—the brother president of the republic, commander-in-chief of the armed forces, and secretary of the General People's Congress, the 1,000-strong body equivalent of a government party.

In the competition for revolutionary legitimacy and loyalty to the values of Arab and Yemeni nationalism combined, 'Ali 'Abdallah Salih leaves little to chance. His picture is everywhere. Yet a less likely champion of revolutionary and nationalist values could hardly be found. 'Ali 'Abdallah Salih, born in 1943 of a minor sheikhly family in Sanhan, south of Sana'a, served as an artillery officer in the armed forces, and won his reputation fighting the left-wing opposition in the 1970s. In 1977, when the Saudis and their tribal allies accused President Ibrahim al-Hamdi of increasing relations with the South much too rapidly and overtly, 'Ali 'Abdallah Salih was widely credited with personally having slain al-Hamdi. With the death in 1978 of al-Hamdi's successor, the conservative Ahmad al-Ghashmi, Salih became president. Few people here or outside the country expected him to survive for long. He is no orator: His first speeches were, in the words of one foreign observer, "extremely painful." Several military uprisings and assassination attempts followed in 1978–79, but he survived them all; he routed his opponents and appears now to have consolidated his position. The Eighteenth Brumaire of 'Ali 'Abdallah Salih has created a Yemeni Bonapartism. His tight security, epitomized in a sprawling and electronically fortified official residence on the hilly outskirts of Ta'iz, leaves little to chance. His bodyguard numbers several hundred, mainly members of his own Sanhan tribe. Salih has grasped the reins of government and built a rudimentary state system below him.

The YAR state, weak as it is, is considerably stronger than it was a decade ago. Salih has expanded and strengthened the army and other security forces, relying on personnel from his tribe and on military officers close to him. One brother, Muhammad 'Abdallah Salih, is deputy minister of interior. A national army now exists for the first time in North Yemen. In 1982, it was allocated 1,810 million Yemeni riyals compared to 580 million for health and education. At the same time, the president has brought considerable numbers of civilians, including many southerners with no tribal loyalties, into the state, and he has won the grudging acceptance of many who fought for the republic in the 1960s. The prime minister, 'Abd al-'Aziz 'Abd al-Ghani, is a US-educated economist who has held the post for most of the years since 1975. The foreign minister, and former prime minister, 'Abd al-Karim al-Iryani, comes from one of the most powerful republican families. The lower echelons of the apparatus are laced with kin networks and corruption. But for many people, Salih at least offers one thing: peace, internally and with South Yemen. There is now the possibility for the YAR to catch its breath after the civil war of the 1960s, in which up to a quarter of a million people lost their lives, and the fighting and assassinations that punctuated the 1970s. Their calculation on government consolidation and a prudent Yemeni nationalism has led many Yemenis to support this hybrid regime, a fusion of tribal faction, military apparatus and civilian recruitment.

The Twenty Years' War

The apparent consolidation of the YAR state underlines the degree to which the politics of this region, albeit greatly influenced by external forces in the Arab world and beyond, also have their own special character and dynamic. The Yemens as a whole are a rather special part of the Middle East, separate and distinct, even as they participate in and are influenced by the turmoils of the larger Arab world.

The two Yemens have been the site of some of the most momentous upheavals of the modern Arab world. But the outside world, including the rest of the Arab states, tends to take notice of the two Yemens only when these acquire, or are invested with, broader international significance. The Egyptian intervention in North Yemen from 1962 to 1967, the turmoil of the British withdrawal from South Yemen and the growth of Soviet influence there after 1967, and the strategic implications of conflict between the Yemens—these have provided focus for external concern and attention. In fact, though, the dynamic of regional politics in southwest Arabia has a lot more to do with local issues and changes than most observers realize. The rest of the world looks very different from Sana'a (and Aden) once this is taken into account.

Three general considerations can help to place the region in a more accurate focus. In the first place, the two Yemens form a natural and historical unity, a region of settled agriculture and civilization that has existed for over 2,000 years. Like the Nile Valley and the cities of Mesopotamia, they represent one of the historic cores around which the contemporary Middle East is built, long predating nationalism or the modern state. This is often obscured if we attend only to the divisions of recent history, especially those of colonial rule, which separated Aden from the Yemeni hinterland and later devolved into two separate, often hostile states disputing the claim to represent Yemeni legitimacy.

The degree of unity is, at the same time, overstated by contemporary nationalists. They not only underestimate the local and tribal divisions that still divide Yemeni society from within, but also the degree to which two separate and unassimilable states have now arisen in this single cultural historical region. The ratchet effects of post-colonial state formation cannot be easily reversed. The practical implications of this historic unity are still significant, though. There is, for one thing, a deep popular sense that the Yemenis are a people with a single history and identity who must seek cooperation as well as peace. There is also a popular sense of what they, as Yemenis, are not, a sense that the Arabian Peninsula has long been divided between the settled and the nomads, between the sons of 'Adnan and those of Qahtan. In today's political terms, this means in particular that the Yemenis sharply distinguish themselves from Saudi Arabia.

This historic division of the Peninsula has been compounded by oil, the second general factor in evaluating the regional and international position of the two Yemens. Some oil deposits have been found recently in both states, but no oil in major quantities has yet been conclusively identified. Despite the great differences in the way the two Yemens are organized, both depend to a considerable extent on income from the oil states. Both are, in a certain sense, tributary of the other Peninsula countries. This bond is maintained in two ways. One is via official aid, a vital factor in the economy and state finances of North Yemen, and a significant one in the budget of the South. In the YAR, foreign aid accounted for 17 percent of GNP in 1982. The other means by which oil wealth flows to these states is through the remittances of emigrants. More than one million Yemenis, out of a population of 7.5 million, live in the other Peninsula states (mostly in Saudi Arabia), and their earnings make up much of the two Yemens' foreign exchange income. (According to YAR statistics, in 1981, the nearly 1.4 million Yemeni workers outside the country actually outnumbered the active male labor force of 1.2 million inside the country.) YAR remittances, at some $1 billion a year, come to around 40 percent of GNP.

This proximity and link to the oil states also has negative consequences: Needed labor is attracted by the higher wages available abroad. Local wages have risen spectacularly, as have land prices, and sections of the economy have become dependent upon foreign income or foreign imports, to the detriment of other priorities and local production. The decline of food production in North Yemen has made this potentially rich agricultural country reliant on imports for 30 percent of food supplies. This is one example of the warping effect of the link to the oil-producing economies. The abandoned terraces that litter the mountains of the interior tell their own tale.

This link is also closely related to the third common and distinctive feature of the two Yemens: In a peninsula of six monarchies, these two states are republics, a result of the revolutions both countries went through in the 1960s. No revolution makes a clean sweep of the old order and its culture, but these continuities should not obscure the fact that very widespread political and social changes did occur, involving the mobilization and combativity of significant parts of the population in both states.

As nearly always happens, these Yemeni revolutions acquired an international character. For one thing, they sought to encourage like-minded political forces elsewhere in the Peninsula. 'Abdallah al-Sallal, the first North Yemeni president, opened an Office of the Arabian Peninsula in 1963 and called for the overthrow of the Saudi monarch and the creation of a united socialist Arabia. His republic also gave support to the guerrillas in South Yemen. The National Liberation Front in the south came to power committed to encouraging the guerrillas in neighboring Oman, and to supporting the radical republicans in the North opposed to compromise with the royalists and with Saudi Arabia.

The opponents of these revolutions were equally concerned to internationalize them, by aiding the opponents in North and South. Saudi Arabia, in particular, has sought to contain and, if possible, reverse the upheavals in the two Yemens. This internationalization of the Yemeni revolutions has had a powerful divisive effect as the two independent states differed more and more after 1967. They fought two border wars, in 1972 and 1979, and until 1982 each repeatedly gave support and encouragement to opponents of the other.

The North Yemeni revolution of September 1962 set off a process of political and social conflict in southwest Arabia that spread from the north to the south and then to the Dhofar region of Oman. It was only in 1982 that this 20-year war came to an end, with the cessation of the guerrilla war in North Yemen and the establishment of diplomatic relations between Oman and South Yemen. (The Omani guerrillas, active in Dhofar, had been effectively crushed in late 1975.) The policies of the two Yemens can therefore be regarded as located within this specific and in some ways novel environment—of consciousness of the Yemens as a distinct and regional entity, of a difficult and yet inescapable dependence on the oil-producing states, and of a revolutionary past that has, at least temporarily, given way to a new period of peace and consolidation.

The View from Sana'a

The end of North Yemen's civil war in 1970 produced a coalition government in which elements from the royalist camp joined with the republicans. Conflict emerged within the republican camp, as some left-wing groups refused to accept the peace and others on the right thought that the government was going too far in enforcing central control of the tribes. President al-Iryani was ousted in June 1974; his successor Ibrahim al-Hamdi was assassinated in 1977; and al-Hamdi's successor, Ahmad al-Ghashmi, was killed by a bomb apparently sent from South Yemen in 1978. The left-wing forces fought a guerrilla war from 1971 to 1973, and again, after the death of al-Hamdi, from 1978 to 1982. President 'Ali 'Abdallah Salih's consolidation of power with a more effective central state apparatus and a stronger central army, and the defeat of the left-wing National Democratic Front, has been offset by a serious economic problem. Foreign revenues have stagnated. The YAR budget deficit makes up 30 percent of GDP. The republic's exports are minimal. Workers' remittances have leveled off and are expected to decline in the period ahead. The crisis of October 1983, when a new cabinet was installed and stringent import controls imposed, signaled the end of North Yemen's easy reliance on wealth from the oil states. The discovery of some oil in July 1984 by Hunt Oil may alleviate these problems, but the scale of the discovery is as yet unclear, and in any case would not be productive for at least half a decade more.

For reasons of economy, therefore, as well as because of influence which it wields within North Yemen, Saudi Arabia remains the main point of reference for YAR foreign policy. The Saudis have in the past suspended payments to YAR governments when these have pursued policies of which they disapprove. Through their direct links to the northern tribes, and in particular to the Hashid group of Sheikh 'Abdallah al-Ahmar, they have an alternative to direct financial pressure upon the government itself. The Saudis are aware that overt pressure will only antagonize the Yemenis, and so they have kept their influence steady but indirect. The Saudis' primary aim is to keep a friendly government in power in Sana'a, and to prevent it from establishing too close relations with either the USSR or the PDRY. But Saudi Arabia has also to contend with other Arab influences in the YAR—Egypt in the past, and more recently Iraq and Libya have sought influence within the armed forces.

No political parties are permitted in the YAR. The official government political body is the 1,000-member General People's Congress, 700 of whom are elected and 300 nominated by the president. It acts as a surro-gate ruling party, channeling political action and patronage, and its char-ter is used for two-hour political orientation classes in government offices every week. Censorship is extremely tight, and none of the major upheav-als of recent years—even the 1979 war with South Yemen—was mentioned at all in the government press.

Shadowy political coalitions, involving the military, tribal and urban intellectual elements, have existed since before the days of the civil war. Many believe that the pro-Iraqi Baathists still have some influence. South Yemen has, until recently, supported the National Democratic Front. In recent years, a tendency close to the Muslim Brothers, known locally as the Islamic Front, has gained influence, to a considerable ex-tent via the 23,000 Egyptian teachers in the country. The Islamic Front has gained ground in the university, and many women now wear the nun-like headdress pioneered by Egyptian fundamentalists. This consti-tutes a new political force friendly to the Saudis and hostile to the PDRY and its supporters in the north. Four of the ministers in the cabinet of October 1983 are believed to be members of the Islamic Front, and the Saudis must see in it a new channel of influence. The president's brother and deputy minister of interior, Muhammed 'Abdallah Salih, may be a potential candidate for the loyalties of this group.

North Yemen has been careful to cultivate relations with the vari-ous factions of the Arab world. It has been critical of the peace initia-tives taken by Egypt, but has not fallen into the rejectionist camp that has severed all ties with Cairo. It has from the start supported Iraq in its war with Iran, and has supplied some of its Soviet equipment to the Iraqis in return for payment. It has received substantial aid from Kuwait and the Emirates, but it is not a candidate for membership in the Gulf Cooperation Council, the grouping of six Arab oil producers of the Peninsula set up in May 1981. As one high-ranking government official put it to me: "There are reasons why we will not be allowed to join. First, we are a republic. Secondly, we are poor. And thirdly, if they let us in, then they would have to let the Iraqis in as well."

[...]

Unity or Coexistence?

Both the YAR and the PDRY talk of unity at some time in the future. Both are too suspicious of each other, and have too great an investment in their separate state structures, to risk that.

The "unity process" does bring some concrete benefits to each side. It encourages a sense of non-belligerency between the two governments, and a reining in of the elements within their own states which seek to overthrow the government of the other. The National Democratic Front remains an organized force in South Yemen, and the National Coalition, a gathering of exiles from the South, maintains a position in the North. But after 20 years of conflict, a more durable coexistence between the two Yemens does seem to have emerged.

Unity involves certain forms of cooperation—in joint companies for tourism, shipping and insurance, and in collaboration between the educational ministries and writers of the two countries. A Yemeni Council, composed of the presidents of the two states and selected ministers, meets every six months to discuss "unity," and a 136-article draft constitution has been prepared: But the meetings of the council so far have yielded no specific decisions, and the unpublished text of the constitution is being "studied" by the two presidents. Unity in the sense of a merger of the two states is almost inconceivable. Like all neighbors, the two Yemeni revolutions are condemned to living with each other.

The problem of unity between the two Yemens is nevertheless posed as sharply by the impossibility of a real unification as it would be by any prospect of a fusion of the two states. The YAR and the PDRY are locked into a relationship that is both close and conflictual, because of their shared characteristics and because of the divergent and competitive outcomes of their two revolutions and the two state structures that resulted from them. Each needs the other, and needs to sustain a politics of Yemeni nationalism, to balance their international alignments and maintain domestic legitimacy. Yet, albeit now in a more peaceful form, the competition between them continues. "Peaceful coexistence" in Southwest Arabia has all the contradictory interaction of its more global East-West version, since it is the coexistence of the two social and political systems that must continue while both have to avoid an outright war.

[...]

Catastrophe in South Yemen: A Preliminary Assessment

Fred Halliday • *MER* 139, Mar./Apr. 1986

How can social tensions be managed and policy differences resolved by ruling socialist parties in poverty-stricken Third World states? On January 13, 1986, this question defeated the Yemeni Socialist Party (YSP) in a devastating spasm of civil war. Parallels can be drawn between the South Yemeni trauma and the equally tragic collapse of unity within the New Jewel Movement in Grenada, although the regional conjunctures were different and the geopolitical context of the Yemeni Republic precluded a Reaganite outcome.

The South Yemeni state emerged out of the victorious struggle against British colonial rule in 1967. A population of some 2 million people live in a land that is almost totally barren; only 2 percent is cultivable and only 1 percent cultivated. Expanding the agricultural area is almost impossible because of the lack of water. Two land reforms after the revolution have brought most of the land into about 60 collective farms and 50 state farms. Some private peasant plots have been allowed, but under stricter limitations than, for example, in the Soviet Union. Despite efforts to achieve self-sufficiency, only about half the country's food requirements are met domestically. Lack of capital inputs and of trained agronomists and managers has caused severe problems, especially in the state farm sector, where a great deal of investment has been wasted. In 1984, only three of the 24 crop-growing state farms operated profitably. Since the late 1970s, fishing has developed as the one non-industrial sector able to expand successfully. Fish has become the country's major export, both to the Soviet Union and to the Far East. Per capita income in 1982 was $460. In 1985, agriculture accounted for 10 percent of output, but 42 percent of employment; the figures for industry were 16 percent and 11 percent respectively.

For almost all of its 18 years of existence, the South Yemeni state has been a focal point of continuous war between revolution and counterrevolution in the region, but it has gained a measure of strategic security through its continuous close relationship with the Soviet Union. Politically, the Soviet view has been that it is absolutely premature to speak of a transition to socialism in a country with such a weak natural endowment, massive illiteracy, great shortage of cadres, and so on. Right from the beginning, Soviet advice has been strongly against what it sees as domestic adventurism, favoring caution, accommodation to Islam, liberalization, a conditional opening to the oil states, and the loosening of control on the peasants and fishermen. Thus, Soviet views have always been more moderate than many of the indigenous South Yemeni political currents both on internal social policy and foreign policy. The Soviets have argued that, in the long run, efforts to "normalize" relations with the Saudis and Oman would weaken the position of imperialism more than a position of support for movements against those surrounding regimes.

The Soviets have sought to avoid becoming too deeply involved in the internal politics of the country, and it is only in the last few years, under the government of 'Ali Nasir, that Soviet and South Yemeni views of how to proceed internally and externally have drawn closer together. Moscow has given South Yemen some $270 million in aid over the past 18 years, accounting for about one-third of the total aid received since independence. The non-Soviet contributions have come from China ($133 million), other socialist states, the Arab states and multilateral agencies.

The Soviets do not maintain a military base in the sense of a sovereign area or permanent troops, but Aden is valuable as a naval port and depot more secure than any others in the region, and they no doubt maintain some intelligence-gathering facilities there.

Ruling Party

The South Yemeni ruling party was founded in 1963 as the National Liberation Front (NLF), which carried the guerrilla war against Britain to victory in 1967. In 1978, it transformed itself into the Yemeni Socialist Party. It has a membership of about 26,000, some 20 percent of whom have been army personnel. Less than 15 percent are members of the working class (by their own criteria) and most of the rest are peasants, intellectuals or party officials of one kind or another.

Throughout its existence the organization has been marked by factionalism. First of all, the liberation struggle itself was at least as factional as that in Angola or Zimbabwe: The NLF's victory in 1967 was won not against the British alone, but also against the Front for the Liberation of South Yemen (FLOSY), the rival, more pro-Egyptian group with whom it had been impossible to achieve unity. More people were killed in the conflict between the NLF and FLOSY—a mixture of personal, political and regional issues—than either group lost at the hands of the British.

After independence, there was an initial rivalry between a quasi-Nasserist faction under President Qahtan al-Shaabi and those regarded as the "Marxist-Leninist" left. The latter came to power in a bloodless coup on June 22, 1969. (Al-Shaabi remained under house arrest almost until his death in 1980.) The Front then began transforming itself into a "party of a new type," following what it regarded as a Leninist model. It united with two smaller political groups—a pro-Syrian Baathist faction and a small, pro-Soviet communist party, the Popular Democratic Union (PDU). This was a fusion in some ways similar to that between Fidel Castro's movement with the Partido Socialists Popular in Cuba, but the Cuban PSP was a much larger political force than the PDU had been.

In 1978, just before the first congress of the YSP took place, another major factional conflict broke out. On June 26, 1978, President Salim Rubai 'Ali tried to seize power against the majority on the Central Committee. Though not a Maoist in a strict sense, 'Ali was opposed to an orthodox party and advocated spontaneity. He believed in appointing people on the basis of political principles rather than functional competence and in the early 1970s he had tried, with catastrophic consequences, to imitate the Chinese Cultural Revolution in South Yemen. But he remained a popular leader, with a larger following than the party leaders who defeated him in 1978.

The man who emerged as president in 1978 was 'Abd al-Fattah Ismail. After less than two years in office, he was ousted in a bloodless change of government in April 1980, on the grounds that he had promised too much from the alliance with the Soviet Union and had mismanaged the economy. His opponents dubbed him derisively with a Khomeinist label, the *faqih*, the interpreter of religious law, a dogmatic Marxist who buried his head in the books but was technically and administratively incompetent. In the mid-1960s, 'Abd al-Fattah proclaimed the need for a Marxist-Leninist line, by which he meant a struggle against the "petty bourgeoisie." This entailed combating the small traders on whom Aden's prosperity depended, and those whom he called the "kulaks" in the countryside. This dogmatic view of economic and social development scarcely equipped him for managing the country's affairs competently, yet many people remained loyal to him. He went into exile in the Soviet Union, but was able to return in 1985. He was a prominent figure leading the movement against the government this January, and he died in the conflict.

'Abd al-Fattah's successor in 1980 was 'Ali Nasir Muhammad, who remained in power until the January crisis. Continuing tensions during these last five years indicate that factionalism, not just a left-right conflict but various shifting alliances and currents, has been an endemic feature of the Socialist Party. One source of this factionalism has been two divergent forms of radicalism: an indigenous, Yemeni trend and a more orthodox, bookish radicalism. The revolution's origins lie very much in the first; the second, regarding itself as orthodox "Marxist-Leninist," flourished in the late 1960s and early 1970s.

Controls and Markets

Under 'Ali Nasir's presidency, these contrasting trends did not apparently diverge over relations with the Soviet Union or China or the West. They clashed over two partly interrelated issues: internal economic policy and policy toward the region.

The dominant internal question was: How far does domestic economic development require the loosening of state controls? The first ten years of highly centralized economic regime did not yield many results. As state controls loosened in the late 1970s, and even more so under 'Ali Nasir Muhammad in the 1980s, living standards rose. There was more foreign aid, private traders were given greater leeway, peasants were allowed to sell about a dozen different products at prices ranging up to 150 percent above those in state markets, and controls on fishermen's sales were also relaxed. This was not a case of completely free markets, such as exist for peasants in the *kholkhoz* [collective farms] of the Soviet Union. It was a controlled liberalization, nothing more.

There was also an attempt to encourage Yemeni workers abroad to send back more money. These workers amount to perhaps one-third of South Yemen's able-bodied young men. They send back over $300 million a year, which amounts to between 60 and 70 percent of all South Yemen's foreign exchange earnings. In 1982, for example, exports of $21 million contrasted with imports of $747 million. The contribution of the workers abroad came not only in foreign exchange but also in imports of consumer goods. By the age of about 35 such workers are worn out and have to be replaced by younger workers going abroad in search of jobs.

Economic liberalization was a source of tensions. When the private sector began to have higher incomes, people on party salaries became nervous. The result was the classic pattern of growing party privileges: in the mid-1970s, special shops for members of the Central Committee; then privileged access to certain goods; then increased license as to what people could bring back from foreign trips, special allowances for state functionaries to buy foreign exchange goods, the provision of air conditioners, video machines and cars. This was done from the top downward. During this time, for example, the army had been completely reequipped by the

Soviets, so the old leadership decided they would get rid of superfluous British arms by selling them to smugglers at the Saudi frontier in return for Toyota cars. The arms most likely ended up with the Afghan mujahidin, probably the only people in the world looking for Lee-Enfield replacements. The Toyotas were allocated to officers in the army and members of the party. In a very small and very visible society, this created rifts. When everyone had been poor, there was less tension; when more goods became available, competition became greater.

To all this must be added the dimension of class forces within the country and outside. There were clearly internal social groups who realized that such developments increased their leverage, and there were both émigrés and foreign governments who realized this was a wedge for undermining the socialist experiment. Just as people living in Havana are aware of Miami, so Adenis know the very high living standards in the Gulf. Such acquaintance comes not only from the migrant workers but also from people being able, since the late 1970s, to pick up television programs from North Yemen, with their idealized picture of North Yemeni life.

So this economic loosening certainly created social tensions and instability, as it did in Cuba in the late 1970s. And insofar as ʿAli Nasir promoted this policy, differences within the party focused upon him. There was no doubt an increase of corruption in official circles as well.

The second broad source of policy struggles within the party concerned relations with neighboring states. In the Dhofar province of Oman there had been a decade of war from 1965 to 1975. There had been border clashes with Saudi Arabia. It is only very recently that the South Yemeni government has established diplomatic relations with neighboring states. In the cases of Saudi Arabia and Oman, there is no dispute that South Yemen has to find ways of living with its conservative neighbors. But in the case of North Yemen, the South had, until 1982, supported the National Democratic Front there, the successors of the radical republicans of the 1960s. This decision to stop supporting the rebels and to press for normal relations with the Sanaʿa government involved bringing some 2,000 Northern rebels south and settling them in camps. This undoubtedly aggravated the internal situation even more, reflecting 20 years of revolution and counterrevolution in South Arabia.

A Tale of Two Families: Change in North Yemen, 1977–89

Sheila Carapico and Cynthia Myntti • *MER* 170, Summer 1991

Virtually every aspect of life in North Yemen has changed dramatically since 1977, including those aspects of Yemeni society which represent continuity with the past: tribalism, rural life and the use of qat. The driving force for change has been economic. By 1975, Yemen was caught up in the dramatic developments that affected all Arab countries. Rising international oil prices generated enormous surpluses in the producing countries, enabling them to initiate ambitious development plans and forcing them to import workers.

The Yemen Arab Republic was in a good position to provide those workers. In the late 1970s, one of the jokes around the capital city, Sana'a, was that Yemen had neither an "open door" nor a "closed door" but a "no door" policy with its oil-producing neighbors. Ill-defined and sparsely settled borders allowed easy movement of Yemeni workers to Saudi Arabia and of their remittances and goods back home.

In addition to geographical proximity, Yemenis enjoyed a certain social proximity to the Saudi job market. Until August 1990, Saudi Arabia allowed Yemenis to live and work in the Kingdom without visas. Many Yemenis owned businesses in Saudi Arabia, while other foreigners were not granted such rights. In the early years of the oil boom, many older Yemeni migrants found a good market for the skills they had learned in Aden when it was a British colony: knowledge of English; and commercial, domestic or secretarial skills. These advantages placed Yemenis ahead of their competitors for jobs, at least in the years prior to the arrival of highly organized work brigades from South Korea and elsewhere in Southeast Asia.

This movement of labor had a phenomenal impact on North Yemen. Some Yemeni regions lost up to half their male labor force to the Gulf, and the national total may have reached as many as 1.23 million. By 1982, remittances reached an annual record high of $1.4 billion. It was a time when Yemeni citizens, on average, vastly increased their spending power. Yet the government, unable to effectively tax these remittances, was forced to rely on friendly countries for aid to meet its basic fiscal commitments. Officially recorded foreign aid reached $401 million in 1982, mainly from wealthy Arab states and to a lesser extent from multilateral and other bilateral donors.

[...]

These conditions affected the lives of virtually every Yemeni family over the years 1977–89. We examined the cases of two families that occupied very different positions in the old social hierarchy. The first is an urban family from the Old City of Sana'a, members of the *sayyid* strata, reputedly descended from the Prophet. The second is a peasant or *ra'iyya* family living in rural Ta'iz.

Both families had prospered during the short-lived period of affluence only to find themselves now unable to maintain the same standard of living despite their hard work. Lacking the economic and political currencies needed in contemporary society, by the summer of 1989 they each found themselves in a precarious position. These cases show the extent to which family fortunes are connected to the national economy, and illustrate the replacement of old status rankings by factors related to class. Whereas in the old days a Zaydi *sayyid* family related by marriage to the royal family was considered part of the pampered Sana'ani "elite" and the Ta'iz family were smallholder peasants, both were now self-employed at the margins of a national market economy. Neither family possess the prerequisites for success or even security in this new economy: the right educational certificates, the right political connections (or "backing") and money.

The household perspective also reminds us that through this tumultuous period women in particular held tenaciously to traditional Islamic and cultural values, modified only superficially by the introduction of new commodities into their daily lives. Living by traditional ethical values, however, seems more difficult than before.

In the Heart of the Old City

The Sana'ani family today includes a relatively young matriarchal figure and widow, Amat al-Karim, her son 'Abd al-Rahman and daughter Khadija, their spouses and ten young children.

In Amat al-Karim's eyes, Khadija and 'Abd al-Rahman were born into nobility. Though neither rich nor politically active, they lived in a fine quarter inside the northern gate of old Sana'a, between a mosque and its garden, just off a main street, the markets and a square with a school.

Amat al-Karim loved her husband, Muhammad, a gentle, honest scribe who traced his ancestry directly to the Prophet. She was grateful to her parents for the good match, for her sister's marriage to a branch of the royal family, and for her own modest inheritance of several farming terraces outside town. Her son and daughter, toddlers at the time of the 1962 revolution, grew up proud and pious like their parents. She herself was able to half read, half recite the Qur'an, and so enrolled them in school. By the time of Muhammad's death in 1970, Khadija had completed five years and 'Abd al-Rahman had finished intermediate school.

Neither Amat al-Karim nor her neighbors could anticipate the fantastic changes of the 1970s, as secondhand affluence from the oil boom and continuing upheaval within Yemen transformed the world around them. Through this tumultuous period, Amat al-Karim and her children held closely to the family and religious values she learned as a child, but their own choices and the changing environment left them in a very different position 25 years after the revolution. Whereas the status position of a Sana'ani *sayyid* previously ranked the family among the elite, nowadays it is their economic class that situates them socially.

Amat al-Karim found spouses for her children through the network of her aunts and sister. Both literate and demure, Khadija was not wanting for suitors. In the end, Amat al-Karim accepted as her son-in-law a military man, who was often stationed in Cairo during the early years of their marriage. Because of his frequent travels, Khadija continued to live in her mother's home. For her son, Amat al-Karim selected from their wide kinship network a bride nicknamed Ghafura, who also moved into their crowded house.

Their house in the old city consisted of three stories. Goats, chickens, fodder, fuel and grain were kept on the ground floor. Amat al-Karim shared the second story flat, containing a large *diwan* (sitting room), two bedrooms, a traditional bathroom and a large ordinary room used for baking, cooking and eating, with 'Abd al-Rahman and his family. Khadija and her children occupied the smaller top flat.

In the late 1970s, the family enjoyed the benefits of Yemen's new affluence, although none of them joined the flood of workers going to the Gulf. 'Abd al-Rahman, whose educational qualifications were rapidly becoming insufficient, had become bored with his routine, low-paying government clerkship. Somewhat idly at first, he began painting Islamic verses on colored glass, of the sort commonly embedded in the plaster around interior windows and doors in Sana'ani houses. With the flurry of new residential construction taking place in Sana'a at the time, sales were soon so brisk that 'Abd al-Rahman matched his government salary and more in his afternoons. He rented a neighborhood shopfront and quit his government post about a year before his marriage in 1977.

Through 1980 'Abd al-Rahman scarcely kept track of his daily earnings, but often grossed 500–1000 Yemeni rials a day ($111–221). Much of the income went toward buying appliances. As they became available on the market, the family bought a tape recorder, washing machine, refrigerator, television and video. They paid gladly for water and electricity hookups and purchased better quality meat, qat, household items, jewelry and clothing, although their tastes remained quite traditional. Their courtyard goats and chickens were replaced by milk, eggs and meat purchased from the market.

Khadija and 'Abd al-Rahman's wife, Ghafura, turned their attention wholeheartedly to motherhood, enjoying almost annually the 40 days of festivities and relaxation that follow childbirth. They passed their time at home with the children or celebrating the marriages and births of others. Khadija bore five children in the first decade of marriage (one of whom died); Ghafura had six. The three-story house resonated with the sounds of children.

In 1982, members of the family decided to pool their resources (Khadija's bridewealth, savings from the men, cash traded in from jewelry and loans from relatives) to purchase a fashionable new one-story house outside the walls of the old city. It cost 220,000 riyals ($48,888 at the new, lower exchange rate). They spent a further 50,000 riyals on decoration and a Western-style bathroom. The kitchen was a separate open room in the courtyard, a more healthful arrangement than in their old house. Khadija and a widowed aunt continued to live in the increasingly decrepit house in the old city.

By the summer of 1989, the family retained neither the prestige of the old era nor the affluence of the oil-boom years. 'Abd al-Rahman now earns less than half what he made in the peak years. The slowdown in housing construction has meant less demand for his religious verses and patriotic designs. The devaluation of the Yemeni riyal has increased the cost of his paint and glass. Many other necessities and niceties of daily life also cost more, and family demands surpass what he brings home. Ten-year-old appliances are breaking down, and need to be repaired or replaced.

'Abd al-Rahman's wife and sister now tell him that had he stayed in his secure civil service job, he would probably be a director by now and that surely a decent position awaits him still. He checked into the possibility of returning to the government, but learned that his intermediate education would gain him only an unskilled, entry-level position and a meager salary. The traditional familial ties that yielded good marriages in the old city are of limited value now in the world of government. In his late 30s, he is the model Sana'ani son, husband, brother and father—loving, sober, hard-working and pious. Yet the smart Western suits of today's successful men are not his style, and his nieces call him old-fashioned. Like his old neighbors and friends, he manufactures artifacts linked to the lifestyles of an earlier generation. His children prefer imported goods.

Khadija has by now joined her husband in Cairo. They live in a fourth-floor, four-room suburban apartment. There is no place for her children in overcrowded Egyptian schools. Ghafura, for her part, lives with her family in the one-story suburban house, now surrounded by workshops, a lumber yard and the smaller houses of recent arrivals from the country-side. Both women longingly recall the old days in the old city, with its fa-miliar social network and the never-ending cycle of afternoon parties for new brides and mothers. They both fear that their children are not being taught the proper old city manners, respect and piety that they want them to have. They are keenly aware of the importance of school certificates, yet they remain more concerned about their children's moral education.

In Rural Ta'iz

Far away from Sana'a, in a village outside Ta'iz, the Qasir family repre-sented the epitome of success. Theirs was an extended family in which all except Mustafa, the father, resided in the tall stone house in the vil-lage and worked in agriculture. They worked on lands they owned or rented in a sharecropping arrangement (*shirka*) common in that part of Yemen. Like other families with excess labor, they took in rented lands to maximize production.

The grandfather, 'Ali, had spent his youth as a stoker on steamships moving from Aden to Southeast Asia, Suez, Europe and beyond; he re-turned to farming after his retirement, doing what men do in agriculture in those parts of Yemen—the plowing and threshing. Grandmother Sybil worked alongside him, and tended to the farm animals. 'Aziza, their daugh-ter-in-law, managed the household; she organized maintenance tasks such as shopping, cleaning, cooking and fetching water, arranged agricultural work, and helped her father-in-law decide about expenditures. In the af-ternoons or during agricultural slack periods, she was a seamstress. In the 1970s, 'Aziza's three sons and three daughters were in school but they also helped with cooking, cleaning, fetching water, running errands and shop-ping in the market town, and with agricultural work.

'Aziza's husband, Mustafa, was in Saudi Arabia, where he held down two and sometimes three jobs. As a boy he had lived with his father in Aden, where he learned some English, how to be a houseboy, cook and servant, and how to read and write Arabic. In Saudi Arabia, he worked variously as a construction foreman, a cook, a clerk and a shop attendant. To keep down costs, he shared living quarters with other Yemeni migrants, sent a small remittance to his father each month, and scrupulously saved every riyal of the rest. When he returned to Yemen after four years away, he brought with him luxurious gifts: a fake fur coat for 'Aziza, a color television, new and fashionable ready-made clothes for his children, imitation Persian carpets, a washing machine, a Butagaz-fueled stove with oven, a blender and other household appliances. He took his parents on the pilgrimage to Mecca. The bulk of his savings went toward the cost of building a new house, a one-story bungalow, for 'Aziza and their children.

Mustafa returned to work in Saudi Arabia, but in 1983 he lost one job after another. After an extended and fruitless search for new work, he returned to Yemen.

Since then he has drifted from one unsuccessful venture to another. At one point, he was unable to repay a bank loan he had taken out to start a small restaurant; 'Aziza sold and pawned her jewelry to make the bank payments. It has been difficult for Mustafa to settle into business because he now needs certificates and permits for everything, and must bribe officials to get them. He has become exceedingly discouraged about the possibility of earning a decent income honorably.

He has also become disheartened about his own children, especially his sons, who do not appreciate the value of hard work, spend more than they earn, and seem ashamed by his lowly work and powerlessness. Some call the new generation the "Nido generation"—spoiled on the Nido powdered milk so plentiful in the affluent 1970s.

Mustafa's and Aziza's eldest son Hamud works in a civil service job in Ta'iz. Like many other village men, he lives in town during the week and returns to the village on weekends. Nearly 30 years old, father of three, he spends more than he earns on his personal habits: smoking cigarettes and chewing expensive qat daily.

Chewing qat has taken on enhanced functions in Yemen in the 1980s. Nationally, consumption is on the rise because more people—men and women—are chewing daily. Average daily chews cost about 100 riyals ($10). Together with the cost of cigarettes, expenditures on this recreational drug can easily exceed a household's income. There is new evidence that some men are inadvertently "starving their families" to support their qat consumption. That fathers like Mustafa, who in an earlier era would have reached middle age and been supported by their sons, are instead finding

themselves covering their sons' debts, means that somehow, begrudging-
ly, they appreciate the important social function of the qat chew for their
sons. Yemen is a more complex place now than it was in their youth. To
get things done in Yemen today, one needs "backing." Backing assures individuals of jobs, certificates, perquisites, "justice" and business opportunities. If one does not have a tribe to turn to, as is the case for many of the
southern districts of the country, one creates and reinforces one's backing
through daily social intercourse around qat.

It is not surprising, then, that Hamud has failed to relieve his parents
of their burden of work by providing regular cash support. His irresponsibility has become the major source of conflict in the family, particularly
when he runs up large debts that he expects his father to pay. Yet everyone
knows that his irresponsibility is the necessary price of keeping in with
friends and in the know. Men who do not chew qat are stigmatized as mi-
serly, negative and anti-social.

In 1988 the second son, Salih, a university student, pressured his parents into coming up with enough money to allow him to marry a cousin.
When Mustafa and 'Aziza finally acknowledged that it would be impossible, he left for town and refused to visit them until a year later, after they
had made arrangements to finance the marriage. When the marriage finally took place in 1989, with an installment brideprice and "no frills,"
Salih only complained that things were not good enough for his bride and
himself.

Other aspects of family life have changed as well. When 'Aziza and
Mustafa moved into their own house, they insisted on reducing the
amount of rented lands taken in by the extended family. They would work
on their patrimonial plots, but no more. 'Aziza also looks after six sheep,
but no longer keeps more demanding animals such as cows. Nor does she
sew clothes for her daughters and herself; it is more economical to buy the
cheap imported clothes from Southeast Asia which are now available in
the village shops, the Turba market and Ta'iz town. 'Aziza and her daughters derive great pleasure from their leisure time, something unknown to
them a few years ago. They spend their afternoons and evenings sitting in
front of the television, watching Egyptian soap operas or Saudi religious
programs.

'Aziza worries about her daughters and their future marriages. She
wants them to marry close so that she can keep an eye on them, but views
the pool of desirable bridegrooms as distressingly small. She questions
the sincerity and ultimate motivation of the youthful converts to religious
fundamentalism, and wants her daughters to have nothing to do with

them. "These religious men say that everything is shameful ('*ayb*): We shouldn't go out with uncovered faces, we shouldn't educate our daughters. This isn't real religion," she says. Yet, as 'Aziza has seen with her own sons, the current situation forces many ambitious young men in the direction of excesses: irresponsible financial management, corruption, and overconsumption of qat, cigarettes and even alcohol. As she puts it, "Life nowadays is unstable."

As the prosperity and satisfaction of the 1970s gave way to the austerity and relative deprivation of the 1980s, a sense of frustration and alienation developed. We noticed it especially among these women and their friends who, always quick with a quip, grew increasingly cynical about the political order. Though both families enjoyed the security of home ownership, they each now relied mainly on the precarious earnings of one man with nothing of material value to pass on to his sons. The women worried about this, about the erosion of the moral fabric of society, and about the contradictions between what they still felt was right and the kinds of action that seemed necessary to get ahead.

Authors' Note: Names have been changed. While the details of the families' lives are true, the general opinions that were expressed were gathered in Yemen at large.

The Economic Dimension of Yemeni Unity

Sheila Carapico • *MER* 184, Sept./Oct. 1993

To the outside world, the unification of the two Yemens in 1990 resembled the German experience in miniature. North Yemen (the YAR) was considered a *laissez-faire* market economy, whereas the South (the People's Democratic Republic) was "the communist one." When, weeks ahead of Bonn and Berlin, Sana'a and Aden announced their union, Western commentary assumed that in Yemen, as in Germany, capitalist (Northern) firms would buy out the moribund (Southern) state sector and provide the basis for future economic growth.

In theory—and in Germany—capitalism and socialism are distinguished by patterns of private and public ownership of the means of production. In North and South Yemen, however, differences in ownership patterns were largely evened out by comparable access (and lack thereof) to investment capital. Disparities in the relative weight of private and public enterprise were far more subtle than the designations "capitalist" and "socialist" indicate. Indeed, available data on private and public participation reveals common patterns of spending. The North's state sector invested more than did the private sector, while the South's socialist policy statements belied the increasing role of domestic and foreign private firms.

Relatively poor countries situated on the periphery of the Arabian Peninsula's oil economy, both Yemens relied on labor remittances and international assistance. Both Yemens faced austerity when falling oil prices, compounded by a drop in Cold War–generated aid, reduced access to hard currency—until the discovery of oil in the border region in the mid-1980s attracted a third type of international capital from multinational petroleum companies. These forces cumulatively reduced the differences between the two systems and added an economic dimension to the political incentives for unification. In contrast with Germany, their marriage was more a merger than a takeover, for neither was in any position to buy the other out.

Two Economies

Historic Yemen was a cultural entity rather than a political unit; its formal division stemmed from British imperialism in the South. Unlike the relatively isolated, independent North, where a semi-feudal agrarian society persisted, the South developed capitalist classes, markets and enterprises. The major port between the Mediterranean and India, Aden's modern infrastructure and services attracted a small indigenous capitalist group, a working class of stevedores and industrial labor, and a small urban middle class, including shopkeepers and intellectuals. Sana'a, by contrast, was a center of Islamic conservatism ruled by a Zaydi Shi'a imam. Strict trade and investment restrictions protected a few monopoly importers and large landowners. Would-be bourgeoisie and working-class aspirants escaped this restricted environment for the free port at Aden. The North was ripe for a kind of bourgeois revolution, opening the door to capitalist development, just when the South's radical anti-imperialism slammed the door to foreign investors.

After the 1962 revolution and 1962–68 civil war, the North (the YAR) became a "no doors" economy, with few legal barriers to either trade or investment. Revolutionaries in the South after 1968 nationalized or collectivized many foreign enterprises, large estates and fishing boats. Whereas the South was subsequently governed by a single Soviet-style Marxist party, in the absence of legal parties politics in the North were dominated by fluid tribal, Islamic and leftist "fronts" covertly supported by other Arab regimes.

The two Yemens shared a physical environment where household-scale cereal and livestock production employed most men and women. Both governments were unsure of their authority in the countryside, and each backed elements of the other's opposition. The economies remained intertwined. In the early 1970s, the Southern bourgeoisie, some of them originally Northerners attracted to Aden's port economy, moved back north to Ta'iz, Hudayda and Sana'a, where they established businesses and held government posts. After the rise in oil prices in 1973, worker remittances fed consumption (imported goods, residential construction) rather than productive investment, despite both regimes' efforts to mobilize these funds for agriculture and industry.

The more affluent North enjoyed higher consumption of imports, but ran far worse current account deficits. Although the labor force was still predominantly agricultural, especially in the North, over half of gross domestic product in both systems was generated by services; the rate of new investment in services, especially government services, indicated that this trend would continue. The level of education and health services—slightly better in the South, especially for women—put both countries among the world's least developed nations. While central planning was a goal of the leadership in the South, in the North planning was not an ideological commitment but rather part of the documentation required by the International Monetary Fund and the World Bank.

Property Relations

The South, with its colonial legacy, entered the 1960s with many more capitalist enterprises than North Yemen. South Yemeni nationalizations and land reforms created a modern state sector, and dramatically equalized land ownership, but retained many features of a traditional agrarian economy comparable to that of North Yemen, which was just embarking on its first commercial and industrial projects.

Production systems in the South included subsistence agriculture on family land mixed with herding on commons, sharecropping on pre-capitalist estates, and wage labor on modern farms. In Aden and Lahij, where ownership was most distinctively class-divided, the revolutionary regime expropriated the largest holdings as well as religious endowments (*waqf*). The number of expropriated estates increased from 18 to 47 between 1975 and 1982 with the addition of some smaller properties of unpopular landlords. These state farms, with modern equipment and wage labor, managed most farmland in Aden governorate and nearly a third in Lahij just to the north. Redistributed land, nearly two-thirds of the South's cultivated area, was classified as cooperative. Over a quarter, mostly in the east, remained private.

By contrast, the revolution in the North nationalized only the royal family's prime tracts. Over half of the large farms were private and were conservatively managed, frequently employing sharecrop labor and moving only slowly toward capitalist farming. Most dry land in both systems consisted of family-cultivated parcels or open range. Well into the 1980s, at least half of Yemeni farms produced cereals and livestock for cultivation. The only popular, profitable cash crop in the highlands was the narcotic leaf, qat, outlawed in the South and discouraged by the North's Ministry of Agriculture.

Both regimes advocated farm mechanization, yet typical Yemeni farmers planting sorghum or millet with their own draft animals on small, scattered, often terraced parcels were unable to profitably invest in pumps, tractors or trucks, even with remittance income. Each regime turned to cooperatives around 1974, hoping to combine petty savings and remittances for investment in nurseries, equipment, repair stations, storage facilities and marketing services. Southern holders of redistributed land formed purchasing and marketing cooperatives. Sixty-odd cooperatives helped up to 50,000 members acquire inputs in the mid-1980s, but instead of moving toward full-scale cooperative farms, 29 state farms abandoned group farming and only two produced collectively.

Although Northern cooperatives built stopgap rural infrastructure, the 20-odd agricultural, fishing and craft cooperatives foundered on both credit and marketing. Voluntary participation often made no sense as an investment. While a few cooperatives profitably ran diesel stations or rented drilling rigs, most failed to mobilize and manage share capital.

After nationalization, public ventures controlled 60–70 percent of the value of industry in the PDRY, including power and water and the oil refinery (the single largest employer). Mixed companies produced cigarettes, batteries and aluminum utensils; wholly private firms were either small-scale plastic, clothing, glass, food and paper goods manufacturers or traditional carpentry, metal, pottery or weaving industries.

Whereas the South inherited modern plants and offices, the North embarked on its first modern enterprises only in 1970. Despite liberal investment incentives, private manufacturing grew slowly. An industrial complex near Ta'iz producing sweets, soaps and plastics, owned by the Hayel Sa'id Group, dominated large-scale private industry. The remaining large private factories were mostly food processors or bottlers. Light industry consisted mainly of repair and construction "workshops" and crafts.

Unlike in other Third World countries with a large pool of labor, the proximity to the Persian Gulf's oil economies drove wage levels up. Roughly a third of adult males were absent for at least a year or two at a time during the oil-boom decade (1974–84). The North imported not only teachers and health professionals but construction and hotel workers. While planners and international experts were initially optimistic about the investment potential of remittances, the class that benefited most from *laissez-faire* were Northern-based moneychangers and importers, middlemen to the migration-and-consumption cycle. The North's open import markets attracted a commercial bourgeoisie from the lower Red Sea region, resulting in a predominance of service sector investments. Those with cash to invest—local traders, North Yemeni migrants to the Gulf, and entrepreneurs from Aden, Asmara, Djibouti or Mombasa—were lured to the North's currency, real estate and import markets, where they profited from the hefty share of remittances spent on consumer goods.

Extraordinarily unfettered currency and import markets worked better for the YAR during the boom than the bust cycle. Global recession and depressed oil rents slashed remittance and aid levels, undermining, postponing or eliminating private and public projects by the thousands. The Yemeni riyal, having been kept artificially high at a uniform rate of 4.5 riyals to the dollar for over a decade (stimulating imports), plummeted to 18 to the dollar in the winter of 1986–87. Facing balance of payments and currency reserve crises from 1982 onward, Sana'a temporarily banned all imports, blocked rampant smuggling, reformed and enforced tax codes and, in late 1986, took over currency markets and halted new investment projects. The secondhand bonanza in the North was gone, and with it the "hands-off" policy of economic non-management.

Ownership and Investment

Ideologies differed from plans, and plans from outcomes. At best, the North's capitalist orientation and the South's socialism represented tendencies or goals, for both were really "mixed" economies.

The relative contribution of private and public capital can be measured in several ways. The North experienced a trend during the oil boom away from private capital formation toward public investment. In 1975, the private sector provided two-thirds and the state only one-third, but these proportions were reversed by 1982. By 1987, the North Yemen government financed three-quarters of investments in agriculture, fisheries, transport and communications, and nearly all utilities and mining development—amounting to two-thirds of all investment. Individuals funded most new construction, trade and hotel business, and 70 percent of manufacturing. Private investors' preference for real estate speculation over agricultural production was particularly disconcerting to planners; whereas overall growth was a healthy 6.6 percent, in agriculture it was only 2.4 percent.

Nor was the PDRY ever an entirely state-owned economy. The nationalizations of 1969 affected foreign financial, trade and services businesses. Between 1973 and 1976, consolidation of state and joint industrial ventures continued, reducing the contribution of private domestic firms to industrial production from 51 percent to 38 percent, and the contribution of foreign firms from 36 percent to 10 percent. In fishing, however, foreign investors replaced some cooperative production. By 1976, private domestic and foreign firms held about 40 percent of the construction market, and local private transportation had over half the market. Cooperatives were credited with 71 percent of agricultural output, and the state with the rest, but livestock production was over 90 percent private. This was as "socialist" as the South got.

In Aden's plan for 1981–85 targets for private investments increased, and during the first three years of the plan private-sector participation exceeded expectations by 8 percent, mostly in agriculture and local private fishing. The 1988 census reported that of nearly 35,000 establishments, 75 percent were private, 21 percent governmental, and the remainder cooperative or joint ventures. Just over a quarter of the work force was in the government sector.

All these figures are estimates that probably understate subsistence, smuggling and some informal trade. Cumulatively the evidence is sufficient to conclude that state and private sectors each played significant roles in both economies. There is little sign of sharp contrasts between centralized public ownership in the South and private enterprise in the North. Although their revolutions committed them to divergent paths, 20 years of practice produced convergent patterns. The explanation lies in the development projects supported by foreign donors.

Foreign Finance

Before the first Yemeni oil discovery in 1984, Yemen depended on aid rather than foreign companies for capital investment. International "soft" loans to the public sector represented the largest single source of new

capital formation between 1970 and 1990. International companies participated either as contractors on donor-financed or nationalized state projects, where they earned profits but committed no capital, or as minority
partners in public enterprises, to which they brought both capital and expertise. Once the oil industry began to take off, foreign private and public
firms competed for roles in Yemen as contractors, partners and investors.

The foreign-owned private sector in the PDRY was limited. BP and
Cable & Wireless did contract work for state corporations. BP, Mobil and
a joint Yemeni-Kuwaiti company supplied petroleum. Planners spoke of
foreign firms as a source of capital for development, and a few Arab, Asian
and Eastern European firms entered the market.

In the North, the Arab world's most liberal foreign investment policies attracted only a few foreign ventures, which raised much of their capital locally. Canada Dry, Ramada and Sheraton were the most visible; since
the hotels imported their own staffs, only the locally owned bottler was a
source of significant jobs. Other companies bought shares of Yemeni public corporations: A subsidiary of British Rothman had a 25 percent partnership and five expatriate employees in the National Tobacco & Matches
Company, and the Saudi al-Ahli Commercial Bank and Bank of America
together owned 45 percent of the International Bank of Yemen. Citibank
found an economy where two-thirds of the cash circulated outside the formal banking system to be an unprofitable market. Scores of American,
Arab, Asian and European contractors were active with donor projects:
In roads, for instance, American and European engineers, Lebanese contractors, and South Korean and Chinese work forces (cheaper and more
skilled than Yemenis) were not unusual.

By the 1980s, the overall patterns of external financing in the two
Yemens were remarkably similar. For more than a decade, the West and
the conservative states of the Peninsula had shunned the South while the
Soviet Union, its allies, China, and radical Arab regimes were the main
benefactors of both North and South. The global and regional multilateral agencies did work with the South, however, led by the World Bank's
International Development Association (IDA). After 1980 the easing of
tensions on the Peninsula prompted Saudi Arabia, Kuwait and Abu Dhabi
to offer assistance; by the middle of the decade, Arab funds surpassed assistance from socialist countries. In North Yemen the Arab oil monarchies were the most visible donors in the 1970s, and the IDA exercised the
most influence in economic policy. North Yemen's development assistance
peaked in about 1981 at over $1 billion, and declined to half that amount
in 1985 and to less than $100 million in 1988.

By that time, both countries relied on a similar list of donors and creditors. Grants were normally limited to small-scale technical assistance programs from the UN or European donors, or showy "gifts" from wealthy Gulf monarchs. Most new capital formation came from "soft" loans with low-interest charges and long repayment schedules. Thus debts accumulated against the accounts of international benefactors roughly in proportion to the amount of aid provided. The extent of polarization between "socialist" and "capitalist" trends was mitigated by the fact of Arab, IDA, Soviet, Chinese and European loans for both development programs. Infrastructural projects were the bedrock of government development investment. Bilateral donors chose their own design, engineering and construction firms, and global and Arab multilaterals applied the World Bank bids and tender system.

Utilities—immense industrial plants supplying urban water and power nationwide—were also financed from diverse sources. After studying the South's poorly functioning Soviet-built system, World Bank economists recommended an all-Yemen electrification grid to maximize economies of scale, and IDA initiated financing for this joint grid in the mid-1980s. While not the first joint North-South venture, this involved unprecedented inter-Yemeni coordination.

Integrated rural development (IRD) was the multilateral agencies' strategy to equip rural regions with roads, utilities and some social services. The most prominent IRD projects followed the World Bank model, whereby infrastructure, credit and technical assistance stimulate rural investments by individuals or cooperatives. They were introduced in the areas of North Yemen best suited to intensive cash farming: the semi-tropical Tihama plain and the temperate southern uplands. By 1987 integrated projects, with different components from IDA, UN organizations, several Arab funds and the European Community, at least theoretically covered most rural areas.

These schemes followed a similar pattern in both countries. The South's largest IRD project, the Wadi Hadramawt project, stressing road construction, groundwater studies, deep wells mechanization, and credit through cooperatives for fertilizers and pesticides, was modeled on the Tihama Development Authority project. The only difference was that in the South credit was available exclusively to cooperatives, whereas in the North, private loan applications were also accepted. Had farmers flocked to mortgage their land for bank loans (other than for qat, disallowed from loan applications), this might have been a significant difference; instead, credit officers in both systems bemoaned the lack of applications, and public spending in agriculture far outpaced private and/or cooperative financing.

Petroleum

The latest stage in the convergence of the two economies occurred in the nascent petroleum industry. Here the convergence was literal: Deposits discovered in the border region were jointly developed by the two states in cooperation with international firms.

Both state petroleum companies relied on foreign expertise. Soviet companies conducted on- and off-shore studies for the South, and by the late 1970s concessions were won or under negotiation by British, French, Italian, Spanish, Kuwaiti and Brazilian firms. Thirteen international firms had explored in the North. In 1984, Yemen Hunt, then a wholly owned local subsidiary of Texas-based Hunt Oil, made the first significant discovery, beyond Marib near the joint border. Soon Exxon, and then a consortium of South Korean firms, bought into Yemen Hunt; Texaco, Elf Aquitaine, Total, Canadian Occidental and Soviet firms bought rights to drill. The Soviet company Technoexport made a major find in 1986 at Shabwa, across the intra-Yemeni border from Marib. Discoveries in turn created scores of subcontracting opportunities for suppliers and builders from around the globe, such as the US firm that built a small modular refinery near Marib and a Lebanese-Italian-German group that laid the pipeline. There were new commercial finds in 1987, 1988 and 1989.

Realization of the commercial potential of the Marib-Shabwa basin required both inter-Yemeni cooperation and foreign capital and expertise. Not only was security around oil fields astride the border improved by joint production, but the North hoped to use existing facilities at Aden, including the port and the refurbished BP refinery, which in turn needed the business. Cooperation avoided both conflict and duplication. The two national petroleum companies merged their operations into a joint Yemen Company for Investment in Oil and Mineral Resources, which signed a production agreement in late 1989 with an international consortium consisting of Hunt and Exxon, the Kuwait Foreign Petroleum Exploration Corporation, Total, and two subsidiaries of Technoexport.

This commercial agreement culminated the 20-year convergence of two ideologically different systems on a common, and eventually joint, pattern of public-foreign partnership on the "commanding heights." A more "mixed" venture could hardly be imagined, for the whole package included not just the joint Yemeni corporation but two of the largest capitalist oil giants, Exxon and Total, and Soviet and Kuwaiti state corporations. Destined to overshadow the value of property and investment in other sectors, this technically public venture was shortly followed by the political unity accord.

[...]

Many of the arguments advanced for unity stressed the economic advantages, such as combining Aden port facilities with the North's private transport network, utilizing both the South's professional cadres and Northern-based entrepreneurs, taking advantage of larger markets and economies of scale and maintaining all existing foreign trade and aid relationships. The prospect of economic improvement offered considerable popular appeal because of widespread political unease and economic dissatisfaction in both polities, personal and social ties of the Northern bourgeoisie to families or places in the South, political leaders' cross-cutting ties, and a common sense of nationalism.

[...]

Before any economic benefits of unification could be realized, the Gulf crisis disrupted the flow of remittances and aid from Kuwait, Iraq and Saudi Arabia. Newly unemployed migrants and their families, numbering upwards of a million, streamed into the cities just as operating funds in many social services sectors drained away. By early 1991, the value of the riyal, having stabilized at about 13 to the dollar, collapsed to 26 to the dollar. The government suspended civil service salaries to cover the costs of currency support and vital operations. By that summer, unemployment, inflation and the strains on housing and services prompted public marches and demonstrations. Oil revenues were not only insufficient to cover the losses of foreign exchange, but they were threatened by Saudi claims to oil in the border region. Once again, politics abroad and changes in the world economy disrupted Yemen's economic plans.

3 Yemen After Unification: Elections and Civil War

Some optimists—I confess that in 1993, while on a Fulbright fellowship at Sana'a University, I was one—anticipated that Yemeni unity would introduce a more viable economy with a more democratic political system. As it happened, Yemeni unification all but coincided with the Iraqi invasion and annexation of Kuwait in the summer of 1990 that, in turn, prompted a massive multilateral military operation known as Desert Storm. Kuwait's occupation and liberation constituted a turning point in the history of the Peninsula for many reasons. For the monarchies of the Gulf, it marked a new era for the Carter Doctrine and a deepening American role in guaranteeing their longevity. For people in Yemen, it precipitated a deep economic crisis fueled by losses of both remittances and foreign aid. Comparatively free and fair elections in 1993, however free-wheeling and reflective of popular and elite demands for democratization, did not lead to a viable power-sharing agreement by two former ruling parties. Instead, within 12 months, Yemen became a case of "from ballot box to bullets."

It has been downhill ever since.

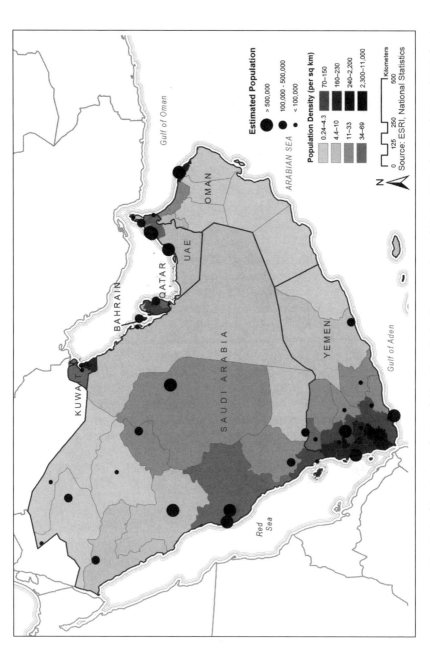

Map 3: Arabian Peninsula Population Density by Governorate and Major Cities by Population. (2014 data) Produced by the Spatial Analysis Lab, University of Richmond

Yemen: Unification and the Gulf War

Sheila Carapico • *MER* 170, Summer 1991

On May 22, 1990, the People's Democratic Republic of Yemen (or South Yemen) and the Yemen Arab Republic joined to become the Republic of Yemen. [...] Unity offered beneficial economies of scale in oil, power, administrative apparatus and tourism. It made political sense, too, reflecting the view of most Yemenis that the division into separate countries was artificial and imposed.

Formal unification heralded unprecedented pluralism and political opening. Televised debates in Parliament, dominated by the former ruling parties of the YAR and the PDRY, the General People's Congress and the Yemeni Socialist Party, exposed bureaucratic corruption. Some three dozen new parties, of Nasserist, Baathist, liberal and religious orientations, began publishing newspapers and organizing for the May 1992 elections. Sana'a University students demonstrated to replace national security police with student workers as campus guards. Military checkpoints virtually disappeared from Sana'a, Aden, and the highway between them. In June and July of 1990, the mood was like that in Prague.

For all its popularity, Yemeni unification is anathema to Saudi Arabia. Although the YAR's more conservative social, economic and political system appeared to dominate the new union, a unified Yemen of 13 or 14 million people posed a potential military threat, the Saudis felt, and its relative freedom of press, assembly and participation, including women's participation, could set a dangerous example. Riyadh tersely congratulated the new republic, but covertly subsidized an opposition "reform" party of conservative tribes and fundamentalists.

Washington has traditionally dealt with North Yemen through Riyadh. Sana'a got a modest $30 million or so annually in US development assistance. The PDRY was on the State Department's list of "terrorist states." Economic plans of the unified state called for freer trade and investment, and Soviet influence seemed on the wane. When 'Ali 'Abdallah Salih became the first Yemeni president to visit Washington in January 1990, two months after being designated to lead the future unified state, the [George H.W.] Bush administration approved $50 million in trade credits. YAR ambassador Muhsin al-'Ayni stayed on in Washington, while the PDRY's 'Abdallah al-Ashtal remained as the new country's UN delegate.

It was against the backdrop of this most important event in its recent history that Yemen responded to the Iraqi invasion of Kuwait. Initially opinion was divided, but the balance shifted after Saddam Hussein, in his first major speech of the crisis, declared that Iraq had been inspired by the Yemeni example to pursue Arab unity by erasing colonial boundaries, and Saudi commentators lambasted Sana'a for refusing to commit troops to the Kingdom's defense. The Saudi request for US troops to confront Iraq prompted extraordinary protest demonstrations, and the consensus at many qat chews shifted decisively against Saudi Arabia. At the same time, pro-Saudi elements formed a Committee for the Defense of the Rights of Kuwait.

Mindful of both the public mood and longer-term interest in maintaining ties with the West and the Gulf, the government declared and held to a policy of neutrality. The Salih regime condemned the invasion, hostage taking and annexation, but did not support sanctions or use of force resolutions. UN representative al-Ashtal became the Security Council's most prominent, consistent advocate for diplomacy.

The al-Saud took this neutrality as an affront. They cut aid in August. Next, they summarily revoked special residence and working privileges for over a million of the Yemenis in the Kingdom, life-long residents as well as short-term sojourners, forcing the majority to sell what they could at distressed prices and head south.

The sudden suspension of Saudi, Kuwaiti and Iraqi aid, the embargo of Iraqi oil shipments, the collapse of tourism and the decline in regional commerce cost Yemen nearly $2 billion in 1990, although a sudden infusion of migrants' remittances cushioned the blow. While ministries struggled to pay faculty and health workers' salaries previously financed from the Gulf, investment plans were scaled back, the riyal's value dropped, prices rose sharply, and a half-million returnees camped outside Sana'a.

Yemen's refusal to join the coalition caused the deepest rift in Washington-Sana'a relations since June 1967, but it also captured US attention. Secretary of State James Baker visited Sana'a but failed to persuade the government to join the US-Saudi axis. President 'Ali 'Abdallah Salih repeated Yemen's condemnation of Iraq's invasion but observed that intervention by a massive multinational force was liable to "destabilize the entire region."

American dependents—the Peace Corps, the US Agency for International Development (USAID), the US Information Agency—their European counterparts and business people gradually evacuated. Once the war began, the remaining 20 US diplomats and Marines moved into the embassy, and oil industry employees stayed off the streets. Yemeni media now carried Baghdad's war coverage, along with denunciations of

Voice of America and the BBC. After some demonstrations, and then a calm, someone threw grenades at the Sana'a International School, there were small explosions at several embassies, and the heavily fortified US compound came under machine-gun fire from a passing car.

News of the US bombing of a Baghdad shelter full of civilians and of the ground assault politicized Sana'a as never before. While the Arab League's minority anti-war faction met at the Haddah Ramada, Tahrir Square overflowed with tens of thousands of enraged students and expelled migrants.

In the confluence of these events—a new nationalism, sudden lifting of political constraints, a war jeopardizing national and individual well-being, and a leading role at the UN—Yemenis and their government feel they have found a political voice. Popular slogans against the war and the Gulf monarchies have helped legitimize a regime which, in turn, tried to play a mediating role in the Arab League and the Security Council. Saudi and US "punishment" has so far only heightened a sense of nationalist self-righteousness. This will deepen if Yemen and other poor Arab states that declined to back the war are forced to pay.

Yemeni Workers Come Home: Reabsorbing One Million Migrants

Thomas Stevenson • *MER 181, Mar./Apr. 1993*

With its moderate climate and terraced highlands, Yemen is agriculturally the most productive part of the Arabian Peninsula. Yet people, not crops, have been Yemen's major export. Migrants from the former North and South Yemen are scattered throughout the world. During the last 20 years, the majority of Yemeni migrants have gone to neighboring oil states. With up to 30 percent of adult men abroad at a time, migration affected virtually every household. The earnings of the roughly 1.25 million expatriates, coupled with heavy foreign assistance, fueled the region's socioeconomic transformation, particularly in the north. This era of prosperity ended abruptly when Iraq invaded Kuwait in early August 1990.

[...]

The invasion immediately forced approximately 45,000 Yemenis and dependents to flee Kuwait and Iraq. When Yemen subsequently took a neutral stance and refused to support the Saudi invitation to US forces, Riyadh rescinded the special status that had allowed Yemenis to enter Saudi Arabia without the work permits and guarantees required of other migrants. Between 800,000 and 1 million people were forced home as a result. Some 2,000 Yemenis were forced to leave Qatar, Bahrain and the UAE. This represented a population increase of about 8 percent. Yemen's ambassador to the United Nations, 'Abdallah al-Ashtal, compares it to the United States suddenly taking in 30 million people. For the fledgling, financially strapped government of Yemen, the crisis was compounded by the disruption of normal relations. Sana'a claimed it lost $1.7 billion in foreign assistance (primarily from Saudi Arabia, Kuwait and Iraq), oil supplies, foreign trade and workers' remittances. Lost remittances were estimated at only $400 million, although in 1987 remittances for the two Yemens amounted to $1.06 billion.

Migrant Context

Yemen's export of workers has been a major source of foreign exchange, and remittances a key factor in socioeconomic modernization of the country. For all Yemenis, migration to Saudi Arabia was easy. They could obtain a visa at any port of entry, often without a passport; they did not require a sponsor for work or residence permits, and could own businesses.

Many migrants used their savings to supplement household incomes in Yemen. With about a quarter of adult men from the north and a third from the south abroad, their families grew dependent on remittances. Both national economies came to rely on migrants' earnings, which accounted for as much as 20 percent of gross domestic product in the north and 50 percent in the south.

In the north, remittances financed a construction boom and the rapid expansion of petty commerce. The easy escape of excess labor opened positions for, and raised wages of, workers at home. Migration from South Yemen, rather than being a safety valve for excess labor and a means of acquiring skills, led to labor shortages and skill deficits. As a result, Aden severely restricted migration after 1973. Those working abroad became, in essence, permanent migrants. Despite government attempts to encourage investment, most money and acquired skills remained abroad. Only since unification and their return have migrants from the south begun spending their savings as had those in the north.

The typical migrant was a single man who stayed abroad two to five years. By the mid-1980s, though, many had brought their families to live with them in Saudi Arabia. In 1990, an estimated one-third of the 285,000 migrant workers in Saudi Arabia were accompanied by their families. The decision to have their families join them seems to have coincided with migrants' shifting from the volatile and competitive construction sector to more secure positions in the services sector.

Yemen's position in the Gulf crisis may have been only one factor in the Saudi decision to expel the migrants. The Saudis were angry with Yemen's unification and, some suggest, sought to undermine the new government, sensing that the unification dynamics made Yemeni migrants potentially more threatening to Saudi internal security.

Another speculative explanation derives from changes in the Saudi economy. In the 1980s, many migrants moved into low-status service positions—taxi drivers, storekeepers, bakers, small business contractors and farm workers—once held by Saudis. Yemenis also began to bring their families, making themselves semi-permanent features on the Saudi economic landscape. As oil revenues declined, the Saudi labor market shrank. At the same time, the number of Saudi vocational school graduates increased, but desirable service positions were no longer readily available. One way to create openings was to eliminate the Yemeni competitive advantage. This was apparently behind the Saudi attempt in the late 1980s to implement a law requiring unincorporated businesses to be Saudi-owned. North Yemeni president 'Ali 'Abdallah Salih interceded then—to secure a special exclusion for Yemenis. This exclusion was canceled on September 19, 1990, and the status of Yemenis reverted to that of other migrants. They were given 30 days to find a Saudi guarantor or majority partner for businesses, and to obtain residence permits. The deadline was subsequently extended for another 30 days.

An unknown but probably small number did arrange to comply with the new regulations. Many, perhaps the majority, seem not to have expended much effort to do so. Some were motivated by nationalist feelings; others felt they could not satisfy the requirements. The result was a rush to liquidate assets, pack or sell possessions, and prepare to return to Yemen.

The Return

Those Yemenis suffering the greatest financial loss and dislocation were those forced to flee Iraq and Kuwait, leaving everything behind. Most migrants in Kuwait were native to Hadramawt, and many returned there.

The losses of returnees from Saudi Arabia were less severe. Although there were reports that the Saudis had detained and tortured hundreds of Yemenis, no migrants with whom I spoke reported being mistreated.

Most returnees, however, did accuse those who bought their property of profiting from their expulsion. Many were forced to sell their property and possessions at absurdly low prices. Hammoud Husayn, a migrant for over 30 years, owned three rental properties in Riyadh that he valued at 275,000 Saudi riyals. He was able to sell them for only 40,000 riyals. Many sellers received a fraction of their invested capital, especially those with tea shops, restaurants or bakeries. Sana'a estimates the returnees lost $7.9 billion in assets.

For Yemen, the greatest impact came from trying to meet the needs of up to 40,000 returning migrants a day. The government sent trucks to the border to transfer returnees and their property to receiving points in Yemen. Customs rules were relaxed so most possessions were duty-free. To defray costs and aid in resettlement, government and private-sector employees were ordered to contribute one day's pay per month for three months to a resettlement fund.

The government pledged to create jobs and provide housing, schools and health centers. The estimated cost of these programs was $245 million, but funds from the World Bank, USAID, Germany, the UN and Yemen amounted to only $60 million. Sana'a made available 60 million Yemeni riyals. Promised programs did not get off the ground. Preliminary funds provided and administered by the UN Development Program set up an Emergency Recovery Program but not much else.

Returnees found more obstacles to resettling in Yemen than they anticipated. Most single returnees were accepted in the homes of kin, as were many returning highland families. Some 11.5 percent owned homes in Yemen. Some returnees with dependents needed assistance. The government provided temporary housing in schools and hospitals. In the hardest-hit areas, Hudayda and Aden, vacant lands were transformed into tent cities. The population of Hudayda tripled to more than 500,000 people. According to the returnees, probably between 75,000 and 100,000 families were directed to camps, where they remain.

Why did hundreds of thousands end up in camps? Many returnees, especially those from the Tihama area along the Red Sea coast, had been abroad more than ten years. They had lived for years in urban areas and were unwilling to return to the countryside.

A second factor is the returnees' status, a key element in Yemeni culture. According to some Yemeni social scientists, many migrants were from the lowest-status group known as the *akhdam* (literally "servant"). Predominately from Tihama, *akhdam* are generally described as having

African heritage. They traditionally performed tasks like street sweeping that others refused. For them, emigration was a way to shed this culturally imposed status. Having severed ties to their birthplaces intentionally, these returnees were unwilling to return to villages where their ancestry was known.

Finally, Yemen suffers from a housing shortage. This is most severe in urban areas of the former South Yemen. The 11.5 percent of migrants who owned houses they could return to in turn forced their tenants into the housing market. Some 32 percent of returnees found housing, often temporarily with kin. The majority of returnees, 56.5 percent, having limited resources and confronted with skyrocketing rents, had no place to go.

In Yemeni culture, family is central and custom demands that kin support each other. In Tihama, though, many returnees had long ago severed any such connections. In Aden, there was simply no space; some men were able to house family members with kin but had to find other quarters for themselves. People reported that their relatives' homes were overcrowded and life stressful. Camps were the alternative.

Broader Impact

Repatriation brought $1.36 billion to Yemen, but the remittance flow slowed dramatically. Once the returnees' resources were exhausted, the ripple effects were many. The lack of foreign exchange drove inflation up.

Migration had created a relative labor shortage and high wages, even for day laborers. The return reversed this trend. Skilled returnees displaced less-skilled workers. The influx of returnees drove unemployment from around 4 percent to 25 percent, with 40 percent unemployment among former migrants.

Peddling and begging proliferated. In addition to adults, scores of children spend their days on the street instead of in schools, helping to support their families. Shortages and inflation pushed food prices up by more than 200 percent between 1990 and 1992. The United Nations Development Program reported the number of people living in poverty rose from 15 to 35 percent. (The official poverty line is a family income of 3,000 Yemeni riyals per month—$250 at the official exchange rate, but in reality less than $100—an amount that would permit only the most modest existence even if one had housing.) Overcrowded conditions and malnutrition became common.

The crisis is nationwide. In October 1991, middle-class protests erupted in Sana'a. Frustrated by high prices, lack of jobs and increasing poverty, demonstrations again broke out in mid-December 1992 in Taʻiz, where thousands reportedly participated in looting and burning. The riots spread to Sanaʻa, where they lasted four days. Smaller demonstrations occurred in Hudayda, al-Bayda and Ibb; unrest spread even to small towns. More than 60 people were killed, hundreds injured and thousands arrested. The government reportedly brought 8,000 armed tribesmen into the capital to maintain power.

[...]

There was talk of job creation schemes such as road and agricultural projects, but this has not happened. Whether it was lack of funds and resources, lack of planning or simply lack of commitment, the government has not done much to alleviate the crisis. In the end most returnees have had to rely on whatever assistance kin and friends have been able to provide.

Elections and Mass Politics

Sheila Carapico • *MER* 185, Nov./Dec. 1993

The Yemeni parliamentary election of April 27, 1993, marks a watershed for the Arabian Peninsula. The multiparty contest for 301 constituency-based seats, and the period of unfettered public debate and discussion that preceded it, represents the advent of organized mass politics in a region where political power has long remained a closely held family affair.

[...]

Yemen's commitment to elections accompanied the unification agreement between ʻAli ʻAbdallah Salih, president of the Yemen Arab Republic, and ʻAli Salim al-Bayd, leader of the ruling party in the People's Democratic Republic. Following formal unification on May 22, 1990, a five-member Presidential Council headed by Salih held executive power, and the two former parliaments were combined in a unified Chamber of Deputies. Under a constitution approved by national referendum in May 1991, political parties organized openly and most restrictions on association, expression and movement were lifted. The 1991 referendum specified that the elections be held within 30 months of unification, but a combination of technical problems, procrastination and conflicts between "ʻAli and ʻAli" (Salih and al-Bayd) postponed polling beyond the November 1992 deadline.

[...]

Arab leaders have promised free elections in the past and not delivered. What made Salih and al-Bayd—neither of whose personal histories indicates a commitment to political liberalism—follow through? The answer lies in societal pressures which took different forms: mass conferences, strikes, demonstrations, political organizations, press commentaries, academic symposia and *maqiyal* or "salons."

Prior to the elections, a series of mass conferences provided outlets for articulate opposition elements. A nine-day Talahum (Cohesion) Conference in December 1991 gathered some 10,000 men; although its banner was the Bakil tribal confederation, urban intellectuals were among the organizers and authors of a 33-point resolution calling for judicial independence, strengthening of representative parliamentary and local bodies, fiscal restraint and management, revitalization of agricultural and services cooperatives, an independent media, environmental protection, free elections within the mandated time frame, peaceful resolution of tribal conflicts and other reforms. At least seven other tribe-based but civic-oriented mass conferences in 1992 each issued written demands for the rule of law, pluralism, economic development and local autonomy. The Saba' (Sheba) Conference of Bakil and Madhaj tribes elected a council of trustees, a council of social reform and follow-up committees to ensure institutional continuity.

This activity culminated with a national conference of representatives of the smaller center and left parties and political organizations, led by 'Umar al-Jawi. This time, the two ruling parties strove to delay, discourage, coopt and eventually offset what promised to be a major event by holding a simultaneous counter-conference and by arranging the ouster of their opponents from the Sana'a Cultural Center to the local Sheraton. Well publicized in the opposition press but ignored by the official media, the center-left conference criticized delayed preparations for the elections and the government's reckless printing of money, and proposed a code of political conduct for political parties. The Ta'iz Conference in November 1992, headed by 'Abd al-Rahman al-Jifri , went even further in attracting faculty, journalists and professionals; challenging Ta'iz's governor; constituting steering and work councils; and articulating explicit demands for civic and human rights, local elections and improved local services. Not to be outdone, the Islah organized a 4,000-strong Unity and Peace Conference in December under the slogan "The Qur'an and the Sunna Supersede the Constitution and the Law."

These conferences, both tribal and urban-based, involving tens of thousands of people, were among the transition period's most important political developments. In response, the regime felt compelled to adopt its own code of political conduct, dismiss the Ta'iz governor, accept the principle of local elections and adopt a rhetoric of electoral rights. There were also several outbursts of popular frustration, most notably in December 1992. Outrage with the collapse of the value of the riyal, inadequate services, mounting unemployment, government corruption and postponement of the elections erupted in mass demonstrations against both the state and private merchants in all major cities. Along with strikes and threatened strikes by groups ranging from garbage collectors to judges, the near-riots reminded the government of the power of popular wrath.

On a smaller scale but a more institutionalized basis, numerous independent political organizations emerged. The Committee for the Defense of Human Rights and Liberties, established by liberal university professors, initiated the National Committee for Free Elections, in turn spurring the formation of other electoral NGOs. Although they failed on their own terms to guarantee the integrity of the balloting process, they did perform a modest watchdog function and met again after the elections to prepare for the next round. Syndicates, charities and interest groups have also been increasingly active in the political process.

The press is also significant within the political arena. More than 100 partisan and independent newspapers and magazines, mostly founded since 1990, covered these events. Although the government daily, *al-Thawra*, and state-run television and radio tend to dominate news coverage, a number of opposition weeklies have a strong readership among the literate, urban, politically active population: *Sawt al-'Ummal* (Voice of the Workers), based in Aden, has the largest circulation of any paper. Party organs, including al-Ra'y, al-Tashih, al-Sahwa and others, provide critical commentary and information about opposition conferences and independent organizations. There has emerged a press corps of scores of men and several dozen women who more and more approximate a fourth estate, conducting interviews, attending Parliament, asking critical questions at press conferences, testing the limits of press law and defending one another against lawsuits.

Related to the mass conferences, political organizing and press activity was a trend toward academic symposia on topics such as the constitutional amendments, administrative decentralization, municipal services and the campaign experience of women candidates. Typically inviting members of each party and independent specialists, such symposia, virtually unheard of in the old North or South Yemen, provided fora for discussion, debate and refinement of ideas which were then reported in the opposition press.

More frequent and informal is an updated variation on the male qat session, or *maqiyal*, which approximates the "salons" of nineteenth-century Europe. Nowadays these customarily informal social gatherings may elect a chair, select a topic, establish rules of order and hold organized political discussion on topics ranging from relations with the Gulf to women's rights to exchange rate policy.

Collectively, these civic activities applied considerable pressure on the regime to fulfill its promises, abide by a code of conduct, address its critics and respect political pluralism. Several Yemeni intellectuals have criticized international observers and reporters for presenting an unduly positive picture of the electoral experience, and many participants in the conferences and seminars are quite cynical about their own influence, insisting that they have been marginalized from the political process. By the same token, it is difficult to imagine the events of the past year taking place had they been passive.

The Yemeni Elections Up Close

Renaud Detalle • *MER* 185, Nov./Dec. 1993

Candidate registration for Yemen's first-ever multiparty elections opened on March 29 in a climate of lively polemics against the president's party, the General People's Congress (GPC). The GPC's permanent committee had approved its electoral program on March 27. That same evening it appropriated an hour of television and radio time to present its proposals, shoving aside the law which stipulated that access to the official media was subject to the provisions of the Supreme Elections Committee (SEC) in the framework of equality between the parties. The head of the SEC's information subcommittee immediately distributed a letter condemning this violation and threatened to resign. The GPC subsequently felt compelled to play by the rules.

The biggest campaign surprise of the week-long registration period was the huge number of independent candidates—3,246 out of the 4,602 who registered—made possible by an electoral law that required candidates only to be literate, of good moral standing, religiously observant and not to have been convicted of any crime. A requirement to submit 300 voter signatures from the electoral district was dropped from the law.

The high number of independent candidates was the result of several factors. Local notables were testing their appeal. Some enlisted only in order to negotiate a rewarding withdrawal. The big parties—the GPC, the Yemeni Socialist Party (YSP) and the Islah—hoped that the distribution of votes among independents would benefit their candidates, who were supported by activists and enjoyed proximity to power. The two ruling parties also had to face candidates originally from their own ranks who ran as independents because the parties had nominated others or because as civil servants and members of the armed forces they could not have a formal party affiliation.

In putting together their slate, the GPC looked for persons well-rooted in their communities, with party affiliation taking second place. Many tribal leaders, of course, but also big merchants and high officials, ran in urban centers if they were not certain of their support at home. In the South, the GPC was able to enjoy the support of partisans of 'Ali Nasir Muhammad, the former PDRY president ousted in 1986, by presenting a number of their candidates under its banner. Similarly, the YSP was able to count on its long-standing presence in the North through the old National Democratic Front. The YSP's superior internal organization and activist tradition accounted for the presence among its candidates of a large number of its Central Committee members and government ministers.

The candidates of the Islah were divided between local notables, mainly sheikhs linked to Sheikh 'Abdallah, and university-educated Islamists in the cities. Al-Haqq's list of 67 candidates was a veritable who's who of the *sayyid* families. The candidates of the League of the Sons of Yemen represented some of the most prestigious sheikhly families of Shabwa and Hadramawt. In addition to the three main parties, the League and the Baath were the only parties to put forward candidates in almost all the provinces.

Most of the parties formulated platforms which, if they had at least ten candidates, they could present on radio and TV (twice for 20 minutes) and in the official daily, *al-Thawra*. The GPC's program detailed, sector after sector, all types of measures that attested to apparently liberal and democratic convictions. The YSP adopted a social-democratic line and presented itself as the champion of democracy, modernization and order. The YSP program's priorities were to establish order and security in the country by suppressing violence and moving swiftly against those responsible for corruption via an independent judiciary. In the social domain, the YSP proposed to improve medical care, develop public housing and improve access to education. The party catered to those who accused them of irreligiosity by calling for an Islamic university which, the Socialists claimed, would be a training center for clerics under the rubric of tolerance. Like the GPC, the YSP called for decentralization and the holding of local elections.

The Islah program focused on the idea that Islam should again have the central role that, according to the party, it had lost in Yemen. Its main slogan—"The Qur'an and the Sunna Supersede the Constitution and the Law"—was manifested in various propositions for reform. So as to reassure its critics, the Islah affirmed its commitment to a peaceful transfer of power and "consultative democracy," but it refrained from mentioning a multiparty system in its program.

The other party programs presented variations on the same key themes: denunciation of corruption, a call for strengthening the judiciary and unification of the two armies and security systems, development of services in the rural areas, and an affirmation of support for the principle of peaceful transfer of power.

The Campaign

The 10-day campaign officially began on April 17. Party and candidate newspapers and broadsheets proliferated, and the walls in all the large towns and even in villages were covered with posters. The Islah had already before the start of the campaign pasted up its many slogans.

Almost all the GPC's posters carried a picture of President 'Ali 'Abdallah Salih. The independent candidates satisfied themselves mostly with posters carrying their picture and some key phrases from their program. These posters typically mentioned a person's profession and featured the candidate's favored attire: head covered or not, Western or traditional Yemeni dress. An independent candidate from Sana'a, a professor of political science at the university who belonged to a *sayyid* family, had taken care to wear a *jambiya*, the curved dagger that signified his affiliation with the tribal world. A candidate from Marib showed his preferences by placing in the corner of his picture a small photograph of Saddam Hussein.

The law allowed for meetings in public spaces made available to the candidates, but it was only in large towns that huge gatherings took place. There were no debates between candidates except perhaps within neighborhoods.

In keeping with Yemeni custom, the period before the elections was marked by outpourings of generosity and hospitality on the part of the more affluent candidates. In the Jebel Yafa, in Lahij province just north of Aden, a Socialist minister candidate organized a daily banquet followed by a qat-chewing session in the late afternoon (qat generously provided). The total cost of organizing the campaign and election emptied state coffers and seriously aggravated the country's liquidity crisis. In addition to their personal generosity and the energy of their poster pasters, the candidates from the ruling parties were able to count on the advantages offered by their control of local government. In the larger towns in particular, neighborhood chiefs, with their links to the security forces, were able to mobilize voters around their respective parties.

The Elections

The day before the elections, the president and vice president addressed the voters, reminding them of the importance of the elections in closing off the period of transition and opening a new stage. The vice president took the occasion to renew offers to resume good relations with the Gulf countries. In a press conference a few days earlier, the GPC's 'Ali 'Abdallah Salih and the YSP's 'Ali Salim al-Bayd had confirmed, a smile fleeting across their lips, that they intended to continue their collaboration after the elections, the results of which they undertook in advance to accept. The quiet confidence they exuded, even more than the withdrawal agreements, suggested the real stake of the elections: to measure the respective popularity of the three main parties that would comprise a coalition. The election results would determine the quotas of ministers of the parties in government, but there was hardly a question of a real transfer of power.

On the morning of April 27, all polling stations opened, a box for every 500 registered voters. Upon presenting their proof of registration, the voters received a sheet on which, in a booth if there was one, they wrote the name of the candidate of their choice. The voter then slid the sheet into the box and dipped his or her finger into ink, intended to prevent a return visit to the polls.

At first light, hundreds of voters began pushing their way into the centers. Many had to wait long hours. The turnout rate, not officially announced, was definitely more than 80 percent. A formidable military presence assured order throughout the day. In the polling stations, though, there were moments of disorder. In one place, women voters fed up with waiting forced themselves inside and cast a collective vote, some filling out a whole series of sheets for their illiterate friends in the presence of passive officials. Elsewhere soldiers at the booths filled out voting sheets for others that no one bothered to check. Multiple voting was made possible by the facility with which the ink could be washed off; more than once, a voter prepared to cast his vote only to discover that his registration number corresponded to that of someone who had already voted. Finally, the deployment of troops made it possible to modify the composition of the electorate of certain districts significantly and at the last moment.

Not even waiting for the vote count, the US Embassy issued a communiqué on the night of April 27 congratulating "the people and government of Yemen for the success of their first multi-party elections" and declaring that "the United States looks forward to working with the government to be formed as a result of these elections." The official media never tired of quoting this and the commentaries of the Western media and of international observers and diplomats, even when the most serious incidents of fraud were taking place in the days of ballot counting. When the official results were announced on May 1, the GPC had won majorities in all the governorates in the North and three seats in the South. In the South, the YSP won an overwhelming victory, which could be interpreted as evidence of its popularity after two decades of Socialist power, but also as an indicator of an effective apparatus of control. In the southern province of Abyan, birthplace of ʿAli Nasir Muhammad, the YSP took seven out of the eight seats, even though YSP relations with the former president have only recently begun to improve. The YSP did not elect any representatives in Sanaʿa, but did well in al-Bayda and Taʿiz provinces, even if the competition with the Nasserists in Taʿiz allowed seats there to be picked up by the Islah and GPC. The two seats won by the YSP in the electoral district of the Sufyan tribe, in the heart of the Zaydi tribal area, and among the Bedouin of Marib, confirm the existence of a tribal challenge to the GPC that the YSP was able to exploit. But the commitment of these elected representatives to the entire YSP platform remains uncertain. Contrary to the GPC, the YSP can pride itself on a largely ideological vote. How else to explain the performance in Sanaʿa and elsewhere in the North of little-known candidates originally from the South who nevertheless came away with encouraging results?

Although the Islah carried not a single seat in the South, it did well in several provinces there. It was only thanks to the withdrawal of the Socialist candidate in favor of the ʿAli Nasir Muhammad faction of the GPC that the two parties were able to block the victory of the Islah's candidate in Mukalla, the Hadramawt capital. This province has been a priority area for Islah proselytizing, with its proximity to Saudi Arabia and strong religious tradition.

Sheikh ʿAbdallah, who was a candidate in the province of Khamir, the Hashid capital north of Sanaʿa, triumphed without difficulty; out of deference, the GPC and YSP ran no candidates against him. Al-Haqq was the only party to compete with him. One of his sons won under less glorious circumstances in Hajjah province, as his victory was offset by several deaths and the destruction, by rocket launcher, of the local Socialist headquarters.

The election results were less auspicious for the smaller parties: The Baath saved face with seven seats, one of which was taken by the son of its leader, the permanent deputy prime minister in charge of tribal affairs, Sheikh Mujahid Abu Shuwarib, who is also Islah leader Sheikh ʿAbdallah's brother-in-law. Al-Haqq naturally carried its two seats in Saʿdah province, the historical Zaydi stronghold. The Nasserists, who had had great hopes, could only join in the concert of complaints against fraud and ruling-party manipulations. The results of other parties were derisory, despite some very active campaigns.

The new Yemeni Chamber of Deputies remains in the hands of the large parties. The electoral struggle hardly helped the candidates representing new modernizing trends in Yemeni society. The notables prevailed, be they the great sheikhly families (al-Ahmar, Abu Shuwarib, Abu Raʾs, al-Shayif, al-Ruwayshan), the big entrepreneurs (Hayil Saʿid and Thabit) or the new aristocracy in the South, the members of the YSP Central Committee. With only two women elected, the diversity of the Yemeni population is less well represented in the new chamber than in the old, which has lost several of its most voluble critics (al-Fusayyil and al-Samʿi, for example).

The parties filed 113 challenges with the constitutional division of the Supreme Court. The three big parties decided, after a number of mutual accusations, to retract in a collective letter the complaints they had submitted against one another's respective candidates, without even consulting their own membership. This locked in place the coalition in the making. Of the 20 cases remaining, the court ratified the initial results.

The various international observer groups gave their imprimatur to the results, which contrasted with the accusations leveled by the National Committee for Free Elections, a Yemeni NGO, and the smaller parties of the National Conference, which charged fraud on the part of the three big parties.

Prudent Democratization

The fact that elections were held constitutes in itself a victory for a process of democratization that started after unification. Whatever one might say about the manner in which the elections took place, everyone sees this as a first step. The coalition government constitutes the best solution to maintaining political stability in the country, despite the reticence of some of the Socialists, like Jarallah 'Umar, who had hoped that his party could regain its virginity as a member of the opposition.

The coalition, though, has left little by way of an opposition. The three big parties have made it practically impossible for opponents to enter the Chamber of Deputies (the Baath, with its seven seats, is very close to the GPC). Now that the opposition parties have been told to take a hike in the desert, they would be wise to hearken to the remark of 'Umar al-Jawi, who lost his election bid in Aden, to "be strong in the streets, because we are not represented in Parliament." (Al-Jawi, head of the Yemeni Union Rally and one of the most vocal critics of the ruling parties, was reputedly on President 'Ali 'Abdallah Salih's list of people to defeat in the elections. The Socialist candidate won in his district.)

Local elections in the provinces may offer hope for the opposition. In the short term, the political agenda appears to be dominated by constitutional reform, which is supported for different reasons by all three coalition partners. The Islah wants to make the *shari'a* the sole source of legislation. The YSP and GPC want to alter the regime's institutional architecture. Three years of experience have persuaded them to renounce the country's collegial form of leadership—a Presidential Council appointed by the Chamber of Deputies. Now a vice president would be elected from a list approved by the National Assembly (YSP version) or appointed by the president (GPC version). The Assembly would consist of the current Chamber of Deputies augmented by the new Consultative Council, some of whose members would be appointed. Sheikh 'Abdallah has already made clear his hostility to a second chamber, which might erode the prestige of the chamber over which he is currently speaker. (Many cited his selection to explain the adjustment of the Yemeni riyal vis-à-vis the dollar in May, as this would facilitate reconciliation with Saudi Arabia and the resumption of Gulf aid.) The opposition, for its part, condemned a project that would further strengthen the executive branch, while calling for a redistribution of power to the judiciary and legislative branches.

It is still too early to predict what Yemen will look like once these reforms have been adopted. It seems likely that the country will remain fixed on a path of "prudent democratization" that will not threaten the elites in power.

—Translated from the French by Joost Hiltermann

From Ballot Box to Battlefield: The War of the Two 'Alis

Sheila Carapico • *MER* 190, Sept./Oct. 1994

Artillery and bombs rather than innocent fireworks marked the fourth anniversary of Yemeni unity and the first anniversary of free parliamentary elections of the Arabian Peninsula. The fight between the armed forces under President 'Ali 'Abdallah Salih and those loyal to Vice President 'Ali Salim al-Bayd was complicated by ideological, tribal and regional politics. In the end, though, it boiled down to both military leaderships' rejection of pluralism and dialogue. Simply put, each side wanted its maximum domain: for the southerners, either a full half of the power in a unified government or an effectively independent administration of the south; and for the north's Salih, control of the whole country, period. Not incidentally, given the acute state of economic collapse, both also had their eye on the Shabwa and Hadramawt oil fields.

When Salih and al-Bayd signed the unity pact in May 1990 on behalf of the Yemen Arab Republic and the People's Democratic Republic of Yemen, a number of critical issues—not least, how to merge the two separate militaries and security apparatuses—remained to be resolved "through the democratic process." A year later, when the constitution was ratified in a public referendum, and three years later, when national parliamentary elections partially redistributed top posts, none of these matters had been dealt with.

The results of the April 1993 elections exacerbated the stalemate over how power would be shared and exercised. If there were still essentially two camps, the north's now included not just the president's political machine but also his effective ally, Islah, the party alliance of Islamists, tribal leaders and some prominent merchants headed by 'Abdallah al-Ahmar, paramount sheikh of the Hashid confederation. Although al-Bayd and al-Ahmar signed a series of reconciliation agreements, in retrospect neither camp really intended to give up its army and security forces. The competition between them opened up political space for four years of pluralist politics whose most remarkable feature was a vibrant free press and dissenting opinion, formal and informal. But this competition became polarized, and the leaderships with their respective military commands resolved to remain in power separately rather than make the compromises that unity and democracy demanded.

The tribal basis of both military commands, especially Salih's, got much critical public attention during the crisis leading up to the civil war. *Sawt al-'Ummal*, the Aden-based Labor Federation weekly, first published the names of the 33 top officers in the northern army, who all happened to be from Sinhan. A pro-regime paper, *22 Mayu*, ran a counter-list of 26 southern officers from Radfan and 29 from Dalaa. *Al-Shura*, a weekly published by a small opposition party, then printed the two lists side by side.

In a country of about 14 million people and (reputedly) 50 million guns, degeneration of the conflict along tribal lines was one gruesome potential scenario. To date, this has not happened. Tribal divisions created rifts within the two camps, not between them. The north's more populous Bakil tribes resented the stranglehold on military command positions by officers from Salih's Rashid subtribe of Sinhan and the selection of 'Abdallah al-Ahmar as speaker of Parliament. To press demands for government reform, local economic development, and the arrest of high-profile swindlers, the Bakil imposed a "quarantine" against Rashid-owned petrol and Butagaz trucks entering Sana'a in April.

Tribal tensions also overlapped with other issues in the south, where 'Ali Nasir Muhammad and his supporters in Abyan lost out to politicians from the Hadramawt and officers from Radfan and Dalaa in 1986. In order to fan the embers of that dissension, Salih threatened in April to replace Prime Minister Abu Bakr al-'Attas with 'Ali Nasir, then still in exile. While most southerners closed ranks against the advance of Salih's army, the tribes of Shawra offered no resistance when the northerners took Ataq.

Whereas the popular culture of Sana'a exudes religious conservatism, Aden has a more relaxed, secular atmosphere. But this is not what the fight was about either. Salih did set the religious right against both northern leftists and the Socialists, helping to propel Islah's Islamist ideologue 'Abd al-Majid al-Zindani—opponent of unity, democracy and constitutionalism—into one of five seats on the ruling Presidential Council. In the lead-up to war, Salih addressed mosques while al-Zindani visited army camps. No amount of prayerful public posturing makes either Salih or Islah party head al-Ahmar into fundamentalists, however. Al-Zindani had actually reached a compromise with the YSP late last year on the wording of a constitutional amendment dealing with the place of *shari'a* in laws and legislation. Outside Aden, the south was no less conservative than the north. Religion was part of the rhetoric of war, but Yemenis were not fighting over religion's role in politics and public life.

The extraordinarily open political climate of the past several years unfortunately also encouraged Salih and the YSP, each still in control of a broadcast station and a daily newspaper, to air their differences in an acrimonious "war of declarations." Salih insisted on a presidency where he can appoint the vice president and all other influential positions. Al-Bayd wanted an independently elected, virtually co-equal president and vice president. Salih's cadre opposed independent local government; YSP Deputy Secretary-General Salim Salih Muhammad called for "confederation." Salih was happy to merge the armies under his relatives' command, and spoke with a straight face of the army as a "democratic" institution; the south invited "reorganization" and "appointment by merit." The YSP, which lost over 100 cadre to assassination during the unity period, called for "law and order," which it claimed to have provided in the former PDRY.

The public often sympathized with al-Bayd's positions but not his tactics. After a private visit to the United States in August 1993, instead of returning to Sana'a he went to Aden and issued "18 points" summarizing his demands. These served as the basis for some bargaining; negotiators for the president's GPC claimed they made significant concessions. One agreement concerned the composition of the five-man Presidential Council: two from each of the ruling parties, and one from Islah. But on October 29, as compromise seemed at hand, an attack on al-Bayd's sons and nephew scuttled the whole deal. He subsequently refused to take the oath of office, effectively depriving the country of a constitutional executive.

The elaborate electoral process to compose a new government that would in turn resolve constitutional, judicial and policy matters was unraveling. The Presidential Council, the cabinet and Parliament, all composed of the three-party coalition, were in deep constitutional and political crisis.

A lot of prominent Yemenis wanted unity and pluralism to succeed. Two leading northern figures took it upon themselves to bring together a group of personalities and then sell the feuding cliques on the idea. Mujahid Abu Shuwarib, for all his complicated past Baath, GPC and Hashid connections, was consistently considered as an "independent personality" and "acceptable to both sides." Sinan Abu Luhum, also a veteran of the 1960s struggle to establish the republic and subsequent political contests, rose during the dialogue efforts from among many competing Bakil sheikhs to a much-admired position of mediator. Backed by an impressive array of past Yemeni leaders, exiled figures and prominent nationalists, they proposed a National Dialogue Committee of Political Forces to discuss the YSP's 18 points, the conditions of Salih's camp, proposals from a recently formed Opposition Coalition, resolutions of dozens of civic meetings, and recommendations of lawyers and intellectuals. The new committee was to consist of five representatives each from the three ruling parties (who sent their most thoughtful and reasonable spokesmen), five from a recently formed Confederation of National Forces, leaders of the Opposition Coalition and smaller parties, and "independent social personalities." All significant factions and regions were represented.

After virtually continuous meetings for three months, 30 respected men produced in early 1994 a Document (*wathiqa*) of Contract and Agreement spelling out comprehensive reforms. Among the most important of these were delineation and limitation of presidential and vice presidential power; depoliticization, merger and redeployment of military and security forces, starting with the removal of checkpoints from cities and highways; administrative and financial decentralization to elected local governments, starting with development budgets; empowerment of an independent judiciary to enforce the letter of the law, starting with the arrest of assassins; election of an upper house of Parliament modeled on the US Senate; stricter auditing procedures; abolition of the ministry of information; and a comprehensive list of other reforms.

Public response to this idealistic document was overwhelmingly positive. College professors called it a "social contract;" their students said the president would now be like the queen of England; a taxi driver in Sana'a chuckled that the Gulf monarchies would be furious. Small wonder that the two leaderships were loath to sign a document that would, if implemented, force them to give up direct control of their armies, their purse strings and their cronies. Within hours after Salih, al-Bayd and al-Ahmar signed the agreement in Amman, Jordan, on February 20, a skirmish broke out in Abyan, where northern and southern troops, forces loyal to 'Ali Nasir, and a small cell of Islamic Jihad zealots were all camped in close proximity. More skirmishes erupted wherever units of the two armies were positioned near one another, more than once ending with the retreat of southern soldiers into Bakil territory.

These low-intensity, low-casualty battles prompted a barrage of seminars, editorials and peace marches under the slogan "No to War, No to Separation, Yes to the Document." Campus sit-ins in Sanaʿa and Aden, a new round of mass regional and tribal conferences from Hudayda to the Hadramawt, and smaller demonstrations in dozens of locations made a powerful statement. Perhaps even more remarkably, they were covered positively by the entire media. Everybody tried to identify with what was clearly the mood of the street.

Still the two sides stalled. Each leadership group contained both compromisers who talked to the other side and military diehards who insisted that the other side fulfill its part of the bargain first. By March, Abu Shuwarib and Abu Luhum left the country in disgust after publicly condemning what they called "preparation for separation."

Along with the remainder of the Dialogue Committee, foreign embassies and regional leaders tried to avert a war. US and French military attachés on the Military Committee went around helping to "put out fires" until artillery broke up their luncheon in ʿAmran on April 27. US Ambassador Arthur Hughes, like the Yemeni cabinet and the Dialogue Committee, shuttled between Sanaʿa and Aden. Several Arab leaders met with or sent personal envoys to meet both sides. King Hussein had hosted the Document signing ceremony in Amman, physically pushing the two reluctant ʿAlis to embrace on television; at talks hosted by Sultan Qaboos in Oman in early April the cameras recorded a warmer hug. Egypt's Mubarak had invited Salih and al-Bayd to Cairo the first week in May, and extended the invitation again and again during the fighting.

All to no avail. Public dissent, elite pressures and the other side's taunts seemed to embolden elements in each camp favoring the bang of a military solution over the incessant din of debate. Would-be outside mediators came away appalled, especially by Sanaʿa's intransigence. As the wing of the YSP advocating secession over a merger of the armed forces prevailed within the Central Committee, Salih's commanders showed him a battle plan "to preserve unity." The president effectively declared war from Sanaʿa's Great Mosque on April 27. After skirmishes ignited into full-scale battle in early May, Salih dismissed the "separatists" from his government. The YSP and some smaller southern-based parties, including ʿAbd al-Rahman al-Jifri's Sons of Yemen League, which had opposed the PDRY from Saudi Arabia throughout its entire history, declared a breakaway Democratic Republic of Yemen on May 21, 1994.

On a popular level, the Yemenis saw the "war between the two 'Alis" as recklessly squandering lives, resources, infrastructure and standards of living on crass and seemingly unwinnable power plays. Outsiders, too, saw both sides as taking unequivocal, rash positions. Both sides tried to marshal the widest possible government coalition, simultaneously silencing critics of their new policies. Salih imposed martial law, detained some critics and suspended all non-GPC newspapers, lest the northern peace forces undermine the drive to conquer the whole country. During the war, scores of rank-and-file socialists were detained in Sana'a in each of three separate rounds of arrests. Aden, for its part, imprisoned hundreds of Islah members.

While the north quickly established military superiority and encircled Aden and Mukalla, the rump Democratic Republic showed that it had one key ally: the Saudis. While the Gulf monarchies had refused to meet Salih and only received his chief diplomat on the eve of full-scale war, King Fahd, a score of Saudi princes, and top-ranking Kuwaiti and Emirates officials granted audiences to al-Bayd and his colleagues during the immediate pre-war crisis. Once fighting began in earnest, the Saudi press reveled in the fulfillment of its predictions that democracy could only come to chaos. When the battle turned against the south, the Saudi ambassador to Washington, Prince Bandar, pressed the Security Council to call for a ceasefire, a halt to arms shipments and a UN negotiator. The Gulf Cooperation Council condemned the north's aggression, claiming it was backed by Iraq.

Saudi support for those it had for decades called "godless communists," after having backed al-Zindani and al-Ahmar's northern opposition to unity a few years earlier, accentuates Riyadh's abhorrence of unity—not to speak of democratization—and its readiness to support whomever might break it up. It also helped that the new southern government included a number of former sultans, sheikhs and other anti-communist dissidents with connections to the Gulf royal families.

While UN mediator Lakhdar Brahimi brokered a series of stillborn ceasefires, and the Military Committee reassembled, the independent half of the Dialogue Committee groped for a "national salvation" government, or at least a committee to sit down with the two sides again. But the northern command showed no readiness to compromise. After the "legitimate forces"—the northern army, 'Ali Nasir loyalists, and some irregular militias—entered Aden on July 7, virtually all government offices and public-sector enterprises were sacked and looted. The southern leadership, having fled Aden for Mukalla in advance of Salih's army, abandoned the fight a week later to seek asylum in the Gulf countries.

On July 14, journalists and intellectuals held a well-publicized, well-attended seminar in Sana'a, reminiscent of many similar sessions over the past couple of years, to discuss the country's future. Three days later, at least a dozen participants were thrown into dungeons of the political security prison for two to six days.

One can already hear the apologists of authoritarian regimes in the Arab world crowing, along with the Saudi princes, that an unusual political opening has failed because even fundamental political liberties and civic participation are incompatible with Arab culture. But it is the regimes, not the cultures, that have proven to be incompatible with these goals, at great cost to society's human, material and cultural foundations.

4 Modern Political Islam in the Arabian Peninsula

Political Islam became a decisive force in the Islamic Republic of Iran, in Afghanistan as resistance to the Soviet occupation, and, as we have seen, in Saudi Arabia with the insurrection at Mecca, all in 1979. Although in the interim Yemeni politics was more driven by distinctly secular political parties and/or personalities, in the decades after 1979 two kinds of fundamentalisms with rival claims to Islamic authenticity gained momentum in the whole Peninsula. In the Sa'dah region of Yemen near the Saudi border, the movement subsequently known as the Houthis (or, technically, Ansar Allah, meaning "partisans of God") clashed with Saudi-style Wahhabism, also known as Salafism. Meanwhile along Yemen's southern coast Salafi-inspired jihadists foreshadowed the movement later called al-Qaeda in the Arabian Peninsula (AQAP). Written against the backdrop of al-Qaeda's spectacular 2001 attacks on the United States and the 2003 US invasion of Iraq, the following selections critically analyze the rise of explicitly denominational Islamist politics in the Peninsula. Of particular interest in terms of explaining the sectarian turn of subsequent events are juxtapositions and conflicts between the official Saudi version of Salafi/Sunni Islam, the Shi'a minority in the Kingdom, Zaydi revivalism just south of the Saudi-Yemeni border and Salafi jihadi guerrillas like al-Qaeda.

In 2001, many Americans imagined a kind of Muslim hive-mind, driven by creed; this was and remains, as Khaled Abou El Fadl writes in a brilliant post–September 11, 2001, essay excerpted below, "anachronistic and Orientalist." By 2015, a new narrative of Sunni vs. Shi'a conveyed a different explanatory paradigm. In the specific context of the Arabian Peninsula, these were both fleetingly useful frames of reference. However, Islam has neither historically nor recently been a monolith. To the contrary there has always been pluralism among various "schools" of both Shi'a and Sunni Islam. Nor, as made clear by this series of dispatches looking at the specific politics of dissent, conflict and Islamism, does the Sunni-Shi'a schism explain contemporary crises. Instead, Shelagh Weir, Iris Glosemeyer, Gwenn Okruhlik, Toby Jones, Toby Matthiesen and I join Abou El Fadl in observing the plurality and politicization of Islamisms in the context of multidimensional struggles over wealth and power. Weir and Glosemeyer recount and analyze the rather obscure origins of the Houthi movement that later became a major fighting force in Yemen's 2015 war. Okruhlik, Jones and Matthiesen look across the border at political tensions inside the Kingdom that also help explain the Saudi-led campaign against the Houthis.

All these essays suggest that sectarian conflict is the result, rather than the cause, of structural and kinetic violence.

Islam and the Theology of Power: Wahhabism and Salafism

Khaled Abou El Fadl • MER 221, Winter 2001

Contemporary Puritan Islam

The foundations of Wahhabi theology were put in place by the eighteenth-century evangelist Muhammad ibn 'Abd al-Wahhab in the Arabian Peninsula. With a puritanical zeal, 'Abd al-Wahhab sought to rid Islam of corruptions that he believed had crept into the religion. Wahhabism resisted the indeterminacy of the modern age by escaping to a strict literalism in which the text became the sole source of legitimacy. In this context, Wahhabism exhibited extreme hostility to intellectualism, mysticism and any sectarian divisions within Islam. The Wahhabi creed also considered any form of moral thought that was not entirely dependent on the text as a form of self-idolatry, and treated humanistic fields of knowledge, especially philosophy, as "the sciences of the devil." According to the Wahhabi creed, it was imperative to return to a presumed pristine, simple and straightforward Islam, which could be entirely reclaimed by literal implementation of the commands of the Prophet, and by strict adherence to correct ritual practice. Importantly, Wahhabism rejected any attempt to interpret the divine law from a historical, contextual perspective, and treated the vast majority of Islamic history as a corruption of the true and authentic Islam. The classical jurisprudential tradition was considered at best to be mere sophistry. Wahhabism became very intolerant of the long-established Islamic practice of considering a variety of schools of thought to be equally orthodox. Orthodoxy was narrowly defined, and 'Abd al-Wahhab himself was fond of creating long lists of beliefs and acts which he considered hypocritical, the adoption or commission of which immediately rendered a Muslim an unbeliever.

In the late eighteenth century, the al-Saud family united with the Wahhabi movement and rebelled against Ottoman rule in Arabia. Egyptian forces quashed this rebellion in 1818. Nevertheless, Wahhabi ideology was resuscitated in the early twentieth century under the leadership of 'Abd al-'Aziz ibn Saud who allied himself with the tribes of Najd, in the beginnings of what would become Saudi Arabia. The Wahhabi rebellions of the nineteenth and twentieth centuries were very bloody because the Wahhabis indiscriminately slaughtered and terrorized Muslims and non-Muslims alike. Mainstream jurists writing at the time, such as the Hanafi ibn 'Abidin and the Maliki al-Sawi, described the Wahhabis as a fanatic fringe group.

Wahhabism Ascendant

Nevertheless, Wahhabism survived and, in fact, thrived in contemporary Islam for several reasons. By treating Muslim Ottoman rule as a foreign occupying power, Wahhabism set a powerful precedent for notions of Arab self-determination and autonomy. In advocating a return to the pristine and pure origins of Islam, Wahhabism rejected the cumulative weight of historical baggage. This idea was intuitively liberating for Muslim reformers since it meant the rebirth of *ijtihad*, or the return to *de novo* examination and determination of legal issues unencumbered by the accretions of precedents and inherited doctrines. Most importantly, the discovery and exploitation of oil provided Saudi Arabia with high liquidity. Especially after 1975, with the sharp rise in oil prices, Saudi Arabia aggressively promoted Wahhabi thought around the Muslim world. Even a cursory examination of predominant ideas and practices reveals the widespread influence of Wahhabi thought on the Muslim world today.

But Wahhabism did not spread in the modern Muslim world under its own banner. Even the term "Wahhabism" is considered derogatory by its adherents, since Wahhabis prefer to see themselves as the representatives of Islamic orthodoxy. To them, Wahhabism is not a school of thought within Islam, but is Islam. The fact that Wahhabism rejected a label gave it a diffuse quality, making many of its doctrines and methodologies eminently transferable. Wahhabi thought exercised its greatest influence not under its own label, but under the rubric of Salafism. In their literature, Wahhabi clerics have consistently described themselves as Salafis, and not Wahhabis.

Beset with Contradictions

Salafism is a creed founded in the late nineteenth century by Muslim reformers such as Muhammad ʿAbduh, al-Afghani and Rashid Rida. Salafism appealed to a very basic concept in Islam: Muslims ought to follow the precedent of the Prophet and his companions (*al-salaf al-salih*). Methodologically, Salafism was nearly identical to Wahhabism except that Wahhabism is far less tolerant of diversity and differences of opinion. The founders of Salafism maintained that on all issues Muslims ought to return to the Qurʾan and the *sunna* (precedent) of the Prophet. In doing so, Muslims ought to reinterpret the original sources in light of modern needs and demands, without being slavishly bound to the interpretations of earlier Muslim generations.

As originally conceived, Salafism was not necessarily anti-intellectual, but like Wahhabism, it did tend to be uninterested in history. By emphasizing a presumed golden age in Islam, the adherents of Salafism idealized the time of the Prophet and his companions, and ignored or demonized the balance of Islamic history. By rejecting juristic precedents and undervaluing tradition, Salafism adopted a form of egalitarianism that deconstructed any notions of established authority within Islam. Effectively, anyone was considered qualified to return to the original sources and speak for the divine will. By liberating Muslims from the tradition of the jurists, Salafism contributed to a real vacuum of authority in contemporary Islam. Importantly, Salafism was founded by Muslim nationalists who were eager to read the values of modernism into the original sources of Islam. Hence, Salafism was not necessarily anti-Western. In fact, its founders strove to project contemporary institutions such as democracy, constitutions or socialism into the foundational texts, and to justify the modern nation-state within Islam.

The liberal age of Salafism came to an end in the 1960s. After 1975, Wahhabism was able to rid itself of its extreme intolerance, and proceeded to coopt Salafism until the two became practically indistinguishable. Both theologies imagined a golden age within Islam, entailing a belief in a historical utopia that can be reproduced in contemporary Islam. Both remained uninterested in critical historical inquiry and responded to the challenge of modernity by escaping to the secure haven of the text. Both advocated a form of egalitarianism and anti-elitism to the point that they came to consider intellectualism and rational moral insight to be inaccessible and, thus, corruptions of the purity of the Islamic message. Wahhabism and Salafism were beset with contradictions that made them simultaneously idealistic and pragmatic and infested both creeds (especially in the 1980s and 1990s) with a kind of supremacist thinking that prevails until today.

[...]

Alienation from Tradition

Of course, neither Wahhabism nor Salafism is represented by some formal institution. They are theological orientations and not structured schools of thought. Nevertheless, the lapsing and bonding of the theologies of Wahhabism and Salafism produced a contemporary orientation that is anchored in profound feelings of defeat, frustration and alienation, not only from modern institutions of power, but also from the Islamic heritage and tradition. The outcome of the apologist Wahhabi and Salafi legacies is a supremacist puritanism that compensates for feelings of defeat, disempowerment and alienation with a distinct sense of self-righteous arrogance vis-à-vis the nondescript "other"—whether the other is the West, non-believers in general or even Muslims of a different sect and Muslim women. In this sense, it is accurate to describe this widespread modern trend as supremacist, for it sees the world from the perspective of stations of merit and extreme polarization.

In the wake of the September 11 attacks, several commentators posed the question of whether Islam somehow encourages violence and terrorism. Some commentators argued that the Islamic concept of jihad or the notion of the *dar al-harb* (the abode of war) is to blame for the contemporary violence. These arguments are anachronistic and Orientalist. They project Western categories and historical experiences upon a situation that is very particular and fairly complex. One can easily locate an ethical discourse within the Islamic tradition that is uncompromisingly hostile to acts of terrorism. One can also locate a discourse that is tolerant toward the other, and mindful of the dignity and worth of all human beings. But one must also come to terms with the fact that supremacist puritanism in contemporary Islam is dismissive of all moral norms or ethical values, regardless of the identity of their origins or foundations. The prime and nearly singular concern is power and its symbols. Somehow, all other values are made subservient.

A Clash of Fundamentalisms: Wahhabism in Yemen

Shelagh Weir • *MER 204, Fall 1997*

During the past two decades, a proselytizing, reformist, "Islamist" movement—mainly characterized as "Wahhabi"—has gained increasing popularity throughout Yemen. Wahhabism actively opposes both the main Yemeni schools—Zaydi Shi'ism in the north and Shafi'i Sunnism in the south and in the Tihama. It is closely connected with the political party Islah, a coalition of tribal, mercantile and religious interests that pursues a mixed social and political agenda.

Though little is known of Yemeni Wahhabism, it appears to have a particularly strong following in the northern province of Sa'dah where some of its leading figures are based. Given that this region is in the Zaydi heartlands of northern Yemen, the popularity there of Wahhabism is surprising. Nevertheless Wahhabism has flourished in the mountains of Razih in the west of the province precisely because it has successfully mobilized a hitherto dormant resentment of key tenets of Zaydism. Wahhabism may have been sown, as some suggest, with foreign finance and encouragement, but it only took root because the soil was fertile.

Wahhabism was introduced into the province of Sa'dah by local men who had converted while studying religion in Saudi Arabia or fighting with the mujahidin in Afghanistan. Upon their return to the Sa'dah region, they set up lesson circles, religious institutes and Wahhabi mosques.

Beginning in the mid-1980s, the tribally organized communities of Razih became riven by sectarian conflict as a fervent and growing minority of Wahhabi Sunni converts confronted the majority of Zaydi Shi'a. The Wahhabis, as others dub them (or Sunnis as they prefer to be called), gained key positions in state schools, opened religious teaching institutes and established or took over a number of mosques. These activists were mainly young men (*shabab*) from a wide range of families, including tribal (*qabili*) and those belonging to a low-status group of so-called "butcher" families. These youths were attracted to Islah (which they equated with Wahhabism) because of its effective social welfare programs, and to Wahhabism because of its opposition to the Zaydi religious elite (*sayyid*), its direct, unmediated relationship to God, its egalitarianism and what they saw as its clear, logical doctrines. A major factor in their conversion was literacy; these *shabab* were among the first generation to attend secondary school. They had the skills, therefore, to study the plethora of religious publications flooding Yemen at that time.

In addition to the *shabab*, a minority of older men—mainly tribal leaders (sheikhs and others)—tacitly supported the Wahhabi-Islah movement in part because their traditional political positions were bolstered by Islah and its powerful leader, Sheikh 'Abdallah al-Ahmar, and in part because they approved of the anti-*sayyid* thrust of the movement. The relationship between tribal leaders and prominent *sayyids* has always been one of intermittent rivalry. *Sayyids* are, predictably, aligned entirely on the Zaydi side of the conflict and are supported by the national political party, al-Haqq, which was formed primarily to defend Zaydism against the Wahhabi challenge.

Although *sayyids* have not been revered indiscriminately in Razih, they and their claim to descent from the Prophet Muhammad through his son-in-law 'Ali have been respected by the majority of people. They maintained their high social standing despite the 1960s civil war which had aimed to eliminate their privileges. The Wahhabis primarily resented not the important official posts certain *sayyids* had secured under the republican government, but their religious authority and influence, as well as their religious claims to nobility.

The Wahhabis accused the *sayyids* of blocking access to the "truths" of Sunni doctrine, of propagating superstitious beliefs and practices and of perpetuating social stratification by asserting their divinely sanctioned social superiority. They accused them of reinforcing *sayyid* exclusivity by refusing to marry their daughters to non-*sayyids*—a particularly bitter point of contention. Razih, however, is replete with marriage prohibitions and preferences, and no tribe will yet intermarry with "butcher" families—an Achilles' heel which *sayyids* were quick to exploit with reciprocal taunts of social prejudice.

Sayyids countered by accusing the Wahhabis of propagating their religion for money and of importing a religious school of thought from Saudi Arabia that was inappropriate for Yemen. Zaydism, they asserted, was an authentically Yemeni school, and they were its prime upholders. Although *sayyids* had formerly portrayed themselves as immigrant "northerners" (Adnanis) in contrast to other Yemenis, who were indigenous "southerners" (Qahtanis), in this new context they sought to emphasize their Yemeni identity.

The Wahhabi opposition to *sayyids* and Zaydism also stimulated the emergence of a new generation of Zaydi *ulama* with non-*sayyid* tribal status. These charismatic and ambitious young men vigorously championed the Zaydi *madhhab* [doctrine or denomination] through teaching and religious pamphleteering, and by encouraging Zaydi rituals. In so doing, they predictably found themselves in competition with the *sayyids* of their own sect.

A striking feature of the sectarian conflict in Razih was the tremendous symbolic and emotional emphasis placed on spiritual and ritual matters, with each side accusing the other of heretical beliefs and practices. The greatest source of daily friction was the prayer ritual. Wahhabis made a point of attending Zaydi mosques and, while the majority of the congregation resolutely adhered to the customary Zaydi prayer stance with arms extended, the Wahhabis provocatively prayed in the Sunni manner, folding their arms during the prayer sequence, and, contrary to the Zaydi practice, chanting "*amin*" (like the Christian "amen").

In 1991, a major Zaydi reaction to the Wahhabi challenge occurred during a public ceremony to mark the anniversary of 'Id al-Ghadir, when

Shi'i Muslims believe the Prophet designated 'Ali as his successor. The loud speeches, general clamor and celebratory gunfire of this ceremony, which attracted men from all over Razih, dramatically and defiantly flaunted Zaydi numbers and enthusiasm in the face of the leading Wahhabi activist of Razih, who lived near the ceremonial ground.

The Zaydi-Wahhabi rivalry intensified. Wahhabis attempted to take over the major mosque of Razih, which had become the center for Zaydi activists. The Wahhabis imported skilled preachers from elsewhere in Yemen to deliver Friday sermons, tried to install their own mosque officials and assertively prayed in the Sunni mode—all strenuously opposed by the Zaydis. In one incident, tussles took place over the microphone and when the Wahhabis aggressively intoned "*amin*," the Zaydi congregation defiantly bellowed "*kadhdhabin*" (liars) in response!

As the 'Id al-Ghadir of 1992 approached, the Wahhabis waged a fierce campaign against Zaydi celebrations, threatening violence, and there were armed standoffs in the main mosque. This tense situation reached a bloody climax with the murder of the son of the leading Wahhabi on the eve of 'Id al-Ghadir—a shockingly dishonorable crime by tribal standards, because it was disproportionate to the provocation.

Two years later, the leading Wahhabi on policing duties with the local governor, having pursued his investigation and satisfied himself on the identity of his son's assassin, returned to Razih and shot dead an obscure *sayyid*. Thus he avenged his son's anonymous and secretive murder openly and honorably. Eventually, this was deemed a revenge killing in accordance with *shari'a* and the matter was closed.

After this incident the conflict subsided. Both sides felt things had gone too far and wanted to avoid provoking further government intervention. Local conflicts were also overshadowed by the 1994 war between north and south Yemen, and a deterioration in the Yemeni economy. As people concentrated on economic survival, religious differences were de-emphasized and Wahhabis and Zaydis concentrated on promoting their respective *madhhabs* through religious schools and institutes.

The dramatic and confrontational aspects of this "clash of fundamentalisms" subsided because those divided by religious conflict are linked by economic interests among networks of close neighborhoods and marriage. Leading *sayyids* have marriage links with leading Wahhabi families which predate this conflict. The social status of *sayyids*, however, may be vulnerable unless they modify their conduct and precepts, particularly their adherence to the principle of descent-based social primacy.

In an early sign of such a compromise a female *sayyid* (*sharifa*) recently married a tribesman—predictably a wealthy merchant. The significance of this first small breach in the bastion of *sayyid* exclusivity did not go unnoticed. Crowds of men converged from all over Razih to celebrate, singing the following song:

> *Oh sayyids, you tricked us*
> *With your turbans, remedies and charms*
> *Whenever we proposed marriage, you said*
> *"With a sharifa, a sayyid's daughter? It's not allowed."*
> *God only knows whose book you studied!*

Yemen and the Aden-Abyan Islamic Army
Sheila Carapico • *MERO*, Oct. 18, 2000

One of the leads investigators are following into the October 12 Aden harbor bombing of the USS *Cole* is an obscure network known (or perhaps formerly known) as the Aden-Abyan Islamic Army. Terrorism experts are familiar with this group's past missions, including attacks on Yemeni socialists prior to the 1993 parliamentary elections, the kidnapping of 16 Western tourists in Abyan on December 28, 1998—four of whom died in a botched rescue mission by the Yemeni government—and other bomb attacks in and around Aden over the past several years. But few can tell us anything about the political context in which this group operates. Suspects in the case are Yemeni and/or Saudi dissidents targeting their own governments as well as British and US interests in the Arabian Peninsula.

Background

Once, in its days as a Crown Colony, Aden was among the world's busiest ports and a major United Kingdom naval base. Though traffic is moribund despite recent investments, today Aden stands astride one of the three major "choke points" for the westward flow of the Persian Gulf, the Bab al-Mandab. All ships bound for the Persian Gulf from the Red Sea pass through the Gulf of Aden, within sight of Aden harbor and the minor port of Zinzabar, capital of Abyan. When Marxist revolutionaries drove the British from Aden and the South Arabian protectorates in late 1967, Abyan's sultan and major landowners were dispossessed and went into exile in Saudi Arabia, England or elsewhere. The simultaneous closure of the Suez Canal and the Aden naval base left Aden with few customers.

The revolutionary government of South Yemen, later named the People's Democratic Republic of Yemen, made it onto the US State Department list of state sponsors of terror for harboring Palestinian groups in the 1970s and for its close ties with the Soviet Union. PDRY exiles and migrant workers in Saudi Arabia were among the Arab volunteers for the much-romanticized anti-communist Afghan jihad. Like other mujahidin, they received military and religious training in Pakistan for the guerrilla war against the Soviet Union in the early 1980s. And like other mujahidin from North Yemen and many other Arab and Muslim countries, those from Aden-Abyan returned to their homelands in the late 1980s as "converts" to "*salafi*" (puritan or fundamentalist) or "Wahhabi" (Saudi) versions of Islam.

In 1990, North Yemen and the PDRY unified their two systems, both unstable and poor, and declared democracy. This is how the PDRY got off the State Department terrorist list—it ceased to exist as a state. The remnants of the PDRY army and the ruling Yemeni Socialist Party were defeated in a civil war in 1994 that left the army commanded by former North Yemeni president 'Ali 'Abdallah Salih in virtual occupation of what had been the PDRY. (Salih's regime likes to use the analogy of Northern Yankees versus Southern rebels.) The people of Aden, Abyan and other communities in the southern half of Yemen bristle under the watchful eye of security forces who are less efficient but not more benevolent than those of the PDRY. The dissident current variously described as "Afghani Arab" for its militant elements and "*salafi*" or "Wahhabi" for its contrasts with indigenous Yemeni religious traditions supported Salih's war against the Socialists. A few prominent spokespersons, notably Tariq al-Fadhli, self-identified tribesman, heir to the Abyan sultanate, and crusader for Islam, made alliances with Yemen's ruling party, the GPC. Other self-styled mujahidin are now in opposition to the Yemeni and Saudi governments. This movement is not limited to the southern part of Yemen but extends as far north as the Saudi border, where Wahhabis have clashed with local religious authorities.

Dissident Currents

The neo-Islamist current is hardly the only dissident element in Yemeni politics. Many people are protesting deteriorating economic conditions and the arbitrary powers of security forces. The week before the latest bomb blast in Aden, authorities were again arresting demonstrators affiliated with Popular Committees in Dalaa, inland and north of the Aden-Abyan corridor. There is a lively Yemeni pro-democracy movement. In Sana'a, Aden and other cities, jurists and intellectuals were criticizing a package of constitutional amendments proposed by the ruling party that would enlarge presidential powers while reducing the authority of the elected parliament. Ten years of a sagging economy and frustrated hopes for democratization had demoralized many Yemenis, in the north as well as the south.

Two previously unknown presumed offshoots of the Islamic Army—calling themselves the Islamic Deterrence Forces and Muhammad's Army—both claimed to have attacked the US destroyer with a dinghy or "fiberglass boat" packed with explosives. Of course, all these groups "have ties," via the Afghan-jihad network, to Osama bin Laden—whether or not he is the central "mastermind" of their activities. The network also seems linked to the circles of an imam at the Finsbury Park mosque in north London who until recently praised Yemen as the only Arabian country that had not bowed to Western military force. This connection might explain the bomb thrown at the British embassy in Sana'a, the Yemeni capital, the day after the *Cole* incident. The perpetrators of the 1998 kidnapping, and perhaps the harbor and embassy attacks, included citizens of Yemen, other Arab countries and Great Britain.

The name "Aden-Abyan Islamic Army" therefore connotes an appeal to the right wing composed of deposed aristocrats, mujahidin and religious ultra-conservatives, but also to some extent echoes the frustrations of Yemenis from Aden, Abyan and elsewhere in the former South, including liberals and socialists as well as social conservatives. While the term "Islamic Army" implies an Afghan-jihad strategy, it also has a populist ring to it, as would the notion of a "Christian army" among the American religious right. The organization itself is probably a loose guerrilla network of a few dozen men, Yemenis and non-Yemenis. Zayn al-Abidin abu Bakr al-Mihdar, the Yemeni founder of the Islamic Army and purported leader of the 15–20 kidnappers of British tourists in the Christmas season of 1998, was executed. After having initially denied the existence of any such force as the Aden-Abyan Islamic Army, the Yemeni government claimed to have wiped it out.

Improving Yemen's Image

After Yemen's failure to back the Saudi-US alliance against Iraq in the 1990–91 Gulf war severely strained US-Yemeni relations, the Salih administration, anxious to improve its image in the West, access to international finance, and foreign visits to its still underutilized but potentially world-class port, welcomed the US Navy to Aden with open arms. Sana'a has also taken other steps to meet US conditions for closer economic and military relations. Since 1995, Yemen has accepted the bitter austerity package recommended by the IMF. In the summer of 2000 the government signed an agreement with Saudi Arabia on their mutual border, presumably to ease tensions with the Kingdom. Geographically remote from the conflict in Israel and the Occupied Territories, Salih supports the Palestinians' current struggle but overall is seen as "moderate on the peace process." Recently Yemen began issuing tourist visas to Israeli Jews. The European Union and its member states, especially Germany and the Netherlands, support the government with economic development assistance.

President 'Ali 'Abdallah Salih came to power in 1978 after the mysterious assassinations of two predecessors, and recently won over 96 percent of the vote in the first national referendum to elect a president. Their own reports of arbitrary arrest, prison torture and harassment of journalists and university faculty notwithstanding, Western observers have been rather positively impressed by Yemen's democratic transition, as evidenced by two rounds of parliamentary elections.

Long List of "Suspects"

Anxious to show its cooperation with scores of FBI investigators sifting through marine debris and interviewing possible eyewitnesses, Yemen's national security forces have rounded up "hundreds" of suspects and manned extra army checkpoints at Aden's intersections and highways. Reports of heightened security that may reassure Americans and Britons concerned for the safety of compatriots in Yemen are bad news for the local population, however. In the past few years, the Yemeni government has detained dozens of reporters, scholars and political activists from across the political spectrum, the majority of them unarmed civilian critics who have called attention to corruption and arbitrary use of force. Already the number of those arrested following the double bombing of the *Cole* and the British embassy may well exceed the number of those affiliated with groups suspected of perpetrating the attacks. Hasty action to round up suspects in the *Cole* attack may well serve as a pretext to crack down on peaceful campaigners for democracy in Yemen.

Understanding Political Dissent in Saudi Arabia

Gwenn Okruhlik • *MERO* Oct. 24, 2001

The weeks following September 11 brought to the surface the tense under-currents in the relationship between the United States and Saudi Arabia. In the aftermath of the horrific attacks in New York and Washington, word spread that many of the hijackers were from Asir, the mountainous southwest province of Saudi Arabia, and were linked to Saudi dissident Osama bin Laden, a man who has vowed to overthrow the Saudi royal family, the al-Saud. But the two allies have postured awkwardly over the extent of Saudi Arabia's commitment to the US-led "war on terrorism." The United States resents the Kingdom's reluctance to cooperate fully with investigations of the September 11 attacks and previous incidents, as well as its reluctance to allow use of airbases on its soil for operations over Afghanistan. Among other things, Saudi Arabia resents US reluctance to weigh in on the side of Palestinians in their struggle against Israeli occupation.

More important to understanding the muted Saudi support for the war are internal pressures. The September 11 hijackings followed a long line of attacks tracing backward to the USS *Cole*, Kenya and Tanzania, Riyadh and Khobar, Somalia and Beirut. These attacks do not represent a war between religions. Rather, religion is a means for voicing explicitly political grievances, as is the case with Saudi dissenters and their sym-pathizers in the broader population. Internally, the grievances concern authoritarianism and repression, maldistribution and inequity, and the absence of representation in the political system. The external grievances are about US bases on Saudi soil, US support for Israel, US-led sanctions on Iraq and US backing for repressive regimes in the region, particularly Saudi Arabia, Egypt, Algeria and Jordan. A strong partnership with the United States in the current crisis would only fuel further domestic oppo-sition, something which had finally begun to lessen in the period before the attacks. Due to the widespread resonance of these grievances, the royal family fears the domestic repercussions of aligning themselves with the United States.

But portrayals of internal politics as contests between US-allied "mod-erates" and puritanical "Wahhabis" are grossly oversimplified. So too is a menu that offers two stark choices: an absolute monarchy tilting toward the West or a revolutionary Islamist regime hostile to the West. Internal contests and choices are more complex than that. They stem from three profound political crises to which the ruling family must respond: a convergence of dissent on core grievances, a multiplicity of clergies and socioeconomic distress.

Authoritarian Rule, Sporadic Resistance

Resentment of abuse of state authority has long simmered just beneath the surface in Saudi Arabia, but the regime has historically been criticized only in private. Rarely did criticism erupt into public confrontation. In 1979, Juhaiman al-Otaibi forcibly took control of the sacred mosque in Mecca in an effort to topple the ruling family. He did not garner much popular support because he chose a holy venue rather than a palace, but the incident exposed the vulnerability of the regime. It led to greater surveillance over the population, more power granted to the *mutawwain*—a sort of police of public virtue—new constraints on mobility and expression, and simultaneous promises of reform.

During the 1980s, an Islamic education system fostered a new generation of sheikhs, professors and students. An Islamic resurgence swept the country, but it was not directed against the regime. Several nonviolent Islamist groups took root during this time. The resurgence was also propagated by the newly returned "Arab Afghan" mujahidin. About 12,000 young men from Saudi Arabia went to Afghanistan; perhaps 5,000 were properly trained and saw combat.

Convergence of Dissent

The 1990s were a difficult decade in Saudi Arabia. Festering anger suddenly exploded with the Gulf war of 1990–91. The stationing of US troops in the country transformed what was an inchoate resurgence of Islamic identity into an organized opposition movement. Political criticism was now public—much of it written, signed and documented in petitions presented to King Fahd. The petitions called for, among other things, an independent consultative council, an independent judiciary, fair sharing of oil wealth and restrictions on corrupt officials. Friday sermons became an occasion for political criticism, and several prominent sheikhs were jailed. Demonstrations—largely unheard of under this authoritarian regime—erupted to demand their release, the most significant occurring in Buraydah, the very heartland of the ruling family's support.

A convergence of dissent cutting across cleavages of region, gender, class, school of Islam, ethnicity, ideology and rural-urban settings began to sound calls for redistribution of wealth, procedural social justice and regime accountability, in essence, the rule of law. People are weary of ad hoc and arbitrary personal rule. Because of this convergence, the state can no longer resort to its time-honored strategy of playing one group against another. Private businessmen and public bureaucrats, industrialists and mom-and-pop shop owners, Sunnis and Shi'as, men and women share core grievances.

The incremental response of King Fahd to popular dissent has satisfied no one. In 1992, he appointed a non-legislative consultative council and gave more power to provincial governments, where other family members ruled. These "reforms" disappointed some and angered others. They had the effect of consolidating the ruling family's centrality to political life, rather than broadening meaningful participation.

Multiple Clergies

The al-Saud rule in an uneasy symbiosis with the clergy. This relationship dates back to the 1744 alliance between Muhammad ibn 'Abd al-Wahhab and Muhammad ibn Saud, a sort of merger of religious legitimacy and military might. The descendants of al-Wahhab still dominate the official religious institutions of the state. The official clergy regularly issue fatwas (religious judicial opinions) that justify the policies of the al-Saud in Islamic vocabulary, even when those policies are deplored by the people. For example, they issued a fatwa to justify the presence of US troops during the 1990–91 Gulf war.

Islam remains a double-edged sword for the al-Saud. It grants them legitimacy as protectors of the faith, yet it constrains their behavior to that which is compatible with religious law. When members of the family deviate from that straight path, they are open to criticism since the regime's "right to rule" rests largely on the alliance with the al-Wahhab family. Today, the "alliance" between the regime and official clergy is much contested by dissidents because the parties no longer serve as "checks" on each other.

In the wake of the Gulf war, the state-appointed clergy has been supplemented by a popular alternative clergy that is articulate and vocal. The divide between official Islamic authorities and popular Islamic leaders is great. A dissident explained, "The old clergy believe that the ruler is the vice-regent of God on earth. Advice can only be given in private and in confidence. The new clergy reject the idea of vice-regency. Rather, it is the duty of the clergy to criticize the ruler and work for change." The alternative clergy wrote fatwas during the Gulf war that contested the fatwa of the official clergy and provided reasons to prohibit the stationing of US troops on Saudi Arabian soil. The alternative fatwas drew wider public support than did the official fatwa.

History now repeats itself as competing clergy make their opinions known. Sheikh al-Shuaibi and others have disseminated new fatwas that extend the idea of jihad from fighting foreign infidels to fighting domestic regimes that are perceived to be unjust. Al-Shuaibi's serious elaboration of the idea could be interpreted to target the al-Saud regime.

Socioeconomic Distress

Islamism taps into an already distressed social and economic environment. King Fahd has been incapacitated since his stroke in 1995 and the family wrecked by succession struggles. Since the heyday of the oil boom, per capita income has plummeted by over two-thirds. The birth rate is a very high 3–3.5 percent. The majority of the population is under 15. These young adults will register their demands for education, jobs and housing at the same time. But the Kingdom's once fabulous infrastructure, constructed during the boom, is now crumbling, particularly schools and hospitals. Unemployment among recent male college graduates is around 30 percent, likely higher. Yet Saudi Arabia remains utterly dependent on foreign workers, who constitute perhaps 90 percent of the private sector and 70 percent of the public-sector labor force. Social norms mitigate against the participation of local women in many economic activities. Since the Gulf war, there are reports of new social problems such as guns, drugs and crime. All this provides a fertile field for dissent.

Contentious voices also resonate because the exclusionary structure of governance does not reflect the diversity of the population. Contrary to popular images, Saudi Arabia is not a homogeneous country in ethnicity, religion or ideology. The variety of Muslim practices include Wahhabi orthodoxy, mainstream Sunni calls for reform of the state, minority Shi'a communities, Sufi practices throughout the Hijaz and, most importantly, a Sunni Salafi opposition movement. The Salafi movement opposes the dependence of the official clergy upon the ruling family, and their authoritarian rule. Radicals among them call for jihad today. Reformists prefer to wait until the time and the causes are right.

The Islamist movement—both Shi'a and Sunni—is represented externally by several reformist organizations in London and the United States. Other radical externally based groups like al-Qaeda advocate violence as an appropriate means to achieve their ends. While there is condemnation of the September 11 atrocities inside Saudi Arabia, the grievances articulated by the external Islamist movement do resonate powerfully among most parts of society.

More important than any external organization are the loose underground networks of study groups in Saudi Arabia that can be activated at the appropriate moment. When several sheikhs were imprisoned for their sermons of opposition, popular discontent ran high. In the time since the sheikhs were released from jail in 1999, the Islamist movement has become much quieter. Crown Prince Abdullah did begin to respond to internal and external grievances—he released the sheikhs, limited the business interests of princes, limited the free use of telephone, planes and water by royalty, allowed a freer press and publicly objected to US Middle East policy—but perhaps too slowly for some.

Conspicuous Silence

Other factors deepen the ruling family's conspicuous silence on the US-led "war on terrorism." Several high-ranking members of the ruling family and individuals from prominent families in the private sector have maintained close ties to Bin Laden. Indeed, the United States has been aware for several years of the transfer of funds from Saudi Arabia to al-Qaeda. Intra-familial rivalry also inhibits an unwavering stance. Though Crown Prince Abdallah effectively administers the country as the king's health fails, his succession is still contested by other powerful princes.

Saudi Arabia must, by virtue of its position as guardian of the holy cities of Mecca and Medina and host of the annual pilgrimage, contribute to Islamic charities. This leadership role mandates that the al-Saud, on behalf of the country, fund organizations throughout the international Muslim community. The Muslim duty of alms-giving suggests taking care of the less fortunate—it is an obligation of faith, not a choice. When the United States asked that the regime freeze all Islamic charities, the request put the al-Saud in an untenable position. It may have been acceptable to freeze the assets of Bin Laden's private companies and investments, but a freeze on Islamic charity was unthinkable for this regime whose legitimacy is so intimately tied to Islam. Like George W. Bush, the al-Saud must respond to their domestic constituency first and foremost.

Wide Middle Ground

The al-Saud have long based their rule on conquest, cooptation through the distribution of oil revenues, and Wahhabism. These historic sources of legitimacy are less compelling today because coercion has fostered popular resentment, oil revenues have shrunk dramatically and Wahhabism has never reflected the diverse reality of Saudi Arabia. Now, Saudi Arabians are looking for more inclusive and representative governance. People want freedom of expression and freedom of assembly. They want to participate in the development of their country, particularly in meeting the needs of education, health, employment and infrastructure for a booming population. Saudi Arabians do not want to waste precious national resources on arms purchases from the United States, deals over which they have no control.

The depth of royal coercion has meant that no alternative voices have been allowed to flourish. Today, there is not a viable alternative to the ruling family that could unite the disparate parts of the country, perhaps enhancing Bin Laden's pull artificially. But what many Saudi Arabians are talking about constitutes neither full democracy nor absolute monarchy. Rather, it is a voice in governance, and the rule of law. The challenge before Crown Prince Abdallah is to promote domestic reform that incorporates the diversity of the population. His strong nationalist voice can be used to counter the power of the radical movement. The wide middle ground between a revolutionary Bin Laden and an authoritarian ruling family cries out for cultivation.

Local Conflict, Global Spin:
An Uprising in the Yemeni Highlands
Iris Glosemeyer • *MER* 232, Fall 2004

Clashes between the followers of a Zaydi Shi'i religious figure and security forces left hundreds of people dead in a remote area in northern Yemen in the summer of 2004.

The precipitating incident was obscure, perhaps unimportant. It is hardly worth mentioning these days when worshippers in Arab countries leave the mosque reciting anti-American and anti-Israeli slogans. The Israeli government's violent reaction to Palestinian attacks, the war in Iraq—widely understood as an imperialist invasion—or the pictures from

Abu Ghraib only confirm for many Arabs the impression that Israel and the United States are joined in an all-out assault on the Islamic and, in particular, the Arab world. Thanks to the modern media, even in Yemen the "felt proximity" of events bears no relation to their actual geographic location. As in other Arab countries, and even though the US has never been involved in armed conflict with Yemen, many Yemenis see themselves confronted by an overwhelming American-Israeli force. Demonstrations against what is seen as aggression in Afghanistan, the West Bank and Gaza, and Iraq are part of daily political life, even if Yemen has problems enough of its own.

Nevertheless, the Yemeni police found it necessary, on June 18, 2004, to arrest and temporarily detain demonstrators in front of the Sanaʻa Grand Mosque—reportedly 640 followers of the Zaydi cleric Hussein Badr al-Din al-Houthi.

Two days later, when the governor of Saʻdah, a northern province bordering on Saudi Arabia, attempted to travel into the Marran region (district of Haydan, about 60 kilometers southwest of Saʻdah city), local inhabitants denied him entry. How exactly a local quarrel with the governor, a military appointee, escalated to this point is unclear, though there is precedent for disagreement between the central authority and the population in some parts of the governorate. There were reports that tribesmen from the Marran mountains fired upon police at a military checkpoint, and that the men (probably also tribesmen) blocking the governor's passage were followers of al-Houthi. The governor, rather than letting the matter rest, returned with military reinforcements.

As of mid-August, this local conflict had cost at least 500 lives. Two thousand families are said to have fled the area, while arrests have taken place not only in Saʻdah governorate, but also in ʻAmran, Hajjah and Sanaʻa governorate as well as in the capital Sanaʻa. At least three attempts to mediate the crisis have failed—officially due to al-Houthi's refusal to surrender, though mediators complain that the military resumed fighting during the negotiations—and al-Houthi and his followers have been surrounded in their refuge by thousands of soldiers. Reports that al-Houthi had fled either to neighboring Saudi Arabia or to another part of Yemen were unconfirmed.

In spite of the abundance of weapons in Yemen, it has been years since a dispute between the central government and regional, or tribal, powers has assumed these dimensions. There has been no military conflict between the state security forces and a Zaydi cleric and his followers since the 1960s. So, what is the problem?

One can only speculate about the cause of the troubles between al-Houthi—once a local government official in Saʿdah and, from 1993 to 1997, a member of the Yemeni parliament—and the governor Brig. Gen. Yahya al-'Amri. Nor is it known what took the governor to the Marran region in the first place. It is possible that al-Houthi faced arrest for inciting demonstrations not only in the capital city of Sanaʿa, but also in the governorate of Saʿdah, or that the governor simply wanted to talk to al-Houthi about a recent problem between members of a local tribe and the government. Al-Houthi seems to be attached to and protected by members of the Khawlan Saʿdah tribe whose attitudes toward the government he might influence.

Al-Houthi's leadership is based on his status as a *sayyid*, or a member of the religious elite claiming descent from the Prophet, of the Zaydi school that predominates in northern Yemen. But whereas Saʿdah was historically a stronghold of Zaydi doctrine, lately *salafi* (puritan) preachers who received their training and financial support from neighboring Saudi Arabia have gained quite a following in the region. Violent conflict has even broken out at times between representatives of the two religious tendencies. The local Zaydiyya, adherents of a form of Shi'i Islam that is close to Sunnism, share the belief of the Twelver Shi'a that the imam, or leader of the religious community, should be drawn from the elite *sayyid* families. Zaydis differ from Twelvers in that the Zaydi imam (the last one died in exile in 1996) is a worldly figure, educated, healthy and battle-tested, and always subject to being replaced by a more competent rival. In contrast, the Sunni *salafis*—the ideological archenemy of the Shi'a—lay great stress on the principle of equality among Muslims, gaining as new members ordinary Zaydis who are resentful of the special status of the *sayyids*. In the 1990s, *salafi* preachers vilified Zaydi traditions as elitist in an appeal to the tribal and artisan communities in Saʿdah and elsewhere.

Why the challenge to the government precisely from a Zaydi cleric? First, Arab discontent over Israel and the United States is not restricted to puritan Sunnis. The Iraqi Muqtada al-Sadr, a representative of the Twelver Shi'ism that predominates in the Persian Gulf region, is one signal example. It is possible that Hussein al-Houthi feels inspired by al-Sadr. The latter's resistance to the American occupation attracts attention in the Yemeni highlands not only because of satellite news broadcasts but also because in recent decades many exiled Iraqis have found a new home in Yemen, and many thousands of Yemenis studied in Iraq. Al-Houthi reportedly maintains contact with several Shi'i Iraqis who are located in Saʿdah.

The more interesting question is why the Yemeni government would react so strongly, now, to propaganda from a preacher long an outspoken critic of the US. President 'Ali 'Abdallah Salih maintains that al-Houthi has long been underestimated. Other prominent Yemenis dismiss him as unimportant. The extent of the protest by al-Houthi's followers and the fact that they blocked entry to the governor could have forced the president's hand. For years now, the Yemeni government has faced the same dilemma as other Arab governments: The United States expects cooperation in the hunt for suspected terrorists—and has the means to exert pressure—while the population views this cooperation as proof of the inability or unwillingness of their governments to lessen US influence in the region. The Yemeni press kept a wary eye on the behavior of the outgoing American ambassador, Edmund Hull, whose influence allegedly far exceeded the powers of his office. If the government does not intervene in anti-American demonstrations, the Salih regime loses credit with the US government. If it does intervene, it loses legitimacy in the eyes of the population.

Al-Houthi's following has multiplied since the onset of the fighting. People now speak of thousands of supporters, but it is likely that a view of the massive military presence as an overreaction has drawn more tribesmen into the conflict because they feel the government is encroaching on tribal sovereignties and violating the rules of tribal warfare (which, for example, forbid fighting during negotiations). According to other reports, local tribes are supporting the security forces. The conditions are set for further conflict even after the fighting ends between tribesmen who supported different camps—a situation that evokes memories of the civil war in North Yemen in the 1960s.

The case of al-Houthi probably also promised the opportunity for the government to set an example to establish a monopoly on violence in one of the tribal governorates, while exploiting the conflict as a demonstration of its commitment to the war on terrorism. Parallels to past events like the clashes between the security forces and the 'Abida tribe in the governorate of Marib in 2001 are palpable. This time, however, the government underestimated the difficulties it would face in the difficult mountainous terrain of Marran.

One important factor in the conflict is specific to Yemen. Hussein al-Houthi is a Zaydi *sayyid*, that is, someone technically qualified to lay claim to the imamate and to establish a Zaydi state. Zaydi states existed for more than a thousand years in North Yemen, until the last one was replaced in 1962 by a republic. A scenario in which al-Houthi would declare himself imam awakens memories of the civil war between fol-lowers of the last imam and supporters of the republic, which ended only in 1970. Since that time the Zaydi *sayyids* have maintained a low political profile, even though, with the exception of members of the family of the last imam who fled to Saudi Arabia (and later moved to Great Britain), no one was excluded from the reconciliation achieved in 1970. Only after the unification of the two Yemeni states in 1990 introduced a multiparty system was a political party formed, the Hizb al-Haqq (Party of Truth), to represent the *sayyids*, whose largest constituency is in Sa'dah governor-ate. But this party's platform explicitly renounced the reintroduction of the imamate—one of the major pillars of Zaydi doctrine—and some ob-servers see the party foundation as an act of Zaydi self-defense against the *salafi* currents organized in Yemen's biggest opposition party, al-Tajammu' al-Yamani lil-Islah (Yemeni Congregation for Reform). Al-Houthi him-self was a member of Hizb al-Haqq for the period in which he held a seat in Parliament. Since the end of the 1990s, the former parliamentarian has been increasingly vehement in his statements against US policy, and as early as 1997 he founded a youth organization, the *shabab al-mu'minin* (Believing Youth), which officials now characterize as militant.

The fear that al-Houthi could upset the peace between Zaydis and the other denominations in Yemen—the majority of Yemenis are Shafi'i Sunnis—and threaten the republic by proclaiming himself imam at least contributed to the hard line taken by the government. This can be seen from statements made in the Yemeni and Arab press, accusing al-Houthi of virtually everything that is politically incorrect in Yemen. At times it has been said that he declared himself imam, and he is supposed to have raised his own flag in place of the flag of the Yemeni republic. In anoth-er variant, it was the flag of Hizballah—though it is highly questionable whether anyone in Lebanon had ever even heard of al-Houthi and started to build an alliance with his following before the fighting started. He is supposed to have forcibly confiscated the alms tax—an open challenge to the government. A government official even went so far as to maintain that al-Houthi is supported by the roughly 1,000 Jews living in the gover-norate of Sa'dah, whom the official accuses of working for the collapse of the Yemeni republic—an extremely dangerous transfer of regional con-spiracy theories to Yemeni domestic politics. Most Yemeni Jews emigrat-ed in 1948–51 with the founding of Israel, leaving rather few families who have since refused many offers of relocation. In its August 2, 2004, edition, the *Yemen Times* even suggested a link between al-Houthi and a number of al-Qaeda suspects recently on trial, merely because one of them expressed his sympathy for al-Houthi's case—an interesting twist given the animosity between *salafis* and supporters of Hizb al-Haqq in Saʻdah. This colorful but by no means complete bunch of allegations—most of which were denounced by al-Houthi before his phone lines were cut—indicates how desperately the Yemeni government is trying to justify its line of action domestically and internationally and to prove its commitment to the "war on terrorism" (which one might interpret as a rent-seeking strategy).

In fact, al-Houthi's motivation is simultaneously local and utterly international. In a letter to the Yemeni president, whom he deferentially addressed as "His Excellency, President of the Republic, Brother ʼAli ʼAbdallah Salih," al-Houthi declared his sense of duty to defend Islam and the community of Muslims against Israel and the US.

Unwritten but between the lines was the message that this defense is properly the task of Arab governments, including the one in Yemen. The local conflict in Saʻdah is therefore neither more nor less than the local expression of the crisis of legitimacy confronting Arab governments that are involved in the war on terrorism and whose situation since the transfer of power in Iraq has not improved in the slightest. To be foreseen are further local conflicts—not only in Yemen—sparked by events in other countries in the region. Globalization has reached the most remote areas in the Middle East.

The Iraq Effect in Saudi Arabia

Toby Jones • *MER* 237, Winter 2005

Shi'is in the Kingdom of Saudi Arabia have watched Iraq's political transformation with a combination of horror and optimism. Iraq's slide toward civil war, the carnage wrought by militant violence and the targeted slaughter of thousands of Iraqi Shi'is by Sunni insurgents have sown fears among Shi'a in the Kingdom that they might be the next to suffer bloodshed. Their worries are not unwarranted. They live in a sea of sectarian hostility, where the Sunni government and its clerical backers have long made clear their antipathy for the Muslim minority sect.

The violence in Iraq has led Saudi Arabian Shi'is to distance themselves from the war and the US role in bringing Iraqi Shi'is to power. Even so, the new political dynamic there has fed a growing opportunism, feelings set in motion by both domestic and regional events. Many now believe that with the recent accession of King Abdallah, who is widely viewed as sympathetic to Shi'is, and with the balance of power shifting in the region, resolution of long-standing Shi'a grievances may finally be achievable. Shi'is demand inclusion in formal politics, the right to observe religious rituals and the right to move their struggle against the extreme anti-Shi'ism that permeates society and is condoned by the state into the public sphere.

As many as two million Shi'is live in Saudi Arabia, where they make up between 10–15 percent of the population. Although some live in the cities of Mecca, Medina and Riyadh, the majority of Shi'is are concentrated in the two oases of Qatif and al-Hasa in the Kingdom's Eastern Province, a region that is also home to most of Saudi Arabia's massive oil reserves. Most Saudi Arabian Shi'is are from the "Twelver" branch that claims the majority of the world's Shi'a; they believe that the last successor to the Prophet Muhammad as religio-political leader of Muslims was the twelfth imam who went into occultation in the ninth century. A smaller community of around 100,000 Isma'ilis, who observe an offshoot of Shi'ism that traces imamic descent from the seventh imam, makes its home in Najran near the southern border with Yemen.

The Shi'is' sense of vulnerability is easy to understand. Although sectarian violence has only been episodic in the twentieth century, leading religious scholars in the Kingdom have denounced Shi'a as apostates, and since the founding of Saudi Arabia in 1932 have periodically called for their extermination. Historically, Saudi leaders have done little to tone down anti-Shi'a rhetoric and at times have manipulated the sentiment that fuels it. Until the end of the twentieth century, the Kingdom's rulers preferred publicly to ignore the Shi'is' existence. The nationalist narrative popularized in recent years in various media, including the press, national television, historical texts and most visibly a series of exhibits displayed at an annual Riyadh fair called the Janadiriyya, spotlights the "heroic" efforts of the Kingdom's founder, 'Abd al-'Aziz, in bringing together warring tribes. It scarcely mentions the Shi'a. But recent events have made this erasure untenable.

With Iraq possibly disintegrating along sectarian lines and hundreds and perhaps thousands of Saudi Arabian Sunnis taking part in the anti-occupation and anti-Shi'a insurgency, many in Saudi Arabia fear that the spread of sectarian violence is just a matter of time. Remarkably, the Shi'is' anticipation that they will eventually be targeted by their fellow countrymen and the widely held belief that Saudi rulers have abetted, if not actually supported, sectarian violence have not altered the Shi'is' pursuit of rapprochement and cooperation with the state.

[...]

Even after Ayatollah Khomeini's death and an improvement in Saudi-Iranian relations, the production of anti-Shi'a material continued apace. In the early 1990s, Nasir al-'Umar, a particularly vicious Sunni cleric, wrote a treatise called "The Rafida in the Land of Tawhid." *Rafida*, or *rawafid*, is a pejorative term meaning "rejectionists," a reference to how radical Sunnis consider the Shi'a to be outside Islam. Religious edicts (fatwas) issued by other well-known clerics, including several by Abdallah bin Abd al-Rahman al-Jibrin—then a member of the Higher Council of Ulama—condoned and even mandated the killing of Shi'is. As late as 2002, a leading Saudi Arabia–based charity, the International Islamic Relief Organization, circulated a pamphlet entitled *One Hundred Questions and Answers on Charitable Work in the Eastern Province* that contained passages slandering the Shi'a as apostates and called for efforts to "get rid of their evil."

The Bogeyman Returns

The Iraq war has stoked sectarian ill will. Internet discussion forums popularized by Saudi Arabian visitors are full of vitriolic denunciations of Shi'is inside the Kingdom and out. At least one website supportive of Sunni jihadis reported a widely believed rumor that militants planned to kill the Shi'a cleric Hasan al-Saffar during 'Ashura in 2004. Similar threats may have been leveled at Shi'a communities in Bahrain and Kuwait in 2005.

Most troubling to Saudi Arabians is the appearance of cooperation between the United States and the new Shi'i power brokers in Iraq. Nasir al-'Umar launched a simultaneous direct assault on Iraqi Shi'is and the United States when he denounced the "strong relationship between America and the *rafida*" and argued that they were both the enemies of Muslims everywhere. The appearance of coordination between the United States and Iraqi Shi'is to marginalize and oppress Iraqi Sunnis has produced widespread anger. During the November 2004 US-led siege of Falluja, popular websites published images of Iraqi Shi'i national guardsmen carrying pictures of Grand Ayatollah Ali Sistani alongside photographs of US tanks with rosaries dangling from their barrels, providing symbolic power to arguments about the forces aligning against Sunni

Muslims. Speculation that the United States and Shi'is are actively work-ing to alter the sectarian shape of the region has been further fueled by the widespread belief that Iran, the bogeyman from the 1980s, is actively promoting the establishment of what, in December 2004, Jordanian king Abdallah II called a "crescent" of Shi'i-dominated polities stretching from Iran to Lebanon "that will be very destabilizing for the Gulf countries and for the whole region."

In addition to popular outrage about the sectarian transformation of Iraq, fears that Iran intends to use its influence in Iraq to ignite a wider conflict are evident within the royal family. On September 20, 2005, Saudi Arabia's foreign minister Saud al-Faisal worried aloud at the Council of Foreign Relations that "if you allow...for a civil war to happen between the Shi'a and the Sunnis, Iraq is finished forever. It will be dismembered. It will not only be dismembered, it will cause so many conflicts in the region that it will bring the whole region into a turmoil that will be hard to resolve." The foreign minister seemed most upset by the prospect that the United States was "handing the whole country over to Iran without reason." In apparent disbelief, he said, "It seems out of this world that you do this. We fought a war to keep Iran from occupying Iraq after Iraq was driven out of Kuwait." King Abdallah was more circumspect in comments he made to an American television news program, but he hardly put the issue to rest. "Iran is a friendly country," he said. "Iran is a Muslim coun-try. We hope that Iran will not become an obstacle to peace and security in Iraq. This is what we hope for and this is what we believe the Iraqi people hope for."

[...]

Saudi Arabian Shi'i political leaders are well aware of how fragile the current political moment might be. To be sure, the Iraq war has unleashed a wave of foreign pressure on Saudi rulers to reform and affirmed Saudi Arabian Shi'is in their conviction that they, like the Shi'a of Iraq, deserve more political opportunity. But more importantly, and perhaps tragically in the end, the war has set back the Kingdom's Shi'a in their titanic strug-gle to delink themselves from the politics of sectarianism set in motion by Iran's Islamic Revolution and to assert a sense of loyalty that transcends sectarian difference. Saudi Arabian Shi'is are caught in a delicate balanc-ing act, forced to constantly renew and demonstrate their loyalty to a state that has historically displayed overwhelming animus toward them, while outmaneuvering charges that they are preternaturally bonded with their co-religionists elsewhere in the region. The rise of the Shi'is in Iraq, and more importantly the role that the Iraq war has played in re-politicizing sectarianism in the region more generally, has made their task considerably more difficult.

The Shi'a of Saudi Arabia at a Crossroads

Toby Matthiesen • *MERO*, May 6, 2009

Deep in the morass of YouTube lies a disturbing video clip recorded in late February at the cemetery of al-Baqi' and on surrounding streets in Medina, Saudi Arabia. An initial caption promises images of "desecration of graves." Al-Baqi', located next to the mosque of the Prophet Muhammad in the second holiest city of Islam, is believed to be the final resting place of four men revered by Shi'i Muslims as imams or successors to the Prophet: Hasan ibn 'Ali, 'Ali ibn Husayn, Muhammad ibn 'Ali and Ja'afar ibn Muhammad. The Prophet's wives, as well as many of his relatives and close associates, are also said to be buried here, making the ground hallowed for Sunni Muslims as well.

The clip opens with footage of young boys, Shi'i pilgrims mostly from the Eastern Province of Saudi Arabia, chanting a religious invocation. "O God!" they call out. "Bless Muhammad, peace be upon him, and the House of Muhammad!" The first clause of this prayer is common to Sunni and Shi'i Muslims, but the second—referring to the Prophet's family—encapsulates the key difference between the two main branches of Islam. The Shi'a believe that the succession to Muhammad as religio-political leader of the Muslim community runs through his bloodline, in specific through his cousin and son-in-law 'Ali and 'Ali's son Husayn. This belief is a direct challenge to the juridical authority of the Sunni clergy and, Sunni rulers often fear, political authority as well. The Wahhabi clergy and the Saudi state therefore deem the second clause of the boys' prayer "un-Islamic," if not downright heretical. They have the same attitude toward the Shi'i act of veneration whereby pilgrims collect soil from around the graves of important religious figures, as the boys proceed to do in the video. In fact, the (Sunni) religious police attached to the Commission for the Promotion of Virtue and the Prevention of Vice usually intervene to forestall such acts, but in the clip the boys are allowed to approach a stone marker and gather dirt. Then, as a subsequent caption boasts, "After they had wreaked havoc upon the grave, the security forces removed them."

The government version of events, advanced in openly hate-filled fashion by the video clip, asserts that the pilgrims "trampled upon" the graves of the Prophet's wives and companions. The clip claims that this alleged offense, as well as the pilgrims' other "Zoroastrian rituals" and insults to the Prophet's companions, led security forces to disperse them and provoked local Sunni worshippers into clashing with their Shi'i countrymen. As triumphal music plays, the videographers brag that a "lion-hearted" local youth stabbed "one of those who rejects true Islam" and joke that only the "merciful" presence of security forces protected the "grandchildren of Khosraw" from further harm. These imprecations—that Shi'is are practitioners of pre-Islamic faiths, apostates, followers of ancient Persian emperors—are old standbys of anti-Shi'i prejudice in Saudi Arabia and elsewhere. The second commenter at the YouTube site fumes: "Every apostate Zoroastrian should be expelled from Muslim lands." Another clip even calls the Shi'i boys "little devils."

The Shi'i pilgrims' version of events is quite different. They had arrived in Medina on February 20 to mark the anniversary of the death of Muhammad, which in 2009 fell on February 24. On the same day, Shi'is commemorate the passing of Hasan, the second imam. Pilgrims said that the religious police videotaped the women among them, affronting their piety and modesty. When a group of men, some of them husbands of the taped women, asked the police to destroy or hand over the tapes, clashes broke out. Armed policemen confronted hundreds of protesters chanting slogans in reverence of Husayn. In the following days, the religious police arrested and injured dozens. According to Shi'i reports, many pilgrims gathered on the evening of February 23 to commemorate the death of Muhammad but were not let into the cemetery. They moved to the square between the cemetery and the mosque of the Prophet. There, they say, they were attacked by Sunnis exiting the mosque and by the religious police.

Comments made after the Medina clashes by Prince Nayif, the interior minister who was named deputy crown prince in March, are highly suggestive about whose version of events is closer to the truth: "Citizens have both rights and duties; their activities should not contradict the doctrine followed by the *umma*. This is the doctrine of Sunnis and our righteous forefathers. There are citizens who follow other schools of thought and the intelligent among them must respect this doctrine." In other words, the Shi'i citizens of Saudi Arabia should not express their religious beliefs in public out of deference to Sunni sensibilities, which the prince casually equates to those of the world Muslim community as a whole. Throughout the Kingdom's history, indeed, the Shi'a, who make up 10 percent of the total population, have been subject to discrimination at the hands of the state. The Medina disturbances are part of a pattern of rising Shi'i militancy in response to that discrimination around the country, and particularly in the oil-rich Eastern Province, where Shi'a form a slight majority. Parts of the Saudi regime, at least, seem to have an interest in escalating the confrontation.

5 Water, Oil and Workers

The Arabian Peninsula is known for an abundance of carbon resources, acute water shortages and a fluid labor force. The excerpts in this section highlight those features of the region's political economy. In the first, Robert Vitalis analyzes the roles of American companies and workers inside Saudi Arabia. Following that piece are three entries abridged from an issue of *Middle East Report* entitled "Running Dry": an opening vignette from the introductory essay by George R. Trumbull IV, Toby Jones's explanation of the interplay of oil and water politics inside the Kingdom and Gerhard Lichtenthaeler's account of Yemen's water woes, particularly those in 'Amran in the central plateau. The collection concludes with Enseng Ho's humorous vignette about Yemenis colonizing Mars. In light of earlier and subsequent events, these essays shed light on the material underpinnings of political struggles.

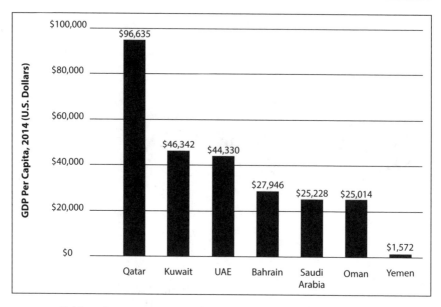

Table 1: Gross Domestic Product Per Capita of Arabian Peninsula Countries
Source: World Bank data

The Ghosts of American Camp

Robert Vitalis • Originally published as "The Closing of the
Arabian Frontier and the Future of Saudi-American Relations,"
in *MER* 204, Fall 1997

The Air Saudia flight approached Dhahran from the water, banking sharply above the causeway that links the Eastern Province to Bahrain. During the drive from the airport, I began to match the landscape before me to the one drawn from extant records of life and work on the early 1940s and 1950s oil frontier, which centered on the fenced-in Aramco company enclave then known as "American camp." Recent retirees and the handful of third-generation Aramco-Americans ("Aramcons") still working in the Eastern Province continue to refer to the sprawling expatriate housing complex and administrative offices of the state-owned oil enterprise, Saudi Aramco, as "camp." Thus, unaware, they draw on a tradition going back more than a century to the mining communities founded on the trans-Colorado border lands, the original model for Dhahran.

It is in the world oil frontier of the Eastern Province where the American empire was made manifest. Oilmen and managers exported a system of race and caste segregation to its zone of operations in Dhahran and the satellite settlements and pipeline stations. These were institutions and norms of separate and unequal rights and privileges, of crude racism and progressive paternalism ("racial uplift"). In going to Dhahran I harbored the slim hope of adding to the archive I have been collecting of the migrant workers, Arab nationalists, communists and tribesmen who mounted the demonstrations and strikes that began the process of overturning Jim Crow in the Eastern Province.

The keepers of the official history of the Saudi-American partnership today appear zealous about preserving the myths of the oil frontier intact. The American embassy in Riyadh recently celebrated the golden anniversary of the special relationship, dating back to the 1945 meeting between 'Abd al-'Aziz and Franklin Roosevelt on a US destroyer in the middle of the Suez Canal. The Saudi embassy in Washington has mounted twin enlargements of the *Life* magazine photo of the meeting, lit from behind, on the wall of its in-house theater. Kneeling between the two frail but noble chiefs is Col. William Eddy, the Sidon-born and Princeton-bred missionaries' son who translated for the king and FDR.

A dissident history, pieced together from other relics of the period, casts images of the old days in different light, beginning with Eddy, who is remembered as one of Saudi Arabia's best friends in America, and the "only official who actually resigned" from the Truman administration in protest of its Palestine policy. The reality is that Eddy joined the CIA using the cover of Aramco "adviser" in Dhahran and Beirut in the 1940s and 1950s. More important, his own secret reporting to Washington on the famous Saudi workers' strike of 1953 contrasted the "primitive land of low pay, slaves, eunuchs and harems to the comfortable conditions of US residents in Dhahran."

Decades later, Saudi Aramco's public relations staff continues to censor material that even hints at the racial discrimination and other forms of injustice that workers once faced in the Eastern Province. The reasons are clearly spelled out in the archives: The country's own labor policies are vulnerable to similar criticisms. In private, officials with the firm recalled for me the period when they still had to drink from fountains in American camp, designated for Saudis only. Others complained that, given the way Americans once treated Saudis, the Kingdom's labor policies receive far too much scrutiny.

The transformations in the oil market in the 1970s associated with OPEC are well known. Western multinationals gave up their control of the producing companies like Aramco, which is now owned by the Saudi state. They also were beset by the phenomenal oil rents produced by the price rises of past decades. These changes in turn altered many dimensions of the US-Saudi relationship if not the global position of the US "hegemon." Even those dissenting theorists like Bromley, who caution against exaggerating the extent of decline of American power in the world economy, recognize these shifts. Firms lost the capacity to call out the gunboats to protect themselves from expropriation, and geostrategists lost the means for direct control of the region's resources. From Nixon on, US administrations have confronted the reality of sharply reduced leverage over Saudi rulers.

The story of the dismantling of the Jim Crow system in Dhahran is part of the same era of momentous change in the world economy, the equivalent of decolonization in the Saudi case, which was effectively completed with the "transfer of (Aramco's) power" to the al-Saud and its agents. Nonetheless, the story has no place in the Kingdom's public history today. The many Saudis and migrant laborers who built the oil industry and transformed the landscape are invisible to visitors of Dhahran's new interactive "Saudi Aramco Exhibit." There are no photos of the king's visit to Aramco when he was besieged by protesting workers, or of the first Saudi oil minister, 'Abdallah Tariki, Aramco's greatest foe whose alliance with the Venezuelans paved the way for OPEC, or of the wild pro-Nasser demonstrations in Dammam, or of the posters of 'Abd al-Karim Qasim that circulated throughout the Shi'a community on the heels of the 1958 Iraqi revolution.

[...]

In Riyadh, US representatives work in a fortress on the city's outskirts, in a quarter reserved for embassies. The arms dealers, bankers, brokers and ex-CIA agents turned consultants who represent US investors in the Kingdom lease homes and live in compounds scattered across the sprawling metropolis. A handful have lived there long enough to be able to chart the capital's remarkable expansion, decade by decade, shopping mall by shopping mall. For most Americans, however, a sense of history barely exists.

[...]

The Kingdom does subsidize jobs in the United States, through the $60 billion in US weapons and support services ordered by the house of Saud between 1990 and 1995. For the region known as the Gun Belt, the Persian Gulf represents a critical market at a time of crisis in the arms industry. These enormous orders mean more than just jobs and therefore votes for politicians or a way to cushion the pain while the Clinton administration oversees the consolidation of the new weapons and aerospace mega-firms such as Lockheed Martin and Boeing-McDonnell Douglas. Sales to Saudi Arabia and other foreign clients have kept whole production lines running—for example, the M-1 tank—which lowers the price of equipment the Pentagon needs for its worldwide forces.

American officials are candid about the weapons themselves being useless for the Kingdom's defense. The expatriates who sell Saudis planes and tanks by the shipload say the same thing. "The Saudis can't use and don't need what they buy," one executive in Riyadh said during dinner, delivering the punchline with pinpoint accuracy: "Ours are the exception, of course." Defense industry people anchor the US business community in Riyadh today, flanked by the transnational banks and services and technology exporters such as AT&T, General Electric and Bechtel. Princes and other entrepreneurs benefit as middlemen and brokers in these deals. Meanwhile the opposition grumbles and opposition watchers in Washington wring their hands about the crisis looming on the horizon when the regime is forced to choose between guns and butter.

Fighting the Next Oil War

Led by Exxon and Chevron, the old owners of the Aramco oil concession remain fixtures of the Saudi oil and petrochemicals sectors, competing for licensing and management deals. It is a far cry, however, from the 1940s and 1950s when Aramco was in effect the Kingdom's public works agency and oil ministry and America's private diplomatic and intelligence operation rolled into one. An American ambassador once described the firm as "an octopus whose tentacles have extended into almost every domain and phase of the economic life of Saudi Arabia." Back then, it was also relatively easy to see through the private interests behind the sudden discovery of a strategic interest in Middle East oil, an idea that some US officials apparently came to believe in as they managed the transfer of millions in rents to Aramco's owners. Decades later, it is virtually impossible to find dissent from this commonsense view that US security and prosperity are inextricably bound up with access to the Gulf's oil resources. The Pentagon for one is deeply invested in defense of this interpretation of the national interest as part of its own post–Cold War survival strategy. The proposition that markets can be relied on to supply the industrial sectors of the West with their energy needs at reasonable costs, without the need for troops, is a serious threat to their interests. US forces instead remain in place in the Gulf to wage the continuing war against Iraq, deter other hypothetical invaders looming over the horizon, and not least, secure the defense budget.

Speaking of Water

George R. Trumbull IV • *MER* 254, Spring 2010

Life After People, the History Channel's plangently alarmist imagined documentary series on the vestiges of civilization after an unspecified catastrophe, forecasts an end for Dubai's infamous Burj Khalifa, the tallest building in the world at 2,625 feet. The desert location of Dubai, coupled with the persistent engineering challenges of building there, proves the undoing of Burj Khalifa in the History Channel's scenario: Desiccation of cables, pulleys and other such quotidian technologies causes the failure of the tower's automated window-washing equipment, which, in the imagination of cable television, swings free, damaging the building and plunging to the ground below.

The metaphor in the History Channel's vision for Burj Khalifa, once a symbol of Gulf wealth and economic mastery, and now of overreach and architectural hubris, comes from the plunging to earth of Dubai World, the emirate's sovereign wealth fund, amid the global recession beginning in late 2008. Dubai's debt crisis was both of its own making and a result of general financial drought, the drying-up of wells of cash and income in a fundamentally altered world landscape. Nevertheless, the global financial media told their audiences that Dubai could tap another source of wealth, another well, through its connections to oil-rich Abu Dhabi, the federal seat of the UAE.

The History Channel series does not explicitly link the fanciful, imagined failure of Dubai to the financial, immediate one. But, back in the real world, the blithe reassurances of Dubai's recovery reflected an assumed tie between oil and water: Oil wealth can compensate for the hubris of building a self-cleaning "superscraper" in one of the driest regions on earth. At a deeper level, water poverty and oil wealth are assumed to be divorced, incompatible, yet nevertheless locked in to a peculiar relationship in which abundance of one resource can make up for profligacy with the other. The assumption is ill founded. At some point, the oil or the water will run out.

The definition of entire states, and indeed entire regions, as "oil economies" implies that hydrocarbon exports alone keep the economies afloat. But the oil industry—its machinery, laborers and managers—relies as much upon the steady supply of water as global industry, commerce and consumers do upon oil.

Saudi Alchemy: Water into Oil, Oil into Water

Toby Jones • *MER* 254, Spring 2010

The abundance of oil in Saudi Arabia is staggering. With more than 250 billion barrels, the kingdom possesses one-fifth of the world's oil reserves, affording it considerable influence on the international stage. At home, oil has secured the fortunes and political primacy of the al-Saud, the country's ruling family. And it has helped cement the nature of the country's political system, fueling autocracy and ensuring that the kingdom's citizens remain, in many ways, subjects. Their exclusion from the political arena has been justified as part of a bargain whereby oil wealth trickles down in exchange for quiescence; patronage has served as a substitute for political and civil rights. The bargain has basically worked, although even during the 1970s oil boom, the royal family faced trenchant criticism and, at times, violent opposition. For the most part, however, disenfranchised Saudi citizens have been content with oil-funded consumption and comfort, confident that they could forever expect their social and economic welfare to be cared for by the state. Oil's power has often appeared boundless, an engine of such considerable riches that it was capable of anything, at least as long as the political bargain remained in place.

Nowhere has this power been more apparent than in Saudi Arabia's pursuit of fresh water. Saudi Arabia has no natural lakes or rivers. Rainfall is rare, providing only meager succor in the arid environment. Ancient underground water reserves have been tapped and relied on heavily since the 1950s. Since at least the early 1970s, efforts to provide, manage and even create fresh water, and to do so cheaply, have been important elements of the Kingdom's attempts to redistribute its vast oil wealth. Through massive engineering works and infrastructure development, including the design and construction of dams, irrigation and water management systems, oil wealth has been used to build a modern techno-state, one of the principal aims of which has been to provide water for household, agricultural and industrial use. In 1970 a subsidiary of the Coca-Cola Company completed the first massive desalination plant near Jidda on the Red Sea coast, a facility that turned seawater into fresh water. With plenty of oil to fuel the plant's operation and with skyrocketing revenues from the sale of oil to subsidize the cost, Saudi Arabia has effectively been turning oil into water for the last four decades. Today more than 30 desalination plants are at work, each one costing tens of billions of dollars to build and operate.

In the last few years amid rising food costs and anxieties about depleted aquifers, Saudi Arabia began looking for secure sources of fertile land and water abroad. The government purchased sprawling tracts of farmland in far-flung corners of the developing world, including in places like Sudan, Pakistan, Egypt and Ethiopia. War-torn, impoverished or both, many of the countries that have emerged as objects of investment and development are hardly stable, calling into question just how much security they will be able to provide the Saudis.

The result appears to be the creation of a new kind of imperialism, in which wealthy oil producers are looking beyond their own shores to secure foreign natural resources, supporting and developing partnerships with sometimes murderous regimes, with the effect of disrupting local social and economic relations, all justified through the legal acquisition of property and through the mechanisms of the market. Just as resource scarcity served as a pretext for British imperial expansion in the Middle East in the early twentieth century and US dominance after World War II, water scarcity is being offered as justification for the projection of Saudi influence abroad. The charge of imperialism is tempting in part because of the rich irony of oil producers seeming to act the part of neo-imperialists. But it is more appropriate to see Saudi Arabia's political and economic behavior as consistent with the rise of neoliberalism in the late twentieth century; rather than seizing and controlling territory directly, open markets and global institutions have been used to capture resources, shape political systems and establish dominance. Use of such mechanisms enables the Saudis to deny responsibility for the various material and political consequences that their adventures engender.

While the Kingdom's quest for foreign resources seems to mark a new mode of behavior, water and agriculture have long been central to power and empire in Saudi Arabia. A look at Saudi Arabia's past domestic agricultural and hydrological practices hints at what current ventures may have in store for those countries on the receiving end of Saudi agricultural investment.

Water's Imperial Past

In the early twentieth century, water and agriculture played critical roles in Saudi imperial expansion and the consolidation of the modern Saudi state.

The forces that drove the expansion of Saudi power from central Arabia in the early twentieth century were complex. Best known, and perhaps most overemphasized, was the role of religion and particularly Wahhabism, the interpretation of Islam that encouraged conquest, exhorted violence and came to serve as the official orthodoxy of the Saudi state. The clergy possessed considerable social and cultural power, helped police the public sphere and lent credibility to the ruling family's claim to temporal political authority. But Saudi Arabia was not only an Islamic power. It was also an environmental power. Capturing natural resources and establishing centralized control over nature was a key political objective for the Saudis over the course of the twentieth century.

The connections between the environment and Saudi political power were established early on. In 1902 'Abd al-'Aziz ibn Saud wrested control of Riyadh from a political rival and established the seat of what would become modern Saudi Arabia. Almost immediately Saudi leaders set to work expanding their political and territorial power. Arid and rugged, with only a few small oases, central Arabia was impoverished and isolated. There were, however, lush natural prizes on Arabia's coasts, particularly in the east, which was home to the two large oases al-Hasa and

Qatif. There, millions of date palm trees and sprawling verdant gardens were nourished by some of the largest water resources in the Peninsula. Covetous of both the water resources and the revenues generated by the date trade, the Saudis laid siege to the region in 1913, forcibly occupying it and incorporating it into their expanding political realm. Similar calculations went into Saudi conquests across Arabia, including along the Red Sea coast. The treasure was often the rich natural resources available in the targeted lands, keys to commerce and power.

The country's imperial generation understood that their ability to recruit and maintain what turned out to be an imperial army depended in significant measure on their ability to master and manage Arabia's scant water resources. Religious zeal went only so far in convincing those who joined the forces of the Ikhwan, the militia that laid siege to much of Arabia and helped forge the Saudi empire, to take up arms on behalf of the rulers in central Arabia. The Saudis enticed the Ikhwan with the promise of permanent and secure access to water, significant booty for the itinerant warriors. Access to water came at a cost as the Saudis dictated that the Ikhwan give up their nomadism and settle in agricultural communities called *hujjar*. The Ikhwan proved disinterested farmers and the *hujjar* ultimately failed to keep them in place. Nevertheless, the Saudis' environmental impulse was already evident. Throughout the twentieth century, leaders in Riyadh would periodically attempt to settle other Bedouins, who through their movements sometimes troubled oil operations and even called into question the sovereignty of the state itself, by enticing them with secure water and subsidized agriculture.

Power over water and agriculture meant power over space and territory, as well as over human bodies, their labor and their movements. Although the country was arid and water-poor, the vast majority of Saudi Arabian citizens derived their livelihoods from some form of agriculture or herding into the late 1960s. Starting in the 1930s, oil merchants, geologists, mining engineers, social scientists and a network of experts arrived in the Kingdom, ostensibly charged with the responsibility of exploring, prospecting, extracting and marketing Saudi oil. They did that and much more. From the Arabian American Oil Company (Aramco) to individual experts to private consulting firms, American and European investors and experts were intimately engaged in not only the oil industry, but also in exploring for water and other natural resources, in the creation of knowledge about the natural environment, its place in local and regional economies, in the social lives of cultivators and in the creation of agricultural markets, and, most importantly, in the construction of the institutions that would be responsible for overseeing and managing all of them. Science, technology, social science, expertise and knowledge of the environment all became important instruments of power, symbols of authority and a means by which to enroll millions of subjects into the orbit of the centralized state.

[...]

Exporting Insecurity

Saudi Arabia's long struggle to control and remake its environment has come at considerable expense. Politically, the Kingdom's environmental imperative succeeded in helping shore up central authority. But it also produced an array of costly failures, often destroying or depleting the very resources that scientific and technical work was supposed to secure. The ill-fated al-Hasa Irrigation and Drainage Project was but one dramatic example. There were others. While food security, agricultural self-sufficiency and resource scarcity seemed to offer reasonable justifications for environmental interventions and massive engineering efforts, the reality was that concerns about scarcity and security served more to distract from the political calculations that also went into the planning, design and engineering work.

While the considerations driving Saudi Arabia's turn to securing farmland and natural resources abroad are different from those that drove the early consolidation of empire and the processes of state building, there are important parallels. Overcoming scarcity and the pursuit of security continue to frame and justify Saudi Arabia's domestic environmental imperative, even as it has been transformed into a global imperative in the early twenty-first century. Oil wealth continues to make possible the pursuit of and even the creation of other natural resources. It also makes possible a range of potentially devastating political and environmental costs in those places where the kingdom is doing business.

Saudi investment in militarized authoritarian regimes will strengthen them and help secure their own political pathologies. It also threatens to displace local cultivators or bind them to increasingly global networks of investment and expertise that could relegate their personal needs and interests to those of foreign powers, businesses and states. Seen this way, Saudi Arabia has arrived as a neoliberal power, willing and able to bend the policies of impoverished states and communities to its economic will. Perhaps most worrisome, as efforts to re-engineer the largest and most verdant oasis in the kingdom itself demonstrated, foreign farmland, foreign water and other natural resources, so vital and precious locally, will almost certainly be viewed as disposable assets. They have served and will serve as sites of investment, all justified in the name of the food security of foreigners, to be dispensed with when no longer profitable or desirable. Given the potential for considerable environmental damage like that which occurred in al-Hasa, it should be a source of concern that little will be left when the Saudis decide to leave.

Water Conflict and Cooperation in Yemen

Gerhard Lichtenthaeler • *MER* 254, Spring 2010

Yemen is one of the oldest irrigation civilizations in the world. For millennia, farmers have practiced sustainable agriculture using available water and land. Through a myriad of mountain terraces, elaborate water-harvesting techniques and community-managed flood and spring irrigation systems, the country has been able to support a relatively large population. Until recently, that is. Yemen is now facing a water crisis unprecedented in its history.

The Middle East is an arid, water-stressed region, but Yemen stands out for the scale of its water problem. Yemen is one of the world's ten most water-scarce countries. In many of its mountainous areas, the available drinking water, usually drawn from a spring or a cistern, is down to less than one quart per person per day. Its aquifers are being mined at such a rate that groundwater levels have been falling by 10 to 20 feet annually, threatening agriculture and leaving major cities without adequate safe drinking water. Sanaʿa could be the first capital city in the world to run dry.

[...]

Race to the Bottom

Agriculture takes the lion's share of Yemen's water resources, sucking up almost 90 percent. Until the early 1970s, traditional practices ensured a balance between supply and demand. Then the introduction of deep tube wells led to a drastic expansion of land under cultivation. In the period from 1970 to 2004, the irrigated area increased tenfold, from 37,000 to 407,000 hectares, 40 percent of which was supplied by deep groundwater aquifers. The thousands of Yemenis working abroad often invested their remittances in irrigation. Other incentives to expand farmland came in the form of agricultural and fuel subsidies. Farmers began growing less of the local, drought-resistant varieties of wheat and more water-intensive cash crops such as citrus and bananas.

The emerging cash economy also led to a dramatic increase in the cultivation of qat. It is estimated that qat production now accounts for 37 percent of all water used in irrigation. In the water-stressed highland basins of Sanaʿa, Saʿdah, ʿAmran and Dhammar, qat fields now occupy half of the total irrigated area. Groundwater levels in these highlands have fallen so precipitously that only the lucrative returns from qat justify the cost of operating and maintaining a well.

[...]

One-third of the 125 wells operated by the state-owned Sanaʿa Local Corporation for Water Supply and Sanitation for supply of the capital have been drilled down to a depth of 2,600 to 3,900 feet. The combined output of all these wells barely meets 35 percent of the growing city's need. The rest is supplied either by small, privately owned networks or by hundreds of mobile tankers. In recent years, as water quality has deteriorated, privately owned kiosks that use reverse osmosis—a water filtration method—to purify poor-quality groundwater supplies have mushroomed in Sanaʿa and other towns.

Future supply options include pumping desalinated water from the Red Sea over a distance of 155 miles, over 9,000-foot mountains into the capital, itself located at an altitude of 7,226 feet. The enormous pumping cost would push the price of water up to $10 per cubic meter (roughly 35 cubic feet). Yemen may be willing to pay this price for household demand. For agricultural water, however, the elevated cost is out of the question since the quantity required per capita is at least one hundred times greater. Other options to supply Sanaʿa from adjacent regions are fraught due to perceived water rights. Islam teaches that water is a gift from God and cannot be owned. Land, however, can. When a person digs or drills a well on his own land, he obtains the right to extract and use as much water as he can draw. The increasing awareness of the country's water scarcity has resulted in a race to the bottom—every man for himself. Well owners are trying to capture what remains of this valuable resource before the neighbors do.

[...]

'Amran

The 'Amran basin is located 30 miles north of Sana'a at an altitude of 6,560 feet. In 2008, the province established the 'Amran Basin Committee, headed by the governor, to regulate water use. Other members include the directors of the districts that make up the basin, representatives of ministries and authorities concerned with water and agriculture, the local police chief and, importantly, farmers and local interest groups. Meetings are held every two months to discuss water-related issues and consider new applications for drilling wells.

Dwindling water resources are cause for alarm among both basin committee members and area farmers. Over 2,600 pumps now tap the catchment's meager groundwater deposits. As a result, wells are being drilled to prohibitive depths, as low as 1,200 feet in places. Between 1991 and 2005, most wells had to be deepened by an average of 295 feet. At the same time, well yield—the quantity of water obtained per second—has plummeted. The period between 1991 and 2005 saw the number of wells increase by 120 percent, while the water supply rose by only 26 percent.

Villagers, increasingly aware of the need for collective action, are angered by the discovery that over 100 new wells were drilled in 2009, almost all of them without a permit. The arrival of a drilling rig sows tension between the farmer and the villagers, who raise their concerns with the basin committee. Bakr 'Ali Bakr, the deputy governor and tribesman who handles the day-to-day operations of the committee, has been a key negotiator in defusing water crises in the 'Amran basin.

Perched on the crest of an inactive volcanic cone is the village of Bani Maymoun. It belongs to the district of Iyal Surayh, home to the Bakil tribe and the watershed between the Sana'a and 'Amran water basins. The predominantly volcanic soil is ideal for growing high-value qat, cultivation of which has boomed. Bulldozers can often be seen leveling slopes for new fields, while truckload after truckload of additional soil is then hauled from afar to fill in the reclaimed terraces. With the unpredictable rainfall often not exceeding six inches per year, irrigation water has to be transported over rough tracks by Mercedes tankers. The result has been new water markets just for the cultivation of qat. Early in 2007, the price increase for irrigation water sparked a conflict that tested the community. Well owners from the village were starting to charge 5,000 riyals ($25) for a one-hour share of irrigation water. Up to that point, the commonly accepted rate paid by farmers with no well of their own had been just half that—2,500 riyals. The well owners, however, argued that new demand from water tankers queuing up at their wells justified the increase. They had become water traders adjusting to emerging markets.

The dispute soon reached the ears of Bakr 'Ali Bakr. He called the tribal elders, who summoned the village men to reach a tribal consensus. It was agreed that well owners from the community were no longer allowed to fill up tankers for qat fields outside their immediate territory. Also, the price for a one-hour share was fixed at its previous level. "Such regulations reached by consensus are usually honored by all community members," said Bakr. "Later, when one of the well owners tried to breach the decision, men from Bani Maymoun just aimed a couple of bullets at the tires of the water tanker. That put an end to the water business."

Bottom-Up Conservation

Bani Maymoun is small and homogeneous, and in its case a verbal agreement on groundwater trade sufficed. In other conflicts over water resources, tribal communities increasingly resort to a written consensus-based form of regulation, known in Arabic as a *marqoum*. Hijrat al-Muntasir, a village located at an altitude of 9,842 feet at the western watershed of the 'Amran basin, is one such place where drilling imperiled vital drinking water resources.

The drilling rig was blocking the narrow mountain track when I visited Hijrat al-Muntasir in 2007. Qat farmers had gathered around the heavy equipment as if to protect it. On the escarpment above, more than 50 tribesmen had positioned themselves, several with AK-47 machine guns. It appeared as if both groups had been awaiting our team's arrival. The tension eased, and some of the tribesmen climbed down from the ridge to make their views heard. The qat farmers, desperate after yet another of their wells had run dry, were about to drill deep into the limestone. The villagers of Hijrat al-Muntasir feared that more groundwater extraction would wipe out their small spring, the sole drinking water source for the 700 inhabitants. They had mobilized their men to prevent the drilling. They accused the qat farmers and the rig owner of lacking a valid permit.

A short but bumpy drive took us to the village. Women and children with dozens of empty water containers lined the route to the nearby spring, displaying an impressive array of protest banners prepared by the schoolchildren. "We hold you responsible for our future," one of them read in Arabic.

A quick survey revealed the gravity of the situation. The water from the spring was carefully rationed. Salih al-Muntasiri, a village elder, brought out the document that listed the water allotments for each family—roughly ten quarts per person per day. Each quantity taken from the roofed cistern fed by trickle from the mountain spring was meticulously recorded and monitored by 'Ali, the gatekeeper of the cistern.

Trouble for the qat irrigators had started when the people of al-Qarin, a village nearby, banned the sale and trade of groundwater from their local wells to outsiders. A *marqoum*, signed by the village elders, was written to regulate the details of this social contract. Groundwater levels around al-Qarin had fallen noticeably over the previous years, sparking fears about the future. At the same time, influential families from the village had been drilling new wells and were selling water to tanker owners who would then take it to new qat farms in other areas—including the fields near Hijrat al-Muntasir. As the ban came into effect, the qat farmers decided to give drilling one more try. On hearing the news, the men of Hijrat al-Muntasir sent a delegation to Bakr 'Ali Bakr.

After several weeks of negotiations, both parties finally agreed to accept the outcome and recommendations of a government technical study. The various parties to the dispute met several times at the site of the drilling rig. Gradually, the focus of their discussions shifted from technicalities to sustainable management of the village's water resources.

In the spring of 2009, I was invited back for the inauguration of a small village project. It was the first visit for the vice governor and other dignitaries. Hijrat al-Muntasir had slaughtered two oxen for the occasion. Banners leading up to the village welcomed the guests. There was good news—the drilling had been stopped. In addition, each household had built a cesspit to improve overall sanitary conditions. Community organizers working for the Social Fund for Development had paid the village a few visits, teaching the benefits of better hygiene.

But there was also bad news. As 'Ali, the gatekeeper, unlocked the screechy iron access gate to the cistern, a number of village women came rushing down a steep path, each carrying a number of empty bright yellow containers. "No water today—go back home!" shouted 'Ali. "Tomorrow morning, inshallah." The daily flow of the spring had been reduced to a trickle—from ten to just five quarts per person per day. Whether the reduction was due to a temporary lack of rainfall or to permanent climate change, no one can say. "One thing is certain, however," Salih al-Muntasiri told his German visitors. "Without your support in preventing the drilling two years ago, we would blame the slow drying-up of our spring on the qat farmers. There would be trouble and strife and God knows what."

Which Scarcity?

Communities such as Hijrat al-Muntasir are coping admirably with their diminishing spring. In social science terms, they retain a strong adaptive capacity, defined as the sum of social resources available to counter an increasing natural resource scarcity.

Social scientists now make a clear distinction between "first-order" scarcity of a natural resource and "second-order" scarcity of adaptive capacity. The latter, according to Tony Allan of the University of London, one of the world's leading water experts, is much more determinant of outcomes. Developing coping mechanisms at the community level is a step in the right direction.

Coping mechanisms will not be enough to solve Yemen's water crisis, however. The structural problems—among them, the draining of aquifers to irrigate fields of cash crops like qat—must be addressed. As has been stressed by Christopher Ward, a long-time analyst of water issues in Yemen, "a decentralization and the partnership approach can only be viewed as elements of a damage limitation exercise aimed at slowing down the rate of resource depletion, to allow Yemen time to develop patterns of economic activity less dependent on water mining." In other words, Yemen needs to demonstrate adaptive capacity at the national level. A national debate on water is planned for late 2010, involving the president as well as other top opinion and decision-makers. This conference will be a crucial test of political will: The Yemeni political class will need to place a high priority on the development of viable alternatives to agriculture in order to prevent the country from slipping into Malthusian catastrophe.

Yemenis on Mars

Engseng Ho • *MER* 211, Summer 1999

When American social scientists began conducting research in the Yemen Arab Republic in the 1970s, there was a great sense of opening and adventure. This opening up (*infitah*) was also part of Yemen's national mood, as a freshly minted republic emerging from a long civil war. A key engine of this opening and newness was the mass migration of Yemeni workers to Gulf oil-producing countries. The new republic's new mood was encouraged by shiny new cars and shiny new goods packaged in plastic. A common phrase in the 1970s summed it up: Yemen had just been catapulted from the Middle to Modern Ages. In the 1980s, after president Salim Rubai 'Ali's Maoist peasant insurrections, or *intifadas*, of the 1970s had died down, and with improved relations with the Gulf oil-producing states under President 'Ali Nasir, the socialist People's Democratic Republic also experienced an *infitah* thanks to hard currency remittances from the Gulf. It seemed a truism to both Yemenis and Yemenists that Yemen could not turn the clock back.

With the hindsight of 20 years, it now appears that the 1970s was an exceptional rather than transitional period. The 1973 Arab-Israeli war, the power of OPEC, Sheikh Zaki Yamani, Americans shooting each other at gas stations—all these have been forgotten, as America's streets now teem with monster minivans and a gallon of gas again costs less than a dollar. Now it is Yemenis who are shooting each other at gas stations. The initial building boom in the Gulf has ceased and Saudi Arabia faces budget deficits. The impact of these changes first registered in 1986, when oil fell from $30 per barrel to $10. But this was only temporary. Then the Gulf war erupted; but while oil prices went up, Yemenis in the Gulf went home. Again, this was supposed to be a temporary problem. If the working population of Yemen at that time was 4 million people, and a million workers came back from the oil countries, and assuming Yemen's unemployment rate was a hypothetical zero, it immediately shot up 20 percent. The rate continues to rise. The temporary situation is now permanently temporary.

Yemenis in Space

Everywhere in Yemen, one hears this joke: When the Americans landed on the moon, they found Yemeni Rada'is working there. Or Ibbis. Or Hadramis, depending on where one hears the joke. Recently, when the Pathfinder went to Mars, Reuters reported that a couple of Yemenis threatened to slap lawsuits on NASA, claiming they had inherited Mars from their ancestors. They were not joking. In villages throughout Yemen, where people have long been dependent on remittances from abroad, the *mahjar*, or diaspora, is practically considered a birthright. Some Yemeni families are virtual matriarchies. Sons do not know their fathers working abroad, and their sons do not see them when they in turn go abroad. Migrants might as well be on Mars. One begins to see why some people think Mars is a *mahjar* that they have inherited from their grandfathers.

There is a poignant side to the Yemeni lawsuit over Mars. On Earth itself, Yemenis have run out of *mahjars*. Although Yemenis have long experienced migration, its benefits have not been as durable as one might expect. Part of the problem is that successful émigrés generally do not return home, and after a few generations they are lost to Yemen. The high-profile Osama bin Laden and his family of construction magnates are a case in point. Part of the problem is that Yemenis have not made the most of their migrations. They have succeeded most dramatically in countries which were just opening up or booming, such as Egypt and Iraq during the Islamic conquests, Christian Ethiopia besieged by Ahmad Granye in the fifteenth century, India under the Mughals, Hyderabad under Muslim rule, Java and Singapore under colonial rule and, of course, the Gulf countries in the 1970s and 1980s. Under these conditions, Yemenis excelled and developed wealthy communities in the *mahjar*. However, once these places settled down to normal levels of growth and the émigré communities grew and assimilated, the Yemeni homeland would inevitably lose out. But there would always be new *mahjars* to explore.

At the close of the century and the millennium, it is unlikely that Yemeni migrants will find any more new countries about to be colonized or opened. They will have to make do with the *mahjars* they already have: America, Britain, Saudi Arabia and the Gulf, as well as lingering connections with East Africa and Southeast Asia.

6 The Roots and Course of the 2011 Uprisings

The 2011 uprisings against entrenched autocrats in Tunisia, Egypt, Syria and Libya took some people in those countries and many outside observers by surprise. Not so in Yemen, where local and foreign political analysts had tracked widespread, pervasive disgruntlement, gloominess and impatience with the Salih dictatorship for more than a decade. In 2010–11, Salih's forces continued an unsuccessful campaign to subdue the Houthis in the far north; the Hirak in the southern governorates gained widespread popular support there; in the central regions, peasants, ranchers and urbanites were all increasingly fed up. Indeed cliché headlines during that time described a Yemen that was continually "on the brink" of disintegration. The first two excerpts here, by Sarah Phillips and Susanne Dahlgren, give a sense of the partisan, regional, class-based and sometimes sectarian fissures that were festering in the first millennial decade. Those essays set the stage for the mass, nationwide revolt against the Salih dictatorship that began in 2011 and continued into 2012 and 2013. Stacey Philbrick Yadav and I each followed those events as they unfolded; Mary Ann Tétreault and Justin Gengler offered insights from Kuwait and Qatar, respectively, on more limited unrest in the Gulf.

Saudi royalty suppressing Yemeni cries for justice. (April 8, 2013)
By Samer Mohammed al-Shameeri

Foreboding about the Future in Yemen

Sarah Phillips • *MERO*, Apr. 3, 2006

In the early 1990s, Yemen was buzzing with optimism. The long-desired dream of unification between the former North and South had been achieved, oil revenues were increasing and the dramatic political reforms enacted by the new government had Yemen pegged as a vibrant transitional democracy.

A decade and a half later, living standards have plummeted, oil and water are fast running out and the armed rebellion that Salih had initially expected to put down in under a week has entered its 18th month with little sign of fully abating. Corruption has also reached dizzying heights. While it is difficult to quantify, statistics published by the World Bank indicate a dramatic upward trend in the last few years, while Yemen was ranked 112th (with the least corrupt country in first place) in Transparency International's 2005 Corruption Perception Index. Anecdotal evidence also abounds. For example, the man appointed to head the state's anti-corruption body, the Central Organization for Control and Auditing (COCA), was given the post while awaiting trial for fraud allegedly committed during his previous tenure in government. After then being fired again for major fraud while running COCA, he was appointed to head the Judicial Inspection Board to ensure the integrity of judges.

Exasperated by such developments, the foreign donors on whom the Yemeni government depends have begun to withdraw their assistance. In 2004, the government was chastized by the World Bank for its rising corruption and warned that they could not rely on the Bank's continued support if genuine reforms were not implemented. The Bank issued a report stating that "Yemen is clearly slipping into a worst-case scenario" of economic performance. In 2005, the World Bank delivered on its threat and reduced an upcoming loan package by 34 percent (from $420 million over three years to $280 million), citing lack of transparency and good governance. This reduction is combined with a loss of income from the International Monetary Fund, which has been withholding $300 million in concessional finance since 2002, due to the government's failure to comply with its prescribed structural adjustment package. The Yemeni state is almost completely dependent on sources of income over which it exercises no direct control. Together, oil and donor money constitute at least 85 percent of government revenue. As oil begins to dry up and frustrated donors reduce their aid commitments, the government's options contract correspondingly.

The Economist Intelligence Unit estimates that Yemen's gross domestic product growth for 2006 will be around 2.5 percent—insufficient to keep pace with population growth (around 3.5 percent per year), let alone meet the World Bank target of 8 percent required for sustained development. The fact that this slump is occurring in the middle of a prolonged oil price spike further indicates the level of corruption and mismanagement that is the backdrop to the political challenges facing the Yemeni regime. Oil revenue probably makes up some 75 percent of the country's budget and, failing the unlikely discovery of substantial new deposits, the World Bank estimates that Yemen's reserves will be negligible by 2012. This date is ten years earlier than was previously thought and represents the natural limit of the current order. Before total depletion, however, oil exports will drop significantly; they are likely to be halved within just three years. While an appeal for foreign and domestic investment to spur other industries could help reduce Yemen's dependence on oil money, investors have been scared away by the corruption that, time and time again, has lined the pockets of the military and tribal elite.

Dissent Widens

While democratization remains popular, Yemenis no longer seriously discuss it as a short-term possibility. The prospect of state failure has increasingly taken democracy's place as the subject of speculation at private gatherings across the country, where Yemenis often speak as if collapse were a foregone conclusion. People attached to the regime no longer necessarily shy away from such topics either, one estimating that "around 90 percent" of his colleagues give voice to grim expectations for the future: "Five years ago, it was probably only 30 percent." In a country that until recently harbored real expectations of decentralized power, hopes for a reprieve from crisis are now being pinned on the linchpin of any autocratic system: the will of the executive.

It is hard to overstate the urgency of Yemen's situation. In July 2005, the Carnegie Endowment for International Peace's Failed States Index placed Yemen as the country eighth most at risk of disintegration. By this count, Yemen was deemed less stable than war-torn and impoverished Afghanistan, and only marginally more so than Iraq and Somalia, a judgment that was seized upon with an attitude of "I told you so" in Sana'a's political circles. Anger on the streets is obvious and has been directed at the president himself (as opposed to the usual faceless "government"). In the July 2005 riots over the reduction of fuel subsidies, tens and possibly hundreds of thousands of people took to the streets of the capital, some shouting "la Sanhan ba'd al-yawm" (no Sanhan [President Salih's tribe] after today) and that Salih was the enemy of God. These chants were certainly the most open display of antipathy for the person of the president in Yemen for quite some time. Protesters also burned Salih's photo on the street and, in an apparent first, many of the demonstrators attempted to reach his heavily guarded residence.

Resentment of unification in the former South has reached levels unseen since the 1994 civil war. Even the victors in that conflict, the northern elite, have been quoted nervously acknowledging the rising southern discontent. Sheikh 'Abd al-Majid al-Zindani, a popular and powerful Sunni cleric from the former North who railed against the South in the lead-up to the civil war, was quoted by the Yemeni weekly *al-Wasat* newspaper in June 2005 as telling President Salih that "if there were a referendum in the South today on the union, they would all vote against it." Southerners believe that corruption, biased government hiring policies and unlawful confiscation of land by the northern-led regime are taking what is rightfully theirs. Many are becoming less reserved about stating their desire for separation from the northern-dominated regime, an aspiration encouraged by Saudi Arabia the last time around. "We like to be called Hadramis, not Yemenis. Yemen is *shamal* (to the north)," commented one businessman in the oil-rich eastern province of Hadramawt. With about 80 percent of Yemen's remaining oil in the former South (the majority of which is in Hadramawt), secession is a prospect that would all but starve the people of the densely populated northwestern areas. As demonstrated in 1994, the northern-dominated regime would not shrink from a fight to maintain this valuable territory.

Then there is the messy armed uprising centered in and around the northern governorate of Sa'dah. "This is the biggest challenge in North Yemen since [Salih] came to power" in 1978, comments a well-informed official. One of Salih's clearest talents since taking office has been his ability to stay above the fray in local tribal conflicts, in the time-worn tradition of *divide et impera*. This time he is caught squarely between two groups that once provided his regime with its greatest support: the northern tribes and northern Zaydi religious leaders. The uprising is led by the al-Houthis, a *sayyid* family (one claiming descent from the Prophet Muhammad) invoking a Zaydi discourse of just rule and supported by armed followers—many of whom are religious students. The movement is arguably all the more dangerous because of its basis in religious doctrine and the Zaydi political tradition, which considers the overthrow of an unjust ruler to be religiously acceptable. However, also competing in the mix are the tribes of Sa'dah that are fighting the government; the tribes that Salih is paying to fight on the government's behalf; and the (also largely tribal) military. The propensity of tribal fighters to sell their loyalties to the highest bidder, and the readiness of military leaders to facilitate this practice for a cut, are pulling the president deeper into a guerrilla-style conflict than he could have intended.

Accurate figures are still impossible to obtain, but the same well-informed official stated in January 2006 that there were "not less than

20,000" government troops deployed in the vicinity of Sa'dah, and that the army was losing an average of 10 to 15 soldiers per day. Fatalities on the other side are even less clear, but are unlikely to be fewer than those suffered by government forces. If this official's estimate is correct, then an average of 600–900 people are being killed in the fighting each month. There are also indications that some of the support for the insurgents is coming from outside of Sa'dah, from those who are ideologically opposed to the rebels' religious motivations but who sympathize with their broader critique of the government. The government has tried to link the movement to support obtained from Iran, but with little success. "The big thing is that the government does not know how they are supported and who is arming [the Houthi rebels]," observed the official. "They are totally confused. It is probably coming from both [domestic and foreign sources]. How did they get these arms when they are under siege? There are Yemenis supporting them from within Yemen.... There are supporters throughout the country...[from a] wider opposition: the South, the poor and the enemies of the system." In late January, two key leaders of the rebellion escaped from one of Yemen's highest-security prisons. "This was no ordinary prison," he noted. The security of such high-value prisoners would not have been left to underlings, and the escape could not have been carried out in complete secrecy. This incident does not necessarily point to broad support within the system for the insurgents, but it does underline the regime's uncertainty about the nature of their enemy and the fact that questions about their right to rule are perceived to be coming from many corners.

The regime's response to the Sa'dah rebellion has demonstrated just how forcefully it is prepared to counter direct threats to its dominance. But, in doing so, the regime is also demonstrating its ultimate weakness, given the enormous toll on the military and the erosion of the regime's traditional support base of northern tribal and religious leaders. Moreover, the Houthi rebellion has probably revealed to the opposition, and perhaps to those with radical inclinations, that the regime's coercive power is not as insurmountable as once imagined. If a movement that began as 1,000–3,000 angry citizens can tie down a government that, according to the estimates of officials, spends up to 40 percent of its budget on security, what could a more concerted effort achieve? This prospect has been debated in a number of qat chews attended by Sana'a's politically active and aware.

An Uncertain Ally

While there is no relationship between the Shi'a Houthi movement and militant Salafi Sunnis in Yemen, the inability of the government to end the conflict in Sa'dah may be emboldening the latter, whose daring moves of late suggest growing confidence. In early February, 23 suspected terrorists broke out of a high-security prison in Sana'a. (Three and possibly more have been recaptured.) The most famous escapee was Jamal al-Badawi, the alleged architect of the USS *Cole* bombing in 2000, in which 17 US naval personnel were killed. The official story has it that the detainees used broomsticks and sharpened spoons to tunnel a considerable distance to a nearby mosque. It is inconceivable that such an elaborate escape could have been executed without the acquiescence of well-placed members of the Political Security Organization (PSO), the domestic intelligence agency that answers directly to Salih. The United States shares this view. *Newsweek* quoted a US official who described the content of a classified embassy cable: "One thing is certain: PSO insiders must have been involved."

As a key partner in US anti-terrorism efforts, the Yemeni government has been treading very carefully since the USS *Cole* attack, seeking to appease both the United States and the network of militants and their sympathizers, who include members of the military and security apparatus. Since 2003, there has been a fragile truce between the government and members of the umbrella group Qa'idat al-Jihad fi al-Yemen (Base of Jihad in Yemen), which includes the Aden-Abyan Islamic Army and al-Qaeda sympathizers. Under this agreement, a number of militants were released from jail and, according to the September 25, 2003, *Yemen Times*, assurances were made that the government would "terminate its military cooperation with the US." US pressure has also been intense and, accordingly, the government has swung between promises and counter-promises. The prison break is a symptom of this delicate and awkward balance. Anything that escalates the standoff with the Salafis is potentially very dangerous. The February "escape" points to three possibilities: The breakout was staged to prevent the detainees from implicating others; it is to pave the way for further militant operations; or it is simply a show of strength by the radicals. None of these possibilities bodes well for Yemen's already diminished stability—and the United States has taken notice.

In January 2005, the US House of Representatives passed a resolution including Yemen on a list of Arab countries whose "political and economic liberalization efforts" could "serve as a model" for the region. In November, however, Salih was told in Washington that his promises of reform were no longer sufficient. In a rather uncharacteristic message to a partner in the "war on terror," top US officials criticized the regime's failure to deliver on promised reforms and recommended the president quickly do more, lest he lose Washington's support in Yemen's 2006 presidential election. One US diplomat says privately: "Our policy in Yemen has really shifted in the last six months." Another was reported in *US News & World Report* to have said: "We're not going to give [the Yemeni government] a pass anymore."

Two well-placed Yemeni observers report that Salih was shocked by the directness of the message he received in Washington, though his closest advisers counsel him that he need not be alarmed, since the United States does not understand the dynamics of Yemeni politics. Over the course of the events, there have been no reform initiatives from the president since November other than a reshuffling of the cabinet and a promise to release 627 al-Houthi supporters from prison.

Stepped-up US pressure on Yemen to turn over al-Zindani for allegedly supplying arms and funds to al-Qaeda is another indicator of waning patience. Al-Zindani has been on the Treasury Department list as a "specially designated global terrorist" since February 2004, and his location in Yemen is well known. The drive to have him extradited began in earnest following the February prison break, however, and was coupled with a letter to Salih from President George W. Bush, who used the missive to air his doubts about Yemen's "commitment to the war on terrorism."

[...]

The Snake with a Thousand Heads: The Southern Cause in Yemen

Susanne Dahlgren • *MER* 256, Fall 2010

In the summer of 2007, a lively and nonviolent movement sprang up in the southern provinces of Yemen to protest the south's marginalization by the north. The movement was sparked by demonstrations held that spring by forcibly retired members of the army, soon to be accompanied by retired state officials and unemployed youth. The deeper roots of the uprising lie in grievances dating to the 1994 civil war that consolidated the north's grip over the state and, southerners would say, the resources of the country. Southerners soon took to calling their protests the Hirak, a coordinated campaign against a northern "occupation."

What is happening in southern Yemen should be understood as a broad-based popular movement demanding sounder and more just governance. As such, the southern cause commands widespread support (including from some outside the south). The movement encompasses elements that want to secede and, in a country long forecast to become a "failing state," if not the "next Afghanistan," these are the actors who are featured in the international media. To the extent that the Southern Movement has been noticed amidst Yemen's multiple problems, it has mostly been dismissed as secessionist or, following the preference of the government, cast as a potential ally of al-Qaeda in the Arabian Peninsula (AQAP) and a threat to Yemeni stability.

The southern uprising is a completely new type of social movement in this part of the world and, even inside Yemen, old-guard activists often fail to understand it. In a country where about 60 percent of the population is under 25 years of age, the movement reflects the aspirations of youth for opportunity and openness to the outside world. It also advocates peaceful resistance rather than armed struggle. As the protests have proliferated, however, President Salih has vowed to crush them. His security forces and the army obliged with blockades of entire provinces (such as Radfan, where the 1963 southern revolution against British imperialism was launched), use of live ammunition against unarmed demonstrators, air raids upon entire cities, assassinations and arbitrary detentions. Still, the southerners have persisted in attempts to foster a new political culture in the poorest Arab country.

Salih and his regime propagate a narrative whereby the southerners, about one-sixth of the Yemeni population, suffer in equal measure with residents of the more populous north. Because of Yemen's pre-1990 history, however, the southern cause is unique. The southerners yearn for reestablishment of the rule of law they recall from the days before unification with the north. Some hope to remain united with their northern brothers under better rule; others would just as soon split the country once more.

Unified and Divided

From 1967 to 1990, the southern provinces of Yemen—Aden, Lahij, Abyan, Shabwa, Hadramawt and Mahra—comprised a self-declared socialist state known for most of its existence as the People's Democratic

Republic of Yemen. [...] After 1988, the border was opened so that Yemenis on either side could visit the "other part of the homeland." It was not so strange, therefore, when the south entered enthusiastically into unity with the north in 1990.

But southerners' contentment soon turned to worry about the failing economy, rising poverty and abuse of power by Salih and his loyalists. The YSP figure 'Ali Salim al-Bayd was made vice president of unified Yemen, junior partner to Salih in an arrangement southerners felt was mirrored all down the ranks of state. Salih had majority control of the Presidential Council and the Ministry of Finance. Southerners complained as well of clientelism, corruption and centralization of power around personality rather than political institutions in the unified state. The northern and southern army commands, for example, did not merge, but remained loyal to Salih and al-Bayd's faction of the YSP, respectively. Negotiations over the mechanics of unification began to break down amid a "war of declarations" from both sides in Yemen's newly rambunctious press. Meanwhile, "Arab Afghans" returning from the anti-Soviet jihad, among them the Abyan tribal figure Tariq al-Fadhli, were used to assassinate more than 100 of the YSP's cadre—apparently with the northerners' blessing. Southern cries for bolstering the rule of law date from the assassination campaign. Many notables on both sides genuinely desired unity, as did the bulk of the population, but hardliners in Sana'a and secessionists within the YSP prevailed in the internal struggles. A secession front emerged behind al-Bayd and his party colleague Haydar al-'Attas, significantly including two former enemies of the YSP, 'Abd al-Rahman al-Jifri of the Sons of Yemen League and 'Abdallah al-Asnag of the Front for the Liberation of South Yemen. A result was the 1994 civil war, which ended in a decisive victory for Salih's forces. On July 7, 1994, northern forces took Aden, trashing and looting government offices and public-sector companies. The leaders of the secession front, having retreated before the advancing northern army, escaped abroad. To add to the humiliation of defeat, southerners were made to celebrate July 7 as a day of national unity. Today's southern activists have renamed it the "day of rage."

Over the past decade, the rifts in the southern political establishment began to heal as the population soured on the policies of Salih's government. Southerners have protested with special vehemence against what they view as large-scale land theft and reallocation of southern wealth and resources to the northern elite. During the 1994 fighting, 'Ali Nasir, a former president of South Yemen ousted in a 1986 intra-regime bloodbath, had directed his partisans to fight on the side of the north. In 2006, speaking from Syrian exile, he declared that Yemeni politicians had been overly hasty in pursuing the original unification. Two years later, on January 13, 2008, his loyalists and their allies in a tiny communist party joined YSP rank-and-filers and the Hirak supporters in a reconciliation rally held in the Aden district of Shaykh 'Uthman. The following spring, al-Bayd acknowledged and apologized to the southern people for his role in unification. Al-Bayd, who remains in exile, now heads the Supreme Southern Movement Council, one of the many groups that form the Hirak.

[...]

The Southern Movement

In any case, the popular movement in the south is much larger and more diffuse than the councils of politicos. It is built on the idea of fairly autonomous local units, each of whose leaders arises organically. As one Adeni man with roots in Abyan said, "It is a snake with a thousand heads. The authorities cannot stop it, as when local leaders are detained or go undercover, new ones replace them. It is the strength of the movement that it does not have a national leadership that can be liquidated." Many of the local cadres are youth, and the signature tools of the Hirak are new communication technologies and social media such as text messaging, Facebook and independent websites that the government has not been able to close down. To keep up weekly demonstrations amid the army sieges and road closures, activists are flexible about the location of rallies, which they schedule by text message on short notice. This "just-in-time" production of protest is possible because the rallies are local and the demonstrators all live in the vicinity. To obtain information on airstrikes in blocked-off areas, some of which the government claims are home to "al-Qaeda camps," young Internet wizards devise means of circumventing state-censored servers and gaining access to foreign-based websites.

The situation in the southern provinces has started to resemble the independence struggle of the 1950s and 1960s. As the British did then, the Yemeni regime faces its fiercest resistance in Radfan and al-Yafa'. As an old-guard women's activist says she told a dismissive northern official, "Do not think we cannot throw you out of our country. We did that to the British, who had a much bigger army than you do."

Most Hirak activists want to establish an independent state and cancel the unification accord. After independence is reclaimed, it will be up to the political forces to agree on what kind of state the south will be. In January the Yemeni Center for Civil Rights found in a poll that 70 percent of southern Yemenis are in favor of secession. However precise this number is, the proportion of southerners who back secession has certainly grown rapidly, as state violence and suppression of press freedom have escalated.

[...]

Three years into the southern uprising, the regime in Sana'a has learned how to disseminate its version of the truth. The offices of *al-Ayyam*, the premier press outlet for movement sympathizers, have been shuttered. Army blockades ensure that little detailed reporting of any sort leaks out of the south. Government officials in southern provinces are regularly briefed in mass meetings to keep them on message, which the state also propagates via "independent" newspapers with more or less open links to the security apparatus. Foreign reporters, meanwhile, are gulled by seemingly firsthand information about al-Qaeda, which since the failed underwear bombing in Detroit on December 25, 2009, has been easy to sell as the "number one threat in Yemen." Part of regime propaganda tactics is to hint that al-Bayd and other southern leaders are in cahoots with al-Qaeda or—through the Houthi rebels in Yemen's northern highlands—Hizballah and Iran. These insinuations find a ready audience in the United States, in particular, and military aid continues to flow to Sana'a. The regime's manipulation of Western fears of al-Qaeda angers southerners, who know the US-made weaponry is deployed against them, as well as the Houthis.

Privatization Gone Bad

In the 1990s, like developing countries around the world, Yemen embarked upon the privatization of its public-sector industries and agricultural ventures, as recommended by the World Bank and the International Monetary Fund. While neither the north nor the south was a worker's paradise before unification, privatization was more haphazard in the south and social dislocation was more severe. Aggressive privatization started after 1994 civil war. Machinery and raw materials were looted in the chaos that followed the arrival of northern troops in Aden and other cities. In Aden, most industrial enterprises were closed down because looting had left them unable to function and the employees, most of them women, were sent home with a state pension. The factories were then put up for sale. Some of them were simply turned into real estate, affording investors access to huge tracts of land. In actual terms, therefore, privatization meant idling Adeni industries and freeing up market share for producers located in the northern industrial zones of Ta'iz, Hudayda and Sana'a. After a few years, former factory workers in the south lost their pensions and joined the swelling ranks of the unemployed.

There were also several well-connected northerners who showed up in the south after 1994 bearing forged deeds to property. In rural areas, privatization of state farms and cooperatives meant that lands were simply given to members of the northern elite. The workers were left entirely without income. These desperate people and their teenaged children form the backbone of the Southern Movement in the countryside.

Too Much, Too Soon

The southerners' grievances are mostly political and economic in nature, but cultural and religious concerns have also come to the fore. According to common sentiments in the south, northern ways of life have been imposed upon the south by the government, pushing the south 100 years back in time. Tribal customs like child marriages and summary executions are two examples that southerners cite; the official patronage system is another. The idea that the Salih regime is tribal and "backward" is one that many northerners share. As one human rights activist from the northern town of Ta'iz explained his support for al-Hirak, "First the tribal-based rulers of Sanaa destroyed all initiative and marginalized Ta'izz; now they are doing the same in the south."

These alleged cultural differences have increasingly been linked in the popular consciousness to religion. After the 1994 war, the conservative Islah party took over the reins of southern governorates and launched a "re-Islamization" campaign. The campaign has mostly been unsuccessful. When Islamists headed by the ill-reputed Islah leader 'Abd al-Majid al-Zindani proposed a Saudi-type morality police for Yemeni streets, for example, the government was quick to refuse it any authority. Still, the mere attempt at establishing such a religious watchdog stirred Yemeni Women's Union leaders to say it "undermined women and the fundamental role they play in building Yemeni society." The era of unification has coincided with the tide of religious conservatism that has swept over every country in the Middle East. Almost all Yemeni women, for example, have donned cloaks and headscarves, and an increasing number wear the *niqab*, the full-face veil that leaves only the eyes visible. Hardline religious schools have proliferated. In earlier times, these phenomena were certainly present, but they were not criticized in the same terms. Today many men say the *niqab* is too much. As one male government official explained, "If this is religion, I don't want it." Southerners often claim that northerners have a shallow, materialistic view of modernity, rushing to buy the latest model of sports utility vehicle but failing to send their daughters to university.

Modernity, in general, is something that southerners associate with themselves and their region's history of European colonization, nationalist rebellion and Marxist-inspired governance. Many southerners would agree with the view of a YSP official in 1982: that unity with the "backward" north will be possible only when the latter develops to the level of the south. Today the YSP's official stance is much softer, of course. In March, the party endorsed the Vision for National Salvation, the opposition's program for a democratic system of federal autonomy, drafted by the Preparatory Committee for National Dialogue on which the YSP sits. This document has not won widespread support in the south, as many perceive that full unification is premature.

Today more and more families in the south tune in to Aden TV, the satellite channel that broadcasts live from London. Aden TV shows footage of present-day demonstrations, as well as newsreels from the good old days of southern independence, inviting viewers to sing along with the popular entertainer 'Abboud Khawaja's ode to al-Hirak. "People of the south, be ready—this is the revolution of the old and the young." While the opposition parties quarrel with the regime over elections and Salih threatens to make southerners "drink from the sea," the younger generation longs for a fair political system and a sound economy. They will not, it seems, be patient forever. As in the 1960s, when there was no going back to kinder and gentler colonial rule, and hasty attempts to allow locals entry into administration came too late, the time for restructuring unified Yemen into a more equitable system has passed in the minds of these young people. They are eager to take their lands into their own hands.

No Pink Slip for Salih:
What Yemen's Protests Do (and Do Not) Mean

Stacey Philbrick Yadav • *MERO*, Feb. 9, 2011

With cameras and Twitter feeds trained on Tahrir Square in Cairo, a series of large opposition protests have unfolded in an eponymous square in the Yemeni capital of Sana'a, as well as other major cities across the country. The protests have been organized and coordinated by a cross-ideological amalgam known as the Joint Meeting Parties (JMP, sometimes also translated as the Common Forum, and known in Arabic as *al-mushtarik*), and have been identifiable by their careful deployment of protest paraphernalia—sashes, hats, posters, flyers and more—tinted in gradations of pink. At first glance, these protests seem to have generated substantial concessions from President 'Ali 'Abdallah Salih, who, having occupied some form of executive office since 1978, is the longest-serving ruler in the Arab world after Muammar al-Qaddafi. Salih pledged on February 2 to abandon his efforts to amend the constitution so as to be able to run again himself or engineer the succession of his son, Ahmad, to the presidency. Much as these steps might appear to presage far-reaching political change in Yemen, perhaps even a colored proto-revolution, there are good reasons for skepticism.

Nor is it obvious that the rallies in Yemen fit into the media-ready narrative of a latter-day "Arab awakening" dawning in country after country on the heels of the dramatic popular uprisings in Tunisia and Egypt. The demands of the political opposition in Yemen align in some ways with those of the pro-democracy protesters elsewhere, but in many more ways they diverge.

Yemen, to be sure, presents a more puzzling picture than Egypt, where a hidebound state lords it over a population that is more homogeneous than those of many other Arab countries. Forged by the unification of North Yemen (of which Salih was president) and avowedly socialist South Yemen in 1990, today's Yemen remains haunted by regional divisions and the state cannot claim anything like full control over many outlying areas in the mountains and desert. But when the *New York Times* tells its readers that its staff "won't try to game Yemen's politics," it is not a sign of editorial humility, but rather a kind of willful ignorance of the likely determinants of Yemen's political future. The political opposition that is mounting the protests in central Sana'a has clear demands that, as in Egypt, are unlikely

North and South Yemen coming apart at the seams. (April 22, 2013)
By Samer Mohammed al-Shameeri

to be satisfied by Salih's promises. And, like his fellow autocrats, Salih has many tools at his disposal for staving off the sort of reform that would strip him and his inner circle of power.

Common Grievances

A common thread connecting demonstrations across the Arab world in early 2011 is frustration with aging, bloated, yet brittle regimes that have fed for decades at the trough of US military assistance. These regimes are practiced at serving up so-called reforms that are marketed as "political openings" but have mainly reinforced incumbent power. None of the regimes is able to respond effectively to the pressing development challenges—unemployment, petty corruption, poverty, dirty, saline drinking water—confronted by its citizens every day. Contra the prevailing policy logic, opposition activists in Yemen and elsewhere do not see the solution to these problems in stronger states, that is, regimes more capable of mobilizing and monopolizing force. They see the remedy in stronger governments, which can respond to people's needs because they better represent ordinary citizens. In other words, the protesters intuitively reject the argument long advanced by incumbent regimes and their foreign donors that development must precede democracy, and they champion its converse instead. From Tunis to Cairo to Sana'a, activists are seeking to attain the voice that would make both democracy and development meaningful.

The specific grievances of the political opposition in Sana'a are not new, nor are the groups who have expressed them in January and February 2011. The Yemeni opposition has coalesced for nearly a decade around an alliance of leftist, secular-liberal, nationalist and various Islamist trends, the JMP. The programs of the JMP's constituent elements do not match up perfectly, and so it is difficult at times to know exactly which demands are salient. The leadership of the Yemeni Socialist Party, for example, is divided over whether and to what extent to align with the demands of the Southern Movement (also called al-Hirak), the grassroots grouping agitating for greater autonomy for the southern provinces and, increasingly, secession. And Islah, the largest of the Islamist parties in the JMP, is riven by generational and ideological cleavages over, among other issues, the role of women in the party and in Yemen's larger political sphere. Each of these divisions divides the alliance and the parties within it—and the regime deftly exploits the gaps.

As in Egypt, the opposition has been systematically undermined by the government (in this case the Salih regime), thanks not least to rapidly stepped-up US military aid, which has expanded the capacities of the security services for surveillance and coercion. While the Yemeni press is far freer than many in the region, including Egypt's, it is increasingly embattled. The government's assault on the media has intensified, perhaps not coincidentally, as Yemen's domestically unpopular strategic relationship with the United States has grown closer in the decade since September 11, 2001.

Because the JMP is an alliance of parties, each with its own partisan press, a small cadre of independent papers have valiantly resisted the state's encroachment in order to create a kind of "virtual space" for the articulation of common JMP policy priorities and critiques of the regime. It is not uncommon to find members of the Nasserist, Socialist and Islamist trends penning editorials that appear side by side on the pages of these non-partisan publications, holding forth on a shared objective. These papers have come under strain—as, by extension, has the ability of the JMP to craft and propound a common agenda—at the hands of increased state surveillance and outright repression, with new techniques for prosecution on spurious charges enforced through an extra-constitutional "special court" for journalists established in May 2009. In January 2010, government forces surrounded the offices of *al-Ayyam*, an independent daily giving heavy coverage to the southern uprising, before invading the offices, jailing the editor and closing down the paper. Other papers have had their archives and computer servers seized, putting the confidentiality of journalists' sources at risk. As the New York–based Committee to Protect Journalists reports: "Taken together, the government's long-standing practice of violent repression and its new legalistic tactics are creating the worst climate for press freedom since the country's unification in 1990."

The US has registered only weak protests at the establishment of the "special court" and other manifestations of the Salih regime's war on journalists. Indeed, as this war proceeds, the Obama administration has more than doubled US military aid, from $67 million in 2009 to $150 million in 2010, as part of a broad counter-terrorism program. Embarrassing State Department documents released via WikiLeaks show that US aid has been directed to the fight against the regime's domestic opponents, particularly the Houthi rebels in the north, with the knowledge of CENTCOM commander Gen. David Petraeus and, thus, all the major power centers in Washington. The scope of US aid to Yemen falls far short of the billion-dollar annual contribution to Egypt, but its unpopularity—and the purposes to which it can be put in suppressing political freedoms—is a link between the protests in both countries.

Divergent Groups

Beyond the similarities, however, the grievances, ambitions and tactics of the Yemeni opposition differ considerably from those in other states in the region. Indeed, the Yemeni opposition is in fact composed of several groups, some of which are coherent and others only loose formations, and which compete with each other and (importantly) within their own ranks as often as they cooperate.

Most notable in international media coverage are the armed groups. In the northern province of Sa'dah, on the border with Saudi Arabia, the rebellion led by members of the Houthi family has entered into its sixth ceasefire in only seven years, with considerable loss of civilian life caused by the government's indiscriminate aerial bombardment and attacks on displaced persons camps. In the south, what began in 2007 as a peaceful protest movement calling for a more equitable distribution of state resources and political power was met with such repressive force that some of its members have begun to shoot back. What might have been negotiation points less than a year ago have increasingly begun to look like lines in the sand.

And then there is al-Qaeda's regional branch, a franchise of unknown size that has found an attractive location in Yemen's more remote regions, where the state's writ is shaky at best. Many analysts, including those at the Congressional Research Service, have pointed out that the Salih regime's relationship to radical Islamist militants is complicated. Salih has made several formal commitments to Washington that Yemen will be a reliable partner in counter-terrorism operations, but has also maintained close ties to conservative cleric 'Abd al-Majid al-Zindani and his fellows, who encourage vigilante violence and are accused of helping to recruit and indoctrinate militants.

The current round of civil protests, however, is led by none of these groups. The JMP coalition's efforts to construct itself as a "loyal opposition" are in clear contradistinction to the rhetoric of open revolt elsewhere in Yemen, and also bear little resemblance to the diffuse, bottom-up movement in Egypt. With rows of plastic chairs lined up and microphones provided for some of the gatherings, the JMP's protests in Sana'a have more closely resembled opposition rallies, with distinguished speakers enumerating demands to cheering, chanting crowds in color-coordinated costume. Even the hue of pink, the "color of love," was chosen to highlight the civil, warm-hearted nature of the protests. The opposition's demands, however, are substantive, and display little tenderness for the Salih regime.

[...]

For its part, the government has oscillated between guarded tolerance and suppression of the protests. It has arrested key activists like Tawakkul Karman, and in a move from the Egyptian regime's playbook, it has reportedly deployed plainclothes police and hired thugs to harass peaceful protesters, especially women, in an effort to provoke a response that would justify retaliation with brute force. In another echo of Egyptian events, the government has staged counter-protests in support of the regime and called out the armed forces to contain any clash that might just happen to erupt between the regime backers and the JMP. Over the weekend of February 5–6, pro-Salih protesters assembled in Yemen's Tahrir Square, while JMP protesters shifted their procession a safe distance away to Sana'a University. The opposition protests are thus not spontaneous waves of popular sentiment, as in the early days of the Cairo events, but something like animated conversations with an interlocutor who remains unmoved.

Ornamental Promises

Salih's February 2 promises—assayed and abandoned before—are unlikely to convince anyone. In the months before the 2006 presidential campaign, for example, he vowed not to run, so that Yemen could be governed by "young blood," and even reiterated this pledge in an interview with the pan-Arab daily *al-Hayat*. But as the election approached, he made an elaborate show of bowing to a popular will that, supposedly, demanded his return to the presidential palace. Few Yemenis doubt that he could repeat this performance when the 2013 contest rolls around. When Salih announced that he would not run again and would not pass the presidency on to his son, he was answering the calls of protests in Cairo against Hosni Mubarak and family, but not the pragmatic demands of the opposition in his own country. Outsiders should take the announcement for what it is—an effort to link Cairo and Sana'a in the minds of Western policymakers, so that they will fear the spread of chaos and endorse the status quo.

In a January 27 report, the Economist Intelligence Unit identified three main scenarios for Yemen's future, each of them predicated rather optimistically on Salih's departure from the presidency. First, the report mentioned the possibility of a negotiated transition to parliamentary rule, one that would include electoral reforms favored by the JMP, such as a shift from single-member districts, which favor incumbents and large parties, to proportional representation, which could better accommodate diverse constituencies. Such a scenario could absorb members of the General People's Congress. And, indeed, several members of the ruling party have distinguished themselves from the category of down-the-line Salih regime backers by building alliances across Yemen's partisan aisle on issues of import. The report's authors, however, seemed more convinced by two other scenarios: In one, Yemen fragments along regional lines, leaving a vacuum in which AQAP can flourish. Warring tribal factions battle themselves and al-Qaeda over discrete portions of the country, with citizens left to the tender mercies of the combatants. This vision is a version of those engendered by a widely discussed *New York Times Magazine* story that came out in the wake of the failed December 2009 operation of the underwear bomber, the last time Yemen figured so prominently in American headlines. Perhaps this grim outlook is offered to make the remaining option look more attractive: a military coup, with the possibility of secession in the south, but increased stability for the rest of Yemen.

None of these scenarios consider the very real possibility that Salih's promises are ornamental. Particularly as the headlines fade, he could dig in, refusing to yield to protesters' longer-term and more substantive demands, and continuing to govern through managed chaos, leveraging the specter of crisis for more foreign aid. With US and Saudi military assistance at an all-time high, Salih's ability to monitor and suppress the opposition, and then use his large parliamentary majority to further consolidate his power, cannot be dismissed.

Yemen's Fickle Friends

'Ali 'Abdallah Salih's regime is frequently characterized in the Western media as "beleaguered" by a secessionist movement in the south, an armed revolt in the north and the threat of al-Qaeda. It is unclear, though, to what extent aiding such a regime by strengthening its coercive capacity offers a solution to these problems—or even contributes to them instead. The Houthis in the north and al-Hirak in the south are mobilized at least in part against the abusive excesses of the regime. Al-Qaeda exploits the regional dissatisfaction, as well as the outrage that meets the regime's deployment of force against civilian populations.

To date, the scale of US aid tips heavily in favor of military and intelligence assistance, with over $150 million in military aid in 2010, up from only $5 million in 2006. US development assistance, at about $40 million, was focused from 2003 to 2009 on those regions that were viewed by the US Agency for International Development (USAID) as "most at risk of generating political instability and providing possible refuge for terrorists." Of these governorates, only one—Shabwa—is in the south, where acute development asymmetries are fueling opposition demands.

US support for Yemen is now also channeled through the newly established Friends of Yemen, a donor consortium organized by Great Britain in January 2010, whose members include the Gulf Cooperation Council and G-8 nations, as well as the United Nations, European Union, Arab League, International Monetary Fund and World Bank. The efforts of this organization are primarily geared toward blunting the effects of economic restructuring, with some attention paid to reducing corruption. The focus, however, remains economic, not political, thus reinforcing the conventional wisdom that underdevelopment, not unaccountable governance, is the primary source of instability in Yemen. USAID contends that it has now adopted an assistance strategy designed to respond to "the articulated needs and frustrations of communities in the neediest areas," but it is clear that both multilateral and bilateral approaches to development in Yemen have ignored the principal demands of the organized opposition. USAID's Country Strategy for 2010–12 indicates that there is "considerable agreement" over the drivers of instability, yet it does not list the authoritarian state as one of them. Perhaps diplomatic niceties prohibit such a forthright statement, but in the meantime the US does not seem to be listening to the opposition's claim that meaningful political reform is the only sure path to more equitable and sustainable development.

Nor does the US appear to have any illusions about the future of political dialogue in Yemen. Reflecting on her surprise visit to Sanaʻa in January, Secretary of State Hillary Clinton remarked that "at the end of the day, there has to be a willingness on the part of the government and the people to work together toward a common goal. And I'm not sure that any forum or any kind of meeting can produce that." Certainly, as long as foreign donors focus on economic restructuring and US-supplied technology allows the regime to monitor and suppress its opponents, there is little reason to believe that President Salih will be inclined to change.

No Exit: Yemen's Existential Crisis

Sheila Carapico • *MERO*, May 3, 2011

A venal dictatorship three decades old, mutinous army officers, dissident tribal sheikhs, a parliamentary opposition coalition, youthful pro-democracy activists, gray-haired Socialists, gun-toting cowboys, veiled women protesters, northern carpetbaggers, Shi'i insurgents, tear gas canisters, leaked State Department cables, foreign-born jihadis—Yemen's demi-revolutionary spring has it all. The mass uprising in southern Arabia blends features of the peaceful popular revolutions in Egypt and Tunisia with elements of the state repression in Libya and Syria in a gaudy, fast-paced, multilayered theater of revolt verging on the absurd.

Whether the drama will end in glory or tragedy remains to be seen. But indications are not promising. Already, President ʻAli ʻAbdallah Salih has stalled and contrived to avoid signing a late April deal brokered by Gulf Cooperation Council (GCC) neighbors desperate to restore a semblance of stability in the most populous corner of the Arabian Peninsula. The GCC extracted a verbal promise from Salih to resign the presidency after a period of 30 days. But convincing him to make good on his pledge under conditions satisfactory to Yemeni elites, the pro-democracy move-ment and interested foreign parties is a gargantuan task, requiring more diplomatic legerdemain than has been brought to bear so far. On April 30, instead of signing onto the proposed agreement, Salih sent tanks fir-ing live ammunition to clear some 1,500 campers from a central square in the Mansoura district of the southern port city of Aden. 'Abd al-Latif al-Zayani, secretary-general of the six-nation GCC, who had flown to the Yemeni capital of Sana'a to meet with Salih, returned to Saudi Arabia red-faced and empty-handed.

Under the Bush and particularly the Obama administrations, the United States has been deeply implicated in Yemen, which emerged in the late 2000s as a haven and launching pad for the Arabian Peninsula branch of al-Qaeda. Especially since the Christmas 2009 "crotch bomb-er" attempted to detonate an explosive device hidden in his underwear on an airplane in Detroit, the US has spent up to $300 million upgrad-ing counter-terrorism, military and internal security forces loyal to Salih. The Pentagon provided helicopters, armored vehicles, ammunition, sur-veillance technology, Humvees, night-vision goggles and other military equipment, as well as training, to its Yemeni counterparts. Classified ca-bles released by WikiLeaks show that this assistance increased despite the Salih regime's widely recognized backsliding from democratization and toward repression, as well as plentiful red flags in 2009 and 2010 that American-made weapons were being used against domestic enemies. Gulf and French officials were also frank with the State Department in their assessments of the regime's shattered legitimacy. Indeed, as early as 2005, the US ambassador in Sana'a wrote a cable envisioning scenarios includ-ing Salih's fall to the legal parliamentary opposition, plotters among his inner circle or mass popular protests. No one could have predicted the confluence of all three. But Washington, forewarned, might better have hedged its bets. It has yet to do so.

Over $1 billion in additional US military assistance already in the pipeline has been frozen in light of the spring's events. Hesitant to distance itself from Salih and low on sympathy for the protesters, the United States was upbeat about the prospects for the face-saving GCC agreement to be sealed by the end of April. The Embassy in Sana'a announced that it was "distressed" and "disturbed" by the "violence, April 27, that killed [12] and injured hundreds of Yemeni citizens...on the eve of signing a historic agreement...that will achieve through peaceful, democratic and constitu-tional means a transition of authority leading to new presidential elections in July 2011." Its press release urged "Yemeni citizens" to show good faith by "avoiding all provocative demonstrations, marches and speeches in the coming days," adding coyly: "We also urge government security forces to refrain from using violence against demonstrators."

The Central Players

At center stage in the Yemeni potboiler is President ʻAli ʻAbdallah Salih, barricaded in a fortified palace compound in the capital behind Revolutionary Guards and US-armed Special Forces commanded by his son and one-time heir apparent Ahmad. Peeping over the parapets, Salih delivers nearly nonsensical speeches in his trademark not-quite-literate Arabic inveighing against Zionist instigators and fornicating demonstrators. The revolt against his rule is coordinated from "an operations room in Tel Aviv," he ventured on March 1. On April 18 he denigrated the popular movement as an un-Islamic "mixing of sexes." To these and other pronouncements the throngs jeer and hurl their shoes at the giant video screen in the plaza outside Sanaʻa University: In video footage of the scene, the footwear looks like flies buzzing around the president's face.

Defiant if not oblivious, Salih announced in late April the creation of 50,000 new, unfunded civil service jobs and vowed to relinquish power only "through the ballot box," calling, spuriously, for elections monitored by international observers. "People who resign from their posts and join the revolutions are the symbols of corruption and they do not have agendas for reforming the economic, cultural, social and developmental situation in the country," he told military cadets on April 25. Next, presumably enraged by Al Jazeera coverage of the demonstrations, he accused Qatar, one of the GCC states sponsoring the exit deal, of "inciting and financing chaos."

The partners to the proposed exit deal are the leaders of the so-called Joint Meeting Parties (JMP). [...] Comprised of politicians from both of the two Yemeni polities that unified in 1990, this important group has extensive experience in Yemen's unique National Dialogue of Popular Forces and in electoral and parliamentary politics. With its rotating chairmanship keeping any one star out of the limelight, the JMP has played a pivotal yet ambiguous role in the 2011 political crisis, embracing the demonstrations after they were well underway, refusing Salih's belated February offer to form a coalition government and now conferring with the GCC and other international actors to find an exit from the impasse. The JMP leaders accepted the deal whereby Salih would step down in return for immunity from prosecution for his many crimes and the promise that they would gain substantial parliamentary representation.

The Plotters

When Salih accuses his opponents of sedition, he is referring explicitly to defectors from his inner circle. Two were tagged by US Embassy officials who detected dissension within Salih's original "triumvirate" at least as early as 2005 and again in 2009. This fact alone makes the defectors worth noting. One is Gen. 'Ali Muhsin, Salih's henchman since 1978, head of the First Armored Division and the Northwest Military Command who prosecuted merciless campaigns that vanquished southern secessionists in 1994 and scourged Sa'dah province in the far north in order finally to defeat Zaydi Houthi rebels and their tribal allies in 2010. In both battles, the general called upon radical Sunni jihadis to join the fight against godless Socialists in the south and Zaydi partisans in Sa'dah. US Ambassador Thomas Krajeski described him in 2005 as a sinister arms smuggler whose name was spoken in hushed tones because he was feared and mistrusted by the Houthi rebels, southerners, leftists and others. Subsequent cables revealed the rumor that he was assigned the nearly impossible task of fighting the Houthis in order to ruin his military reputation and thus his political ambitions. There is strong evidence, as well, that during its intervention in the conflict in 2010 the Saudi Air Force was given targeting recommendations to strike coordinates that turned out to be 'Ali Muhsin's command headquarters. The general's March 19 defection and deployment of tanks to protect the demonstrators from forces loyal to the president was thus no surprise. Subsequent skirmishes could be the harbinger of a civil war between factions of the military.

In blogs, interviews and Facebook postings, pro-democracy spokespersons made it clear that they were not fooled by cynical turncoats jockeying for power but hardly interested in liberal democracy. When 'Ali Muhsin's troops deployed to the square outside Sana'a University, the demonstrators initially cringed, thinking he was coming to destroy them.

The other power broker, who broke ranks after at least 50 peaceful protesters were murdered on March 18, is Hamid al-Ahmar, the most politically ambitious of the 10 sons of the late 'Abdallah bin Husayn al-Ahmar, paramount chief of the Hashid tribal confederation, longtime speaker of Parliament and stalwart of the original triumvirate backing Salih's rule. Although not his Reaganesque father, as a member of

Parliament, part of the Supreme Committee of the Islah party, a million-aire businessman and a prominent figure in the Hashid confederation, Hamid is able to draw large crowds in the family's hometown of 'Amran. Salih is himself a Hashid.

Cables received by the US embassy and made available by WikiLeaks indicate that Hamid al-Ahmar has been maneuvering against Salih since soon after his father's death in late 2007. One cable from August 31, 2009, quotes him calling Salih "the devil" and his son Ahmad and nephews "clowns." According to the same State Department missive, he promised to organize anti-Salih demonstrations if and when he could persuade 'Ali Muhsin to go along and also enlist Saudi assistance. A second cable dated the same day put al-Ahmar among a small group of insiders blaming Salih for "wrong-headed policies" contributing to "Yemen's myriad problems." The insiders may be "truly concerned about the fate of Yemen, or, smelling blood in the water...positioning themselves for a post-Saleh era." In April 2011, the US Embassy in Sana'a felt compelled to issue a terse denial of rumors of its support for Hamid al-Ahmar.

50,000 Pairs of Clasped Hands

State-run Sana'a television runs continuous tape of people jumping up and down, yelling "the people want 'Ali 'Abdallah Salih," and file footage of marches celebrating his leadership. Yet neither he nor the dissident count-er-elites can contain the unprecedented, sustained, spontaneous grass-roots uprising of the past three months. The crowds clamoring for change (*taghyir*) are diverse, and dispersed among at least a dozen cities and towns. At the core are the youth, the demographic plurality between the ages of 15 and 30 who have never known another government leadership: university students, graduates, dropouts and wannabes grasping at straws of hope for a better future in the Arab world's poorest country. They have turned their daily marches and sit-ins into performance art with music, dancing, skits, caricatures, posters, chants and collective gestures of defi-ance like 50,000 pairs of clasped hands held high. Women, most promi-nently the eloquent and outspoken Tawakkul Karman, head of the NGO Women Journalists Without Chains, have raised their voices more and more, in solidarity with demands for change and lately in outrage at the president's sleazy innuendo directed at "ladies" who march or speak in public. The freedom struggle has now gone viral and virtually nationwide.

A peaceful *intifada* has been in motion since the summer of 2007 in the south. [...] By late 2010, their protests had become commonplace, although Salih and the official media succeeded temporarily in presenting their grievances as secessionist gripes that would destroy Yemeni unity. On April 26, the protesters marked the anniversary of the start of the 1994 civil war in which the former South attempted to reestablish its independent sovereignty.

Whether or not they harbor genuinely separatist sentiments, residents of the former South Yemen have good reason to feel they have been punitively targeted and deprived of basic liberties and entitlements.

Yet, by the same token, many southern tribulations resonate in every province of the republic: the grotesque enrichment of regime cronies at the expense of the many; deteriorating standards of living; obscenely bad schools, hospitals and roads; the skyrocketing price of meat, staples and even clean water; the lack of jobs for college and high-school graduates. Ambassador Krajeski had already seen prospects for revolt in the 2005 riots prompted by the lifting of fuel subsidies. Then, dissatisfaction was particularly acute among the perennially restive tribes of the eastern provinces of al-Jawf and Marib, where truckers and pump farmers consider cheap fuel their lifeblood. Grandiose pageants of presidential power, half-truths in the official media, indignities at military checkpoints, arbitrary arrests and imprisonments—these and other daily insults feed popular alienation, despair and frustration, most notably among the youth. While a privileged few cool off in swimming pools in their luxury compounds, the water table has fallen, decimating the farm economy that remains the livelihood of the rural majority. Farmers and ranchers facing starvation have flocked to the cities where water supplies and social services are swamped. Misery has become the new normal; millions barely survive on the equivalent of a dollar or two per day.

Misery Loves Company

Without a doubt, Yemenis were inspired by the revolutionary movements in Tunisia and Egypt in early 2011. Gatherings in Sana'a and other cities in January, as the spirit of Tunisia diffused in the Arab world, were relatively restrained affairs, replete in some cases with folding chairs for various JMP dignitaries. In February, as Egyptian president Hosni Mubarak began to proffer concessions under the sustained pressure of the street, the timbre of the Yemeni rallies rose in intensity. On the evening of February 11, the date of Mubarak's resignation, thousands of joyful youth converged on Sana'a's Liberation Square. There, they were confronted by uniformed security forces and regime-supporting agitators armed with sticks.

Thus prevented from occupying the central Tahrir Square, the youths nevertheless eventually found their own iconic protest locale: the plaza before the gates of Sana'a University, which they have redubbed Taghyir (Change) Square in homage both to their core demand and the rhyming name of the epicenter of revolt in Cairo. The first tents were set up there on February 21. People who gathered in Taghyir Square echoed the slogans of Egypt's Tahrir Square, which in turn had traveled to Egypt from Tunisia: *Irhal!* (Leave!) and *al-sha'b yurid isqat al-nizam* (the people want to overthrow the regime). Salih's men borrowed the failed tactics of Mubarak, sending thugs wielding batons into the crowds and rounding up known regime opponents. On March 18, in a pitch of fury or panic someone ordered snipers overlooking Taghyir Square to open fire on the assembled protesters. By the following day at least 50 were dead and more lay dying. In disbelief, fury and sorrow, a record 150,000 marched in Sana'a's biggest "day of rage" so far. Ministers, ambassadors, civil servants, members of Parliament and military officers including 'Ali Muhsin declared their sympathies with the protesters. On March 23 a state of emergency was declared. Within a month, a tent city housing men and boys (and sometimes whole families) from around the country stretched, by some accounts, for miles along the streets leading to Sana'a University. Other camps were pitched in other cities and towns.

In provincial cities, where hundreds or thousands had attended rallies, tens of thousands now seized public spaces. In Ta'iz, a large commercial and industrial city in the verdant southern mountains of the former North Yemen, and the neighboring city of Ibb, simmering discontent erupted. The Ta'iz-Ibb area, a rich agricultural zone of peasants and sharecroppers often called the "middle regions," served as a bridge between the southern Hirak and the revolutionary movement centered in Sana'a. People from Ta'iz traveled, telephoned and tweeted with family and compatriots in Aden, Hadramawt, Abyan and other parts of the former South Yemen already in ferment. Youth and parents in Hudayda, the Red Sea port that is the hub of the Tihama coastal plain where Afro-Yemenis suffer the country's highest rates of poverty and political disenfranchisement, filled the public square with banners and chants: *Irhal!* In mid-April protesters were shot dead by security forces in Ta'iz, Hudayda and other cities, as well as in Sana'a. Each funeral—at least 145 to date—provoked more angry or grief-stricken dissenters to call for the downfall of the regime.

Insurrectionary sentiments fueled patriotic solidarities and unify-ing sympathies. These spread to the vast plains, mountains and deserts north, northwest, east and somewhat south of Sanaʻa, in the provinces of Saʻdah, al-Jawf, Marib, ʻAmran and Dhamar. In these rather sparsely pop-ulated, semi-arid regions analogous to Texas or Wyoming, the so-called tribal heartland where ranchers, cowboys, truckers and hillbillies carry Kalashnikovs or even bazooka launchers and historically harbor deep mistrust of the central government, conventional protests were mixed with acts of civil disobedience, such as road blockages and commercial stoppages. In a heavily tribal area further south, al-Bayda, men threw down their arms in April to march to another popular slogan: *Silmiyya!* (Peacefully!) Bear in mind: Armed tribesmen and villagers could resort to open rebellion but have elected to keep their powder dry.

The Impasse

As April moved into May, scenarios were buzzing like the shoes tossed at Salih's visage on the giant screen. The accord that was supposed to be signed May 1 remained a work in progress up to the eleventh hour. The basic plan was for President Salih to transfer power to his vice presi-dent, the relatively impotent ʻAbd Rabbu Mansour Hadi, within 30 days. Under a new power-sharing arrangement, the ruling General People's Congress (GPC) would retain 50 percent of the 301 seats in Parliament, the opposition JMP would acquire 40 percent and 10 percent would go to independents, including, presumably, representatives of the youth movement. Within a week a transitional unity government expected to be led by a JMP prime minister, preferably from the former South, was to be formed. Senior statesman ʻAbd al-Karim al-Iryani, the current sec-retary-general of the GPC, having until recently remained aloof from the fray, was dispatched to the Saudi Arabian capital of Riyadh to par-ticipate in negotiations with the GCC. Crucially, but vaguely, the pro-posal specified an end to the demonstrations. The remaining 70 loyalists in Parliament further demanded that Salih retain his leadership of the GPC. It was not clear if a popular opposition demand that he and family members resign their military posts was really part of the deal.

The arrangement was too ambiguous and riddled with loopholes for either Salih or the protesters to accept by the May 1 deadline. In the end, only the GCC monarchies and the JMP leaders were ready to sign. Salih first offered to have either al-Iryani or Vice President Hadi verify the ac-cord on his behalf in Riyadh, and then promised to sign in Sanaʻa in the presence of the GCC's al-Zayani. At the last minute, he acquiesced to sign in his capacity as head of the ruling party but not as president. This refusal scuttled the negotiation. Salih scoffed at a basket of carrots that left him with his arsenal of sticks.

Although Salih was the one who nixed the deal, it was clear that the GCC plan did not have popular backing, either. It had not been negotiated so much as cobbled together. On April 24, a group signing itself as the Youth Popular Revolution Committee already rejected the provision of immunity from criminal prosecution for the president and his family, which could easily amount to carte blanche for excessive force during the month-long transition. Amnesty International and Human Rights Watch shared these concerns. It was unclear, moreover, how the JMP could disperse the sit-ins and roadblocks; as commentator Jamila 'Ali Raja told Al Jazeera, the formal parties could invite their own members to abandon the barricades, but not give orders to the tens of thousands they do not represent.

The failed GCC push to reach an accord by May 1 turned out to be the opening gambit in a complex negotiation that seems unlikely to be concluded soon. More and more, personalities from bygone dramas are now weighing in from exile: Rebel leader Yahya al-Houthi and former South Yemen leaders Haydar Abu Bakr al-'Attas, 'Ali Salim al-Bayd and 'Ali Nasir Muhammad, to name a few, seek to claim the initiative. If there is to be forward momentum, their views and constituencies, such as they are, will have to be taken into account. And yet these additions to the mix can only complicate matters.

Yemen is now in political limbo and not far from the road to hell. No one believes that the president can continue in office or that he will relinquish power. The popular movement has come too far to back off and yet sees no clear path toward social justice. Gulf monarchies and the Obama administration appear to lack the diplomatic wherewithal, the strategic imagination or the humanitarian decency to envision a solution to the impasse. And yet daily the status quo becomes more untenable. Loyalist patrimonial forces are wont to shoot, and may yet provoke either a mutinous response or a full-fledged rebellion by armed citizens. The spirit of "*silmiyya*," which served Tunisians and Egyptians so well, can persevere only so long in the face of live fire. In March and for part of April, it was possible to envision an orderly transition to a civilian coalition transitional government. The month of May may bring more bloodshed.

Gulf monarchs playing tiddlywinks with a bomb labeled "Yemen." (February 27, 2015)
By Samer Mohammed al-Shameeri

Tawakkul Karman as Cause and Effect

Stacey Philbrick Yadav • *MERO*, Oct. 21, 2011

Political activist Tawakkul Karman has brought Yemen's revolution to New York, speaking directly on October 20 with Secretary-General Ban Ki-moon and organizing rallies at the United Nations headquarters in lower Manhattan, the largest of which is slated for the afternoon of October 21. The purpose of her visit is to keep pressure on the UN Security Council to adopt a resolution that reflects the aspirations of the overwhelming numbers of Yemenis who have sustained peaceful calls for change for the nine long months since protests began in late January. Arriving newly anointed by the Nobel Committee, which named her as one of three recipients of the 2011 Peace Prize, Karman fears—as does much of the Yemeni opposition, in its many forms—that the UN will merely reiterate the approximate parameters of the GCC initiative put forth in April. That plan, which has enjoyed support from the United States, as well as Yemen's GCC neighbors, would allow legal immunity for President 'Ali 'Abdallah Salih, whose crimes against Yemeni protesters have multiplied in the months since the spring. For this reason, Karman will end her week in New York as she has ended so many weeks in Sana'a in recent months—at the head of a protest.

That the Yemeni revolution is now led symbolically by a woman is an attractive concept to many international observers. Karman's biography, however, and her record of activism are more complex than the Nobel Committee's citation would suggest. She is unquestionably worthy of the international recognition attending the Peace Prize, but not necessarily for the reasons given. The Committee recognized Karman, along with two Liberian activist women, Ellen Sirleaf Johnson and Leymah Gbowee, "for their non-violent struggle for the safety of women and for women's rights to full participation in peace-building work." Yet Karman is at the UN demanding trenchant political reform, of the kind that will enhance the political freedoms of Yemeni men, women and children, and produce a new regime more accountable to the public. She is decidedly not calling for "women's rights." In its citation, the Committee reduced the scope of the work of a multidimensional activist whose efforts have been resisted inside and outside the party from which she emerged. Without understanding Tawakkul Karman as both a cause and an effect of change in state-society relations in Yemen, it is difficult to see precisely what she represents or why so many Yemenis from different backgrounds have been so responsive to her call for sustained nonviolence.

Partisan Origins

Yemen's revolution has developed into a post-partisan affair, but its origins undoubtedly lie in the decade of partisan opposition and alliance building that preceded it. Whereas today's revolutionaries are calling, first and foremost, for the end of the Salih regime, the partisan opposition was primarily focused on procedural reforms that would expand their opportunity to hold the country's leadership accountable. There is good reason for drawing this distinction between reformist and revolutionary activism, because the failures of the reformist project fed the frustrations that have sustained the revolutionary movement, even as partisan actors have stepped in to help organize (and, according to some, attempt to coopt) the momentum of the youth.

Why Women Are Essential to the Revolution

In retrospect, despite the fractiousness of the partisan sphere (and, argu-ably, Yemeni society) regarding the rights and roles of women, it should not be entirely surprising that a woman activist has played such an essen-tial role in mobilizing the post-partisan revolutionary movement. As the opposition parties became mired in internal debates over women's rights (among other issues), many Yemeni women—again, including Tawakkul Karman—shifted some of their energies to the associational sector, taking up the cause of reform through their work as journalists or through var-ious civil society organizations, and building dense networks of personal and professional alliances. Growth in the number of women leading such organizations helped to shift the substantive focus of "women's rights" work: Whereas, in the 1990s, this work strove for reforms that would im-prove the lot of women as wives and mothers, the new activities sought to frame women's rights as human rights or to expand the reach of civic and economic freedom in general.

Tawakkul Karman's organization, Women Journalists Without Chains, founded in 2005, reflects this shift in its commitment to freedom of ex-pression and civil rights. Staging weekly protests each Tuesday from 2007 until the beginning of the revolution in 2011, Karman called for inquiries into corruption and other forms of social and legal injus-tice; the lifting of limitations on press freedoms; and more. When the partisan opposition of the JMP came under fire from the government, Karman and her associates rallied to their aid, often working with other Yemeni and international organizations. And when she and other oppo-sition journalists faced pressure, even arrest and detention, the partisan opposition did the same for her. The migration of women into associa-tional sector activism and the ties they forged—illustrated by Karman's own multi-faceted persona as Islahi, journalist and activist—have been central to laying the groundwork for the network-reliant post-partisan opposition movement that has sustained the revolution for these many eventful months.

That Tawakkul Karman is the public face of this movement—and has now become, perhaps, the most recognized Yemeni after President Salih himself—may have a lasting impact on the ultimate inclusivity of con-ceptions of citizenship and equality in the future. At this stage, however, there is no particular reason to view this question as resolved, just as the success of the revolutionary movement itself is still very much in doubt amid the ongoing violence in Yemen and the limited international support for the insurrection. Throughout the revolution, Karman has continued to embody the fraught question of women's rights and roles. She has been a lightning rod for criticism: from Salafis within Islah for her public role and unseemly visibility; from those on the secular left who distrust her Islamist leanings; from those who resent what they see as Islah's effort to dominate the revolutionary movement.

For these reasons and more, the language of unity and the focus on areas of procedural agreement seem to be taking pride of place in Karman's approach to the revolution, as well they must in these movements of great uncertainty and risk. Her work has been essential to the revolutionary movement and she is a resonant exemplar of the vision of Yemeni women. But recognizing her for work on behalf of Yemeni women has been a controversial gesture, one which bypasses the other ways in which Yemeni women have pursued progress for their sisters over the two decades since unification (and still others under the distinct regimes of North and South Yemen before then). Two of these women have died in 2011: Fawziyya Nu'man, who worked within the system to pursue essential reforms in girls' and women's education, and Ra'ufa Hasan, who worked at great personal cost to retain her independence in the associational sector, as both the regime and Islah launched campaigns against her. Both of these women, and the many others who have followed their respective trajectories, might take issue with the idea that Tawakkul Karman is being honored for her work on behalf of women's rights, but they would probably also join Hooria Mashhour and the many others who carried Karman's image at the celebration in Sana'a's Change Square following the Peace Prize announcement. These men and women, in the tens of thousands, admire Karman for the work she has done in transforming Islah, as a party, and advancing the rights of all Yemenis, regardless of gender or political creed.

Looking for Revolution in Kuwait

Mary Ann Tétreault • *MERO*, Nov. 1, 2012

Kuwait's ruling family, the al-Sabah, feared that Kuwaitis would join Tunisians and Egyptians in pressing for their overthrow, despite evidence stretching back to the Iraqi occupation attesting to Kuwaitis' allegiance to the ruling family. Ironically, the Arab revolts probably had their greatest influence in Kuwait on other dissident groups. In the early spring of 2011, stateless *bidun* (residents of Kuwait who are not citizens of any nation) marched to protest their lack of recognition and rights. They were quickly suppressed although gestures were made to extend citizenship to a fraction of the *bidun* population. Later in the year Kuwait was hit by a wave of strikes, mostly settled by generous wage concessions. But the political demonstrations continued along their pre-2011 trajectory throughout. Protesters sought to force the resignation of the prime minister and other ministers from the ruling family, such as the economy minister, Sheikh Ahmad al-Fahd, accused of corruption in awarding $900 million in government contracts. Representatives from professional societies and thousands of other Kuwaitis who wanted corruption curbed were among the marchers, some of whom loudly declared their aspirations for a "constitutional monarchy," one that subscribes to the rule of law.

The demonstrators did take cues from other Arab protesters in some respects, such as by scheduling events on Fridays. Friday gatherings were held in Safat Square, no doubt triggering memories of the first Kuwaiti parliament that had opposed the high-handed governance of the emir's father. In May 2011, the plaza was closed to demonstrators, who were told they could congregate only on the narrow median in front of the National Assembly, now called Irada Square. This move essentially limited the right to assembly by criminalizing rallies taking place in any other venue, although the first Friday demonstration after that decision found gatherings in both places with no interference from police.

The wave of strikes began in September 2011, at about the same time that local banks were reported to be preparing to refer between 15 and 20 members of Parliament to the public prosecutor to be investigated for money laundering. As the investigation proceeded and more MPs were implicated, the suspicious deposits in their accounts began to look like bribes and the bribes seemed to be coming from the prime minister. Protests intensified and on November 17, thousands of mostly young Kuwaitis, including many from the tribes, and led by opposition members of Parliament, stormed the parliament building. Five security personnel were reported as wounded, along with an uncounted number of demonstrators. Although this "black Wednesday" was rapidly designated in the press as a death knell for the opposition, the parliament moved along with proceedings to interpellate the prime minister who, once more, resigned. Finally, in early December, after five years, three unscheduled elections, four cabinet "reshuffles" and a brief period of indecision, the emir accepted Sheikh Nasir's resignation and appointed a new prime minister. When public protests and behind-the-scenes pressures continued, however, the emir dismissed the parliament and called for new elections yet again.

Although some observers might hope for a "real" revolution as a result of the Arab uprisings, Kuwaitis might be better advised to continue their less dramatic, nonviolent pressure to push their reluctant rulers toward constitutional monarchy. Yet this strategy is more difficult to pull off today than in the past, thanks to the frequent resort to abuse by security forces and the mobilization of thousands of angry young men who are no more Legos to be snapped in place by their "betters" than their elders proved to be. If their dignity continues to be assailed on the streets and in police stations, they might well retaliate in kind.

Ansar al-Shari'a

Sheila Carapico • Originally published as
"Meanwhile, in Yemen...," *MERO*, Mar. 6, 2012

War is breaking out between the Yemeni military and a group called
"Ansar al-Shari'a" in the southern province of Abyan—and it is in danger
of spreading. Somewhere between 100 and 200 soldiers are being buried
after battles on March 5 in the provincial capital of Zinjibar, and other soldiers captured are being paraded through the streets of the forlorn neighboring town of Jaar.

Both cities fell to militants affiliated with al-Qaeda in April 2011 when
President 'Ali 'Abdallah Salih withdrew forces from Abyan to protect his
regime against mass demonstrations elsewhere in the country. Now that
Salih has transferred power to his handpicked vice president, the new administration of 'Abd Rabbu Mansour Hadi has launched a new offensive
against the militants. American-trained and -armed government forces
just lost the first battle.

Viewing Yemen not as a place full of popular aspirations for social justice and decent governance but only as a theater of counter-terrorism operations situated in Saudi Arabia's backyard, the United States has helped
to ignite this dangerous engagement and is deeply implicated. Among
many badly informed postures toward Yemen that failed to take Yemen
into account, two from the past year stand out.

Over the course of 2011, as peaceful demonstrations against the
Salih kleptocracy gained momentum only to be met with brute force, a
string of American political actors declared that the Yemen-based AQAP
poses a grave peril, including to the American homeland. New CIA chief
Gen. David Petraeus dubbed it "the most dangerous regional node in
the global jihad" in testimony before Congress in September. AQAP
was the strange acronym given to al-Qaeda in the Arabian Peninsula,
which was actually less a unified command than a motley handful of
preachers, militants and misfits including the Ansar al-Shari'a. It is difficult to imagine a more effective recruitment tool for al-Qaeda wannabes
worldwide than Petraeus's mantra and, sure enough, scores of jihadis
and frustrated youth from Somalia, Pakistan and elsewhere sneaked
into Abyan to fight the good fight against the imperial infidels and their
Saudi-sponsored lackeys.

Adding flame to a tinderbox of fuel, the Obama administration ordered targeted remote-control drone assassinations of individual suspects

including, most famously, the US-born Yemeni cleric Anwar al-Awlaqi, and some weeks later, by way of collateral damage, his teenage son. The lesson to Yemeni officers and infantry acting in close coordination with the US military is clear: Shoot first, ask questions later.

Now, the US ambassador in Sana'a and other officials are complaining loudly about (still unsubstantiated but increasingly likely) Iranian support for the Houthi rebels up near Yemen's border with Saudi Arabia, who have nothing to do with al-Qaeda. So the new Yemeni president's counter-terrorism advisers are sending the message that brute force is warranted in the north as well.

Americans don't hear much about Yemeni politics unless it affects Americans. We should get used to hearing more bad news.

Collective Frustration, but No Collective Action, in Qatar

Justin Gengler • *MERO*, Dec. 7, 2013

In late June 2013, as neighboring Arab states continued their struggles against popular pressure for political reform or regime change, the Gulf emirate of Qatar undertook its own, voluntary transfer of power. Emir Hamad bin Khalifa al-Thani, patriarch of modern Qatar, appeared on state television to name as successor his 33-year-old son, Sheikh Tamim. The outgoing leader was hobbled by serious health problems, it was said, and in any case most observers agreed that a recalibration of Qatar's domestic and international agendas was perhaps just what the doctor ordered.

In the weeks and months prior, Qatar had witnessed a decided backfire of its strategy of greater regional involvement and even interventionism pursued since the beginning of the Arab uprisings. Former Egyptian president Muhammad Mursi, whose brief administration Qatar had supported to the tune of several billion dollars, faced debilitating protests and was but days away from ouster. In Syria, Qatar's year-long competition with Saudi Arabia over patronage and coordination of the opposition was nearing an end, with an overmatched Doha effectively conceding the field to its wealthier and better-organized rival.

And in Libya, protesters burned Qatari flags and effigies of the former emir, while gunmen more than once blocked the arrival of passengers on Qatar Airways. Far from grateful for Qatar's military and humanitarian assistance in service of the revolution, many Libyans accused the Gulf emirate of unwanted interference for its alleged support of *salafi* movements and groups tied to the Society of Muslim Brothers. For fear of retribution from the country's many new enemies, ordinary Qataris now regularly hid their identities while traveling abroad, posing as Emiratis or other less conspicuous nationalities.

Demonstrators, Dialogues, Drones and Dialectics

Sheila Carapico • *MER* 269, Winter 2013

In 2011 Yemenis shared a vision of revolutionary change with protesters in Tunisia, Egypt, Libya and Syria demanding the downfall of cruel, corrupt presidential regimes. Today, like many of their cousins, the peaceful youth (*shabab silmiyya*) of Yemen face a counterrevolutionary maelstrom from within and without. If Gulf sultans were anxious about insurrection in North Africa, they were even more fearful of subaltern uprisings in their own neighborhood.

Compared with Egypt, Iraq or Syria, there is something to be said for the Yemen model of a phased transition predicated on dialogue. In what became known as the GCC initiative, after protracted protests and negotiations the long-time chief executive 'Ali 'Abdallah Salih relinquished power, in exchange for immunity from prosecution; his General People's Congress retained its parliamentary majority while entering into a National Dialogue with the parliamentary opposition and other domestic forces. This mediation, spearheaded by the Gulf Cooperation Council and the United States, may have averted all-out civil war among factions within the divided military establishment in the winter of 2011–12. Meanwhile, however, the American drone campaign and Saudi border policies deepened other tensions and conflicts.

The Dialogue Model

The heart of the Yemeni model is the Hiwar al-Watani, or National Dialogue. In *Civil Society in Yemen* (1998), I described the 1993–94 Hiwar, a far-reaching network of town hall meetings, university seminars, qat chews and tribal gatherings whose collective resolutions were compiled into a constitution-like Document of Pledge and Accord calling for things like the removal of military installations from population centers and constraints on executive power. The central-level National Dialogue Committee of prominent men tried to reconcile power sharing between Sana'a and Aden. This quest failed. After Aden's Socialist leaders declared their independence in April 1994, Salih's army, assisted by *salafi* militias, effectively conquered the south. Notwithstanding the triumph of militarism over mediation, I argued that the nationwide dialogue process epitomized what scholars mean by activism in the public civic sphere.

Several years before 2011, mass protests in Aden, Hadramawt and other parts of the former People's Democratic Republic—known simply as al-Hirak (or the Movement)—prompted Dialogue proponents with ties to both sides to reopen conversations to address legitimate concerns of southerners disenfranchised by Salih's carpetbaggers. When the youth in Sana'a, Ta'iz and other northern cities took up the cries for regime change from Tunisia, Egypt and the Hirak—and especially following scores of defections from the regime after snipers killed at least 50 demonstrators in Sana'a in March 2011—a new Hiwar became all the more urgent.

Salih postured and prevaricated. In a great "comeback kid" performance, after being gravely injured and permanently disfigured in June by a bomb placed inside the presidential compound, he returned alive and kicking after three months of convalescence in Saudi Arabia and the United States.

All the while, the progressive peaceful youth also persevered, combining protest repertoires of the other Arab uprisings with folk performance arts and twenty-first-century social media. Tribesmen threw down their arms; women raised their voices; children painted their faces and danced. Tawakkul Karman, an activist known for her fiery speeches, was co-winner of the 2012 Nobel Peace Prize. Sara Ishaq's film *Karama Has No Walls* about the massacre of March 2011 was later to be nominated in 2013 for the Academy Award for best documentary short subject.

Above and beyond the popular ferment, finally, at a ceremony in the Saudi capital on November 23, 2011, attended by Gulf royalty and Western diplomats—but none of the Yemenis who had called for his removal—a smiling Salih autographed four copies of the GCC plan. Vice President 'Abd Rabbu Mansour Hadi, a nondescript southern native and Salih loyalist who had been acting president during Salih's absence, resumed that role. After an uncontested ballot hastily arranged by foreign donors on February 21, 2012, Hadi was anointed as president. This series of events set the stage, over a year later, for the National Dialogue.

The widely inclusive Hiwar was designed to engage the erstwhile ruling GPC and the parliamentary opposition comprised of the defeated but still credible Socialist Party that formerly ruled South Yemen, the conservative Islah (Congregation for Reform) with its *salafi* and tribal wings, and several small but recognizable Nasserist and Baathist parties. Representatives came from all 20 provinces; major towns; and regions and communities including the Afro-Yemenis of the Tihama or Red Sea coast. A National Dialogue Conference of some 565 individuals including a who's who of veterans of past battles, a robust contingent of women and a smattering of youth put the old guard in negotiations with development professionals and at least some of the new generation. They set about tackling complex problems including the conflict in Sa'dah near the Saudi Arabian border; the southern issue, festering since 1994, and the increasingly irredentist Hirak; transitional justice; state building; good governance; military security, especially counter-terrorism; "independence of special entities" (a catch-all term covering, inter alia, ethnic minorities, the press and religious endowments); rights and freedoms; and development.

Politics of the Peninsula

Most scholars and pundits reflecting on the Arab uprisings have contrasted six repressed and eventually restive republics with the rich, safe, docile (apart from Bahrain) monarchies of the Gulf. The comparative framework examines movements and trajectories within countries; problems are national and domestic. Yet historians and long-time readers of *Middle East Report* will recall the interconnectedness of events in the Arabian Peninsula in the revolutionary 1960s and 1970s, when Samir Amin wrote about the unequal development of capital, class and power across "the Arab nation." Fred Halliday's dispatches from hotbeds of labor, migrant and populist activism in South Yemen, Oman and the Gulf showed how wealth accumulations, contradictions and solidarities transcended national boundaries. As the Gulf dynasties consolidated rentier state comfort, colonial South Yemen joined Third World revolutionary movements, establishing the Peoples' Democratic Republic of Yemen ruled by the Yemeni Socialist Party; and Nasserist Free Officers eventually defeated Saudi-backed Zaydi royalists in the North. During the Cold War, both Yemens' increasing poverty corresponded to the astronomic growth of the Gulf. Only when the old Soviet Union was on its deathbed did the two unstable Yemeni regimes agree to a merger. The republican vision for what became the most populous and populist state on the Peninsula never sat well with neighboring oil dynasties.

The political economies and even social movements of the Peninsula have always been tied together. Historically, European cartographers labeled the Peninsula's southwestern quadrant Arabia Felix for its monsoon-washed mountains, verdant spate-irrigated valleys, walled cities, old libraries and productive farmers. Later, Great Britain's only full-fledged Crown Colony in the Arab region, Aden, a natural harbor between the Red Sea and the Indian Ocean, flourished as one of the world's busiest ports and the hub of commerce and migration for Arabia, East Africa and South Asia. From the mid-twentieth century, oil-fueled monarchies began to eclipse farm economies, building skyscrapers with resource rents and trafficked labor. By contrast with Dubai, Doha and Mecca, Yemen seemed like a slum teeming with protesting masses, corrupt politicians, crony networks and outlaws—a place in need of serious policing and reform.

Transitology and Counter-Terrorism

Diplomats and Western-based think tanks consistently praise the Gulf and Western efforts to manage Yemen's post-uprising transition while at the same time combating the entity known in English as AQAP. Yet many Yemeni intellectuals worry that the process was coopted to contain rather than realize democratic aspirations, and to protect Gulf interests. The Hiwar al-Watani was subsumed under the GCC initiative that Salih signed, and no one pretended that Gulf royals were sympathetic to popular demands for social justice, much less the emancipation of Yemeni women. Instead of fostering bottom-up public consultations, the National Dialogue Conference holed up in the Sana'a Mövenpick and other opulent hotels to hear from a steady stream of foreign consultants. The so-called Group of Ten Ambassadors from the Security Council, the GCC and the European Union, who paid the bills, also seemed to drive agendas under the chairmanship of UN envoy Jamal bin Omar. Various donors "adopted" different committees; the United States, rather obviously, took charge of the committee on military and security affairs. Unlike in 1994 when the National Dialogue Committee was animated by mass public meetings, even the best work of the National Dialogue Conference was mostly sequestered from the public.

While backing all-party talks, security sector reform, anti-corruption measures and socioeconomic development projects, the US and Saudi Arabia also pursue other policies deeply disruptive to Yemen's stability, economy and democratic potential.

During 2013 the CIA and Joint Special Operations Command fired dozens of Predator and Hellfire missiles, often from a semi-secret base in the Saudi Arabian desert, at suspected militants affiliated with al-Qaeda's regional arm, known in English by the acronym AQAP. The last known strike of the year, on December 12, hit several vehicles in a wedding convoy outside the town of Rada' in al-Bayda province, killing a dozen and wounding many more. Missiles launched earlier in the year—including eight attacks during a three-week span in midsummer—did wipe out more mid-level al-Qaeda suspects than innocent civilians. But as the intrepid journalist Farea al-Muslimi and his colleagues on the ground reported, even "successful" drone warfare sowed anger and dismay in communities subjected to overhead surveillance and periodic out-of-the-sky brimstone.

There is substantial evidence that US military action since 2009 attracted more foreign and Yemeni jihadis. Indeed, according to one interpretation, engagement in Yemen is intended to lure militants from Saudi Arabia, AQAP's main target and Washington's main concern. The American drone campaign in a country where there are no "boots on the ground" to protect does not seem to be part of a Yemen policy as such. Rather, Washington views Yemen as a "theater" in the boundless "war on terror," a theater that happens to be in oil-rich Saudi Arabia's impoverished backyard. Yemen's human rights minister, Hooria Mashhour, published an op-ed in the January 14 *Washington Post* observing that the Yemeni public, Parliament and the National Dialogue Conference all object to extrajudicial cruise missile assassinations and the breach of sovereignty they constitute.

The Kingdom of Saudi Arabia's policies exacerbate Yemen's woes, if only as a side effect of domestic economic and security measures. A Saudization campaign is cracking down on illegal migrants and unlicensed businesses and deporting many thousands of Yemenis. A 1,100-mile fence is under construction to prevent illicit border crossings.

Furthermore, decades of public and/or private Saudi financing of *salafi* institutions, most famously the hardline Scientific Institute in Dammaj, in Saʿdah province, site of recent bloodshed, provoked the local Zaydi revival that fired the Houthi rebellion. More broadly, Salih's infamous corruption networks were not purely endogenous; for decades he, his friends, rival politicians and tribal leaders relied on patronage from wealthier Arab countries attempting, in turn, to shape domestic affairs. Gulf aid is not regarded in Yemen as a token of generosity.

Nor is international expertise necessarily all it is cracked up to be. Too few of the technocrats and transitologists flown in to "help Yemen" avoid "state failure" knew even basic history and geography. The main outcome of the GCC initiative seems to be an ill-defined federal system recommended by many UN and other consultants, and derived, incredibly, from the utterly failed US blueprint for Iraqi federalism. This recipe did not percolate upward from the revolutionary youth, the downtrodden masses, Hirak separatists or other domestic constituencies. Responses to a public opinion poll published on the National Dialogue Conference website at year's end were summarized under the headline "Less than Half of Yemenis Know About Federalism and the Majority Don't Favor a Federal System in Yemen." The federal scenario, which would erase existing provincial and past North-South boundaries in favor of new semi-autonomous regional authorities, goes well beyond the original mandate of the Dialogue Committee. Whereas there was a virtue in the Yemeni model of holding talks before elections or constitutional referenda, the new proposal would extend Hadi's term during protracted negotiations and extensive redrawing of administrative maps. In putting forth this plan, the UN and the Group of Ten are inviting further contestation over the spoils of what remains of the Yemeni state(s).

Dialectics

Collectively, Yemenis clocked more peaceful demonstrator days in 2011 than the people of any other Arab country. Since then, the once-hopeful youthful majority has confronted formidable counterrevolutionary forces at home and from abroad. Internally, the Salih family and key defectors from within the regime vie for military command while they, power brokers in the former PDRY, Houthi fighters, dissident tribes and *salafi* jihadis exploit chaos on the periphery. Most people suffer from decades of pathetic misrule from Sanaʿa. At the same time, Yemen's problems are not merely homegrown. Powerful external actors—the GCC's royal families, their domestic rivals, the monarchs' American security guarantor and international civil servants—are deployed to defend the status quo ante in part by containing the Yemeni uprising and various subaltern movements. This is not at all the same as a democratic vision for Yemen.

7 America's Deep Engagement

The media offered conflicting narratives about the 2015 military intervention into Yemen's civil war. Whereas the Anglophone press in Europe and North America and the Gulf media referred to the campaign of a "Saudi-led coalition," some Yemenis, especially in the northern provinces, and some independent Arabic-language news outlets called it the "Saudi-American aggression." Dispatches in this part of the book, predating the massive air campaign in Yemen, explain the deep American involvement in security arrangements in the Peninsula, especially for the protection of the Gulf monarchies. The opening vignette by Al Miskin (a pseudonym used by a few MERIP authors, roughly translating to "the jokester") from 1996, mocks American indulgence of Saudi propaganda. More seriously, Charles Schmitz tracks US efforts to investigate the 2000 attack on the USS *Cole* in Aden harbor. Sean Yom describes American weapons sales to the GCC. Through blog posts, Toby Jones and I react to American policies toward Yemen and especially Saudi Arabia. Chris Toensing and Lisa Hajjar, respectively, criticize the Obama administration's drone campaign in Yemen, including the assassination of US citizen Anwar al-Awlaqi and his teenage son. Given this background (and recalling Stork's 1985 essay from Chapter One on the Carter Doctrine protecting Gulf monarchies) it is hardly surprising that the United States assisted the 2015 Saudi war effort with arms, surveillance and logistical support.

America's Sawt al-Saud

Al Miskin • *MER* 199, Summer 1996

Boldly going where no one has gone before, the Clinton administration is busy renting out its broadcast studios to the Saudi
king's brother-in-law, whose new weekly call-in show, *Dialogue
with the West*, airs inside the kingdom and in neighboring countries. The hour-long program is officially a joint venture of Voice
of America (VOA), Worldnet and the London-based Middle East
Broadcasting Corporation (MBC), owned by Walid al-Ibrahim, a
relative of His Royal Highness, and part of the al-Saud's increasingly visible media empire.

VOA, like other agencies of the Cold War national security
state, is driven to innovate in order to protect its position in post–
Cold War Washington. This has led new director Geoffrey Cowan
to embrace the Saudi-controlled MBC. VOA supplies studio facilities and technical support in exchange for new non-shortwave
outlets for its programming. In the case of the *Dialogue* program,
a VOA personality fills one of the two co-anchor seats while its
executives share "mutual editorial control" with their Saudi partners. This "sharing" has some VOA journalists worried that they
are becoming mere propagandists for "foreign despots." When
Dialogue premiered on January 5, its opening news summary
segment omitted any mention of the day's undeniably important
story, namely, the British government's decision to deport the dissident Islamist Muhammad al-Masra'i.

Dissidents inside VOA began to circulate a petition around the
office. Making good use of the State Department's annual human
rights report, the manifesto begins with a pithy account of Saudi
ruling style (no political parties, torture, administrative detention
and no human rights organizations) and warns that VOA's integrity is threatened "when we partner with dictators who oppose
every principle of freedom." The crux of the matter is that VOA's
royal "affiliate" in this case is able to influence programming, ostensibly against official American journalism's abiding respect for
reporting news "without fear or favor."

Investigating the *Cole* Bombing

Charles Schmitz • *MERO*, Sept. 6, 2001

The investigation of the [October 2000] bombing of the USS *Cole* in Aden continues to irritate US-Yemeni relations. Last week, the agreement worked out between the Clinton White House and Yemeni authorities in November 2000, in which the FBI was allowed to submit questions to Yemeni investigators and observe interrogations, seemed to break down once again. Reports in American papers reiterated US accusations that Yemeni authorities were not cooperating with FBI investigators. "Senior bureau investigators say Yemen has denied them access to prominent Yemenis whom the Americans want to interview in their bid to link the attack to elements of [Osama] Bin Laden's network in Yemen, which became a key base for him in the early 1990's," the *New York Times* stated. Yet this week, reports in the *Washington Post* and the English-language *Yemen Times* say that FBI agents have returned. Earlier reports, published at the beginning of August, of the FBI's return have turned out to be false. Part of the US investigative team apparently arrived only to leave shortly thereafter. The current reports in the *Post* and the *Yemen Times* have not yet appeared in the Arabic-language press in Yemen.

Quick reversals and conflicting statements in the press are indicative of the considerable tension in current US-Yemeni relations. Hot on the trail of Osama bin Laden, its current archenemy, the FBI is treating the *Cole* investigation as an issue of US national security. US investigators remain convinced that the men awaiting trial in an Adeni prison were only part of a wider conspiracy that includes people in the Yemeni government. Last fall, a *New York Times* article on the case featured pictures of several prominent Yemeni officials and political leaders, suggesting that they had some role in the bombing or at least continuing links to Bin Laden. Yet no real evidence to support these charges has been presented. The only possible link to Bin Laden in the *Cole* case is a suspect now thought to be in Afghanistan. US investigators say he is the key to their claims. Yet US officials seem to believe that all political groups espousing Islamic rhetoric in Yemen are suspect, and subject to FBI interrogation. As in the Khobar Towers investigation concluded in June 2001, where US investigators insisted on keeping the case open in hopes of finding a smoking gun implicating Iran, in the *Cole* case the US foreign policy agenda takes precedence over the rule of law in a foreign country.

"Enhanced Observers"

In Yemen, things are seen quite differently. The Yemeni government would like to try the suspects according to Yemeni law—which guarantees a speedy trial—and they resist giving US investigators access to high Yemeni officials based upon the FBI's vague suspicions, or perhaps even prejudices. As Foreign Minister Abu Bakr al-Qurbi put it: "[J]ust because you have an Islamic connection does not mean that you have any relationship to the *Cole* bombing." The Yemeni authorities are particularly anxious to avoid the appearance that they have surrendered national sovereignty to US investigators at a time when the confrontation in Palestine has turned public opinion sharply against US policy in the Middle East. Like the federal indictments in the Khobar Towers case, which alienated Saudi law enforcement officials, FBI actions have caused considerable resentment in Yemen.

Further complicating the issue are apparent tensions between US diplomats in Yemen and the FBI team and the repeated issuance of vague warnings about possible terrorist attacks against US interests in the Arabian Peninsula. In a series of bizarre incidents in June, following the Khobar indictments in Virginia, the FBI team in Yemen withdrew to an "unspecified" country, the consular service at the US Embassy in Yemen was closed, ships of the US Navy's Fifth Fleet in Bahrain were sent out to sea and US Marines participating in maneuvers in Jordan were evacuated. In Yemen, American investigators announced that a group had been caught with plans to attack the US Embassy in Sana'a and asked Yemeni authorities to round up the suspects. Yemeni authorities cooperated with American demands, but then reversed themselves when the Yemeni president said that the local religious group named by the Americans posed no security threat. US credibility was further strained at a meeting for members of the American expatriate community in Yemen where US officials could cite no new evidence of a security threat justifying the embassy closing. Officials merely listed various kidnapping incidents over the last ten years and the *Cole* bombing. Then reports surfaced that the FBI team in Yemen had withdrawn because of differences with the US ambassador, Barbara Bodine, over a request to carry heavier weapons. The head of the FBI team had asked for greater firepower fearing a looming attack. The ambassador refused the request, citing local sensitivities to heavily armed American investigators who were supposed to be mere "enhanced" observers, and the FBI unilaterally withdrew. Needless to say, the FBI team slated to return soon to Yemen has new personnel.

Convergence of Interests

In Yemen, the constant issuance of security warnings is interpreted as po-litical pressure on Yemeni authorities to allow US investigators free rein to pursue Yemeni officials with "links"—however tenuous—to Bin Laden. Yemeni authorities find this line of inquiry objectionable, since they share US interests in a stable security regime in the region. In recent years Yemen has normalized relations with all her neighbors, signing treaties to resolve border disputes and demarcate common borders and submitting to inter-national arbitration to resolve a territorial dispute with Eritrea over the Hanish Islands in the Red Sea. Yemeni authorities have readily cooperated in building a military relationship with the United States. American sol-diers led efforts to remove land mines after the civil war of 1994, US and Yemeni troops have conducted joint maneuvers, Yemeni personnel have received specialized training in the United States, Yemen purchased $5 million in arms from the United States and the commander of the Fifth Fleet recently traveled to Sana'a. The US Navy chose Aden as a port of call for the *Cole* and other ships partly to boost the economy of the Port of Aden while further improving military relations with Yemen.

The Yemeni government also shares the particular US concerns about domestic political challenges from religiously inspired groups. After the two Yemens merged in 1990, many Yemenis who had fought—with US backing—against Soviet influence in Afghanistan returned to south Yemen to continue their cause against the godless communists in the for-mer People's Democratic Republic of Yemen. The trouble these "Afghani Arabs" caused for the Yemen Socialist Party (YSP) of the south was polit-ically convenient for the leadership of the former Yemeni Arab Republic, for it both weakened the YSP and enabled the northern leadership to claim that it was the moderate center between leftist socialists and conservative Islamists. However, after the civil war of 1994 in which the YSP was de-feated, the conservative groups became the sole political rival of the victo-rious northern Yemeni leadership.

Going After "Extremists"

Since the war the Yemeni leadership has moved decisively to weaken Islamist political groups and gain tighter military control over its territo-ry. When Wahhabi groups attacked mosques and other Islamic religious sites in Aden that they considered "un-Islamic" shortly after the war, the government swiftly crushed them with a large military force. Again in late 1998, when militants kidnapped foreign tourists, the government responded with force of arms, killing four hostages in the rescue mission. The leader of the militant group, the Aden-Abyan Islamic Army, was executed after his trial. Yemeni authorities also expelled thousands of non-Yemeni residents suspected of belonging to "extremist" groups after the war. In the elections of 1997, 1999 and 2001, the ruling party presented itself as the moderate center representing tolerance and justice against their erstwhile allies in the Yemeni Reform Group, Islah, whom they now painted as "extremist."

In pursuit of the *Cole* bombing perpetrators, the Yemeni authorities also took the liberty of rounding up whoever they suspect has ties to any group opposing the government. Clearly, the Yemeni government is interested in promoting an image of inclusive tolerance of the widely divergent political, regional and religious groups in Yemen while at the same time increasing domestic stability and security, on its own terms. It has no interest in cooperating with, or even harboring, groups that actually do work closely with Bin Laden. As was widely noted in Sana'a, the *Cole* bombing was aimed at Sana'a as much as it was at Washington. Why US investigators insist upon their right to interrogate the upper echelons of the Yemeni regime, when the Yemenis have been very compliant in their relations with the United States, is a mystery perhaps only the FBI could solve.

Washington's New Arms Bazaar

Sean L. Yom • *MER* 246, Spring 2008

On January 14, 2008, the State Department officially notified Congress of its intent to sell 900 Joint Direct Attack Munitions kits (JDAMs) to Saudi Arabia. Though some in Congress balked at transferring such advanced military technology to a country still in a formal state of war with Israel, their protests soon faltered. The transaction is just the latest phase in the Bush administration's plan to sell at least $20 billion of high-tech weaponry to Saudi Arabia and the five other Gulf Cooperation Council states—Kuwait, Bahrain, Qatar, the UAE and Oman. These sales are part of a massive $63 billion package of arms transfers and military aid to Washington's chief Middle Eastern allies first announced the preceding July. In addition to the GCC sales, over the next decade the US will provide $13 billion of arms grants to Egypt and $30 billion to Israel.

The Saudi weaponry sale was announced during President George W. Bush's January tour of the Middle East, which featured successive stops in Israel, the West Bank, most of the GCC kingdoms and Egypt. The week-long mission reprised a rare joint visit to these states undertaken by Secretary of State Condoleezza Rice and Secretary of Defense Robert Gates in the summer of 2007, shortly after the original $63 billion announcement. In placing huge offers of arms and aid on the table, both trips aimed at strengthening decades-long strategic relationships with these key US allies—repeatedly labeled "forces of moderation" by Rice—in order to contain the threat of regional "extremism." To use the Bush administration's language, the transfer of American-made weaponry will "contribute to the foreign policy and national security of the United States" by helping countries that are "an important force for political stability and economic progress in the Middle East." As Bush colorfully warned, peace and prosperity in the region are now under siege by "violent extremists who murder the innocent in pursuit of power."

In actuality, the ostentatious aid and arms deals signify the latest shift in US Middle East grand strategy. Since 2004, the Bush administration has watched aghast as its stated ambition to plant thriving pro-Western democracies in the arid soil of the Arab world failed to take root. The culprit blamed by the White House and State Department is a legion of extremism whose members are anyone and everyone that has refused to play by Washington's rules—Iran, Syria, Hizballah, Hamas, Iraqi militants and the ever present al-Qaeda. With its grandiose promises of "regional transformation" looking empty, the Bush administration will leave office by falling back on a tried-and-true tactic of hard realism: Shore up client regimes with enormous volumes of aid and arms, not only reminding the world of US military hegemony but also of the benefits of being one of Washington's "moderate" friends, as opposed to its "extremist" enemies.

But the Manichean logic behind the fresh infusions of aid and weaponry cloaks a host of more complex political issues in the recipient states, from the resilience of authoritarianism in Egypt to the rearmament of Israel's formidable war machine to the inflated tensions in the Persian Gulf between the GCC and Iran. Because these states are linchpins of US military strategy, the aid and arms sales are being substituted for critical reflection on these problems, not to speak of the diplomatic engagement that would be required to resolve them. As such, Washington's new arms bazaar highlights the chronic inability of US decision-makers to escape from Cold War–style thinking in which the demands of geopolitical stability outweigh all other concerns.

[...]

Behind the Green Curtain

Overshadowing both the Egyptian and Israeli aid agreements was the dec-laration of intent to sell at least $20 billion of arms to Saudi Arabia and the other GCC member states. Unlike Foreign Military Financing grant-based packages, the State and Defense Departments have long transferred advanced weaponry and defense equipment to the wealthy Gulf kingdoms through cash sales, each of which has to be approved by Congress. While Congress was not circumvented, the announcement essentially preempted lawmakers by publicly committing a large block of American military re-sources to the GCC. Further, the $20 billion figure is considered a "floor" rather than a "ceiling"; the ultimate value of the arms sales could be sub-stantially greater. Nonetheless, at their Jidda press conference on August 1, both Rice and Gates defended the arms sales with their familiar re-frain: "There is nothing new here." And once again, they were technically correct.

Since the Iran-Iraq war, Washington's mastery of the oil-rich Persian Gulf has required not only repositioning its air and naval forces around the GCC but also strengthening the military capabilities of local allied regimes through arms transfers. Several decades ago, oil wealth enabled Saudi Arabia and its smaller monarchical neighbors to rank among the highest per capita military spenders in the world. The severe fiscal crises of the 1980s failed to reverse this addiction. From the end of the Gulf war through the rest of the 1990s, Saudi Arabia allocated a rough average of 40 percent of central state expenditures to its defense sector; Oman and the Emirates, 40 to 45 percent; and Kuwait, Bahrain and Qatar, 20 to 25 percent. In historical terms, through 2005 Saudi Arabia purchased almost $62 billion in US armaments, Kuwait, nearly $7.8 billion; the Emirates, over $2 billion and Bahrain, over $1.8 billion, with the majority of these sales occurring after the 1990–91 Gulf war.

Western defense firms regard the Gulf kingdoms as an especially lu-crative market today, given that record oil prices have them swimming in surplus revenue. The six GCC states spent $233 billion on arms imports from 2000 to 2005, accounting for 70 percent of total armament expen-ditures in the Arab world. But Washington also has a political reason to boost its Gulf arms sales relative to other major suppliers, such as Britain, France and Russia. Because they lack logistical know-how and technical sophistication, when the GCC militaries acquire frontline US weaponry—in the past, centerpiece items like F-16 Falcons, AH-64 Apache helicopters and M-1A2 Abrams tanks—they typically must also purchase secondary support agreements that allow American contractors to provide repair parts, personnel training, specialized data and other vital services. By deepening the dependence of GCC armed forces on its defense industry, the US also ensures greater compliance by these regimes with its geopolitical interests.

Since the $20 billion announcement, the US has wasted little time in expanding its GCC security commitments. From August 2007 through January 2008, the Bush administration notified Congress of 14 different GCC arms sales worth nearly $14 billion. Of these transactions, only the January proposal to sell the JDAMs to Saudi Arabia elicited fierce Congressional opposition; the kits transform "dumb" bombs carried by the Kingdom's F-15 Strike Eagle jets, themselves purchased from the US in the late 1990s, into precise satellite-guided weapons, which some fear would pose a threat to Israel. Indeed, early talk of selling the JDAMs in 2006 so disquieted Israeli policymakers and pro-Israel lobbies that the State Department promised 10,000 more sophisticated versions of the weapon (along with 36,500 other assorted munitions and kits) to Israel, a sale formally announced in early August 2007.

Meanwhile, the other announced GCC arms deals have elicited little controversy. The most prominent are multi-billion-dollar sales of advanced Patriot PAC-3 defense systems to Kuwait and the UAE, which are designed to intercept tactical ballistic missiles and cruise missiles. Lesser transactions include sales of E-2 Airborne Early Warning Aircraft to the UAE, thousands of TOW [Tube-Launched, Optically Tracked, Wire-Guided] land missiles to Kuwait, and upgrades for Saudi Arabia's E-3 Airborne Warning and Control System planes; among the many items under future consideration are the US Navy's new Littoral Combat warships. Notably, such hardware will not transform the kingdoms into efficient fighting machines. The 1990–91 Gulf war revealed that GCC armed forces are technologically top-heavy and lack the numbers, training and doctrine to wage effective offensive campaigns. Similarly, the GCC's near-defunct joint defense force, "Peninsula Shield," has proven useless in regional crises since its formation in 1984. Rather, these items are intended to protect local airspaces and shorelines from foreign intrusion. "When the kingdom gets weapons," Saudi foreign minister Saud al-Faisal chided one reporter at the Jidda press conference, "it gets them to defend itself." In this case, Iran is the intruder in question.

Following the intensification of Iraq's civil war, American hawks began to focus their wrath on Tehran and fanned similar sentiments inside the regimes of Saudi Arabia, Kuwait, Bahrain, Qatar, the UAE and Oman. Fueled also by perennial suspicions of their Shi'i minorities, lingering animosity from previous territorial disputes and trepidation over the looming United States drawdown in Iraq, starting in 2006 Gulf monarchies fostered a climate of anti-Iranian alarmism unseen since the late 1980s. Mainstream voices warned of a radical Shi'i crescent stretching from Tehran to Beirut, an elaborate arc of instability masterminded by Iran's firebrand president Mahmoud Ahmadinejad and his coterie of mad mullahs. Meanwhile, the Bush administration, convinced that the Iranian regime was enriching uranium for use in nuclear weapons, framed the GCC, Egypt and Jordan as the Arab world's moderate bulwarks against Iran and its forces of Shi'i extremism. Indeed, the first stop of the Rice and Gates Middle East tour was at Sharm el-Sheikh, where there were multilateral meetings of these eight allies, dubbed the "six plus two." This was the fifth such US-sponsored gathering. Though the front's official goals initially seemed drenched in honey—a stable and democratic Iraq, a unified and peaceful Lebanon, a state for the Palestinians—each successive conference made clear that the group was an entente against Iran, along with Hizballah, Hamas and Sadrist elements in Iraq, which were portrayed as Tehran's subservient proxies. In addition, in May 2006 Washington enhanced its ties to the GCC by initiating the Gulf Security Dialogue, which brought together diplomatic, intelligence and military officials from both sides for coordinated meetings. It was through this forum that the United States first hinted at the GCC arms package in October 2006.

By the fall of 2007, the containment of Iran had become the predominant theme of US Middle East policy. As one Arab analyst noted, a new regional cold war had been invented, one in which a "Green Curtain" divided the United States and its "moderate" clients from the Iranian-led "extremist" camp. Vice President Dick Cheney decried Iran's ambitions of "dominating this region," while Bush cautioned that a "nuclear holocaust" would result if Iran continued its uranium enrichment program. Were the United States to commence hypothetical airstrikes against Iran's nuclear facilities, furthermore, American strategists were convinced of Tehran's capacity to launch catastrophic reprisals. In a typical war games scenario, the Iranian intelligence services would utilize their connections with Hamas in the Palestinian territories, Hizballah in Lebanon, Sadrist militants in Iraq and even Shi'i minorities in the GCC states to incite widespread violence and instability. Iranian naval forces would interdict oil shipping and US traffic in the Strait of Hormuz with mines and attack boats. Finally, Iran would lob nuclear-armed Shahab-3 ballistic missiles at US bases, oil installations and economic targets in the Gulf countries, and perhaps, in the most excessive scenario, at Israel as well. The result, as Bush warned in October, would be "World War III."

[...]

Embracing Crisis in the Gulf

Toby Jones • *MER* 264, Fall 2012

All claims to the contrary, the Persian Gulf monarchies have been deeply affected by the Arab revolutionary ferment of 2011–12. Bahrain may be the only country to experience its own sustained upheaval, but the impact has also been felt elsewhere. Demands for a more participatory politics are on the rise, as are calls for the protection of rights and formations of various types of civic and political organization. Although these demands are not new, they are louder than before, including where the price of dissent is highest in Saudi Arabia, Oman and even the usually hushed UAE. The resilience of a broad range of activists in denouncing autocracy and discomfiting autocrats is inspirational. As yet, there are no cracks in the foundation of Gulf order, but the edifice no longer appears adamantine.

This state of affairs poses a historic challenge to the order's number-one guarantor, the United States. The task is not, as some might think, to reconcile the Obama administration's professed affinity for Arab democracy with the fact of its firm alliance with the states that the activists are working to open up. Rather, it is to aid those states in managing their domestic crisis so that the regional order can remain intact.

Campaign of Oppression

Gulf regimes have responded harshly to the fresh challenges from below, turning quickly from efforts at cooptation to coercion. At first, when revolts broke out in Tunisia and Egypt, Saudi Arabia, Bahrain, Oman, Qatar and Kuwait hiked public-sector salaries, subsidies and other forms of patronage, literally trying to spend their way out of potential trouble. But there has been a surge in state violence as well, with thousands detained, disappeared and killed. Authorities in the Gulf are not known for their soft touch, but the present repression is both measurably greater and noticeably more out in the open. Typically concerned to hide unrest from view, out of fear of seeming weak or unpopular, the Gulf monarchies now seem disinterested in masking their violent response. In part, the states have lost control; activists can broadcast details of riot police assaults over social media. But the brutality on display is also intentional. The authorities wish to send the message that they can and will crush dissent with impunity.

The repressive turn is collective. Save in Bahrain, where Saudi Arabia and the UAE dispatched troops in March 2011, there has been no obvious collaboration between Gulf militaries. There is, however, a regional pattern. Oman has arrested hundreds and sentenced dozens to jail, including prominent human rights activists, for participating in protests. The UAE has arrested pro-reform demonstrators and stripped them of their citizenship. Saudi Arabia has arrested thousands and killed a significant number of Shi'i protesters in the Eastern Province. Kuwaiti authorities have deployed force against members of the opposition, as well as the *bidun*, native-born residents who do not enjoy the rights of citizenship. The Bahraini state has struck hardest of all, killing dozens, torturing hundreds and terrorizing the majority of the population with tear gas and birdshot. Major opposition and human rights figures, including 'Abd al-Hadi al-Khawaja, Ibrahim Sharif and Nabeel Rajab, have been imprisoned.

It is not just the vigor of local and wider Arab protest movements that accounts for the alacrity of the Gulf regimes' campaign of violence and oppression. The effort is partly driven as well by anxiety, mixed with a sense of opportunity, related to the balance of power with Iran.

Arab Gulf monarchs have summoned the specter of an Iranian threat ever since the 1979 Islamic Revolution. Today, however, anti-Iranian hysteria is at an all-time high, whipped up by Iran's perceived strategic benefit from the toppling of Saddam Hussein, the rise of Shi'i Islamist parties to power in post-Saddam Iraq, Iran's posture of "resistance" during Israel's wars on Lebanon and Gaza, and now the Arab revolts. Riyadh and Manama have been particularly provocative, deliberately poking their rival across the Gulf. Theirs is a conscious effort to discredit Shi'i empowerment—Bahrain's population is majority-Shi'i and Saudi Arabia's some 15 percent Shi'i—and to undermine popular support for domestic protest. For Saudi Arabia, in particular, stoking fear of Iran is one way to keep protests from spreading from the Eastern Province, where most of the Shi'a live, to the rest of the country. No doubt the Saudis, Bahrainis and others also believe that heightened tensions with Iran help to secure the backing of their benefactors, chiefly the United States.

Here, the Gulf regimes appear to have calculated correctly, for to date Washington has paid far more attention to Iranian maneuvering, real and imagined, than to the excessive force used to grind down pro-democracy and human rights activists on the Arab side of the Gulf. Gulf Arab rulers have turned what historically has been a source of US leverage—security guarantees and military might—to their own advantage. Indeed, because containment of Iran is a strategic priority for Washington, the US military has parlayed its withdrawal from Iraq into tighter bilateral relationships with the Arab monarchies to the south, stationing 15,000 troops in Kuwait and pushing for more naval and air patrols of the vital, oil-rich Gulf. Central Command's chief of staff, Gen. Karl Horst, labels this shift "back to the future." And, indeed, the Obama administration's approach in the Gulf—that its Arab allies are strategic partners indispensable to regional commerce, the war on terror and containment of Iran—is consistent with 60 years of US policy. In this regard, the Arab uprisings have changed nothing.

The US in the Gulf

Washington's clear preference for the status quo in the Gulf has come at considerable cost to activists in the region. The United States has enabled the Gulf regimes to behave badly; the regimes, for their part, have exploited geopolitical rivalries to consolidate power at home.

There is a structural weakness in the US position, however, one that has become evident over time. The United States is tied to partners in the Gulf who are politically vulnerable, as clearly demonstrated by the protest of 2011–12 and the failure of the usual buyoffs and blandishments to restore quiet. Washington has long been committed to a set of security assurances that aim to maintain a regional system that is not sustainable on its own. The consequence is a paradox: The United States is by far the strongest power in the Gulf. Its Fifth Fleet, squadrons of warplanes and pre-positioned infantry and armor hold the region together. But its clout is also limited. Neither the White House nor the Pentagon is able to dictate political outcomes, not in Iraq, not in Iran and particularly not in the Arab Gulf states. The Gulf thus becomes no more stable as a result of the heavier and heavier US deployments, the increasingly more direct interventions, in the name of guaranteeing stability. Indeed, since the close of the twentieth century, US security commitments have contributed to the exact opposite trend. The United States has helped to destabilize a region it claims to protect.

Gulf security, notably the "energy security" supplied by the region's oil and gas, is a perennial American obsession. In the early days after the discovery of oil, it was corporate profits that placed the Gulf at the center of US strategic thinking, but commercial and political concerns had converged by the middle of the twentieth century. The US military commitment to the regional order was stepped up in the 1970s, with the closure of British bases in Bahrain and elsewhere. For most of that decade, weary of projecting power directly, the United States attempted to arm surrogates—the "twin pillars" of Saudi Arabia and the Shah's Iran—to do its bidding. That policy collapsed in 1979, with the revolution in Iran and the Soviet invasion of Afghanistan.

From that point on, the United States would not outsource the protection of the oil patch. In his 1980 State of the Union address, President Jimmy Carter was forthright: "An attempt by any outside force to gain control of the Persian Gulf region will be regarded as an assault on the vital interests of the United States of America, and such an assault will be repelled by any means necessary, including military force." Carter's words were directed at the Soviets in Afghanistan, but his vision has guided US strategists long after the Soviet Union's dissolution. It has been demonstrated by the repeated use of military force since the late 1980s, in what should be considered one long war in the Gulf.

Fretting about Gulf security is tied to considerations including terrorism and Israeli military superiority, Washington's chosen method, along with bilateral treaties between Israel and frontline Arab states, for averting another major Arab-Israeli war. Most important, however, is energy. In particular, Gulf security is often framed by the argument that the outward flow of oil, critical to both the American and global economy, demands protection and that the best way to protect it is to underwrite the regional political status quo. When in late 2011 Iran threatened to close the Strait of Hormuz, thus blocking the main oil supply route, it was hardly surprising that the United States scrambled additional planes and ships to the Gulf. Such resolve is entirely complementary, of course, with the stated objectives of the Arab Gulf states, which also insist on the primacy of security. Over time, it has become axiomatic in political and diplomatic discourse, and even in scholarship, that Gulf states are engaged in a "ceaseless quest for security." This phrase, indeed, served as the subtitle of a 1985 study of Saudi Arabia by Nadav Safran, a Harvard scholar who resigned from his administrative job at the university following the revelation that the CIA had funded his research.

Yet while US and Gulf monarchy interests have been served—oil has flowed, the revenues are high and Washington's allies remain in place—it is a stretch to call the Gulf secure, let alone stable. The region has been wracked by war for more than three decades, with hundreds of thousands dead, much of the natural environment laid waste and every prospect of a repeat performance. The reality is that when US leaders iterate their commitment to security in the Gulf, what they mean is that they are committed to the survival of their allies and the political systems that dominate in the region. The result—Washington's blind eye to the Gulf states' repression—is often criticized as inaction.

But the opposite is true. In spite of considerable Congressional opposition, the Obama administration found a way to sell more weapons to Bahrain in 2012. It has also overseen significant sales to other regional allies, including almost $30 billion to Saudi Arabia, all based on the pretense that these states are instrumental in checking a troublesome Iran. The reality, however, is that none of the Arab states in the Gulf are capable of mounting their own defense. They are entirely dependent on the United States for their security. It is something US policymakers know well: Since the beginning of 2012 the US has positioned the USS *Ponce*, a large floating base, in the Gulf, moved a squadron of F-22 fighters to the UAE, doubled its minesweeping presence and deployed the Sea Fox undersea drone. All these moves amount not to inaction to help aspiring democrats, but to forceful and purposeful intervention on the side of some of the most authoritarian states on the planet.

Thrive by the Sword

The upsurge in oppression by Gulf states in 2011 reflected their shared deep disquiet about their own weakness: They have narrow social bases and historically have sought to manufacture loyalty to governments that are corrupt and self-serving. From Riyadh to Muscat, the Arab uprisings induced a sense of looming disaster, one perhaps unprecedented in intensity. It is clear, however, that the regimes believe they have arrived at a winning formula, turning crisis into opportunity. Paradoxically, therefore, the Gulf states have thrived off the very thing—political upheaval—that they have for so very long claimed to fear above all else.

In the mid-2000s, most of the Gulf kingdoms were keen to indulge the pretense of reform. They did more talking about reform than reforming—but even the talk is now passé. Back in vogue today are the police state and the counterrevolutionary tactics that prevailed in the 1970s. Indeed, the

Arab uprisings and local unrest seem to have convinced rulers in the Gulf to offer less accommodation and wield more blunt force. It is arguable that, in the Gulf of the twenty-first century, crises are no longer undesirable, but rather have considerable political utility. In fact, given the arc of history—whereby the redistribution of oil wealth has failed to ensure regime stability or political quietism—the regional system may have arrived at a moment where political survival actually requires the manufacturing of permanent crisis at home and in the region.

To be sure, the uprising in Bahrain and protests elsewhere are potential sources of revolution, but the monarchies have been successful in recasting them as threats to the system (and domestic and regional security) rather than groundswells that reflect the interests of actual subjects. Rather than engage the ruled, the Gulf states feel increasingly compelled to characterize the terms of domestic politics, and especially opposition politics, as destabilizing, inimical to the (fictional) national interest and beholden to a conspiracy of outsiders.

It may be that the embrace of crisis, at least for short-term political gain, represents the latest stage of political development in the oil-rich states of the Gulf. With new grassroots political energy and emboldened demands for change, it is apparent that old patterns of political engagement such as handing out patronage are increasingly ineffective. While the redistribution of wealth has never satisfied everyone, even in times of plenty, levels of political engagement by ordinary Gulf Arabs seem greater than ever. What has not changed, however, is the reluctance of regional authorities to part with power. They remain steadfast in preserving an antiquated and rotten political order. These contradictory vectors, the growing expectation of participation versus intensifying efforts to maintain a closed system, help to explain the power of crisis in shaping regime behavior. To the extent that the United States endorses the status quo, it is complicit not only in the Gulf regimes' efforts to quash citizen protest, but also in the redesign of Gulf security architecture by which crisis becomes the norm.

Rules of Engagement

Sheila Carapico • Originally published as
"A New Green Zone in Sana'a," *MERO*, Jan. 1, 2013

On September 12, amid popular demonstrations in Cairo and other Muslim cities and the death of an American ambassador in Benghazi, all said to be sparked by the *Innocence of Muslims* film trailer released by an Egyptian-American provocateur, a couple of hundred young men stormed the US Embassy in Sanaʻa. They ripped the embassy's sign from the outer wall, torched tires and a couple of vehicles, burned the American flag and breached the outer gates of the security entrance. Yemeni guards returned fire. This gathering was no impromptu assembly of populists: Sheraton Street, a divided highway with no sidewalks or bus stops but several military checkpoints, is far off the beaten track for pedestrians or people traveling by public transportation. While thousands of men and women massed downtown demanding a just resolution to the country's long-standing political crisis, scores of armed militants purposely converged on the embassy in an SUV convoy. There was lots of speculation about who had sent them. *Salafi* extremists? Loyalists of the deposed president, ʻAli ʻAbdallah Salih? Was it related to what had happened in Libya?

The threat level spiked at year's end. In late December, the al-Malahim Foundation, publisher of a irregularly issued online magazine and advertised as al-Qaeda's media arm in Yemen, announced bounties, payable through June 2013, of some $160,000 in gold for the killing of the American ambassador to Yemen and $23,000 for the deaths of American soldiers in Yemen, in order "to encourage and inspire jihad."

Years earlier, in 2000, a second-rate but incongruously prescient feature film called *Rules of Engagement*, based on a story written by Sen. Jim Webb (D-VA), and starring Samuel L. Jackson and Tommy Lee Jones, depicted a mob rioting outside a poorly defended American mission in Sanaʻa. The set designers, anachronistically enough, placed the quaint diplomatic compound in a popular neighborhood. Once upon a time, US envoys welcomed American citizens and Yemeni visa seekers at an architecturally distinguished stone-and-alabaster South Arabian mansion near the city center. It featured charming enclosed gardens of indigenous flora, and opened onto a cobblestone plaza, as in the movie. But after the 1982 explosions in Beirut killed emissaries and spies, a new state-of-the-art fortress was constructed on what had been terraced fields near the upscale

Sheraton (then newly built) and a new gated community to house Yemeni military officers.

Gone were the days when Americans in Yemen could stroll over to the embassy and flash their passports or let drop a phrase of American vernacular to the guards in order to swim in the pool. Gone were the days when diplomats roamed the *suq*.

And yet *Rules of Engagement* depicted Yemenis (actually, the actors, costumes and venues seemed Moroccan), including women and children, mobbing a central destination where a hapless ambassador quivered under his desk until Marines staged a guns-blazing rescue. In the movie rendition, even a girl who appeared to be disabled pulled the trigger of an AK-47 (or Kalashnikov) semi-automatic rifle. There followed courts-martial for the Marines, who were accused of slaughtering civilians. The moral of Hollywood's version of Webb's story seemed to be that the tribunals were wrongheaded: All Yemenis could be crazed terrorists, and the rules meant to inhibit the Marines from gunning them down were foolhardy.

This fictional message has since been internalized as soldierly doctrine. There are few if any rules in Yemen, the theater of operations in the "war on terror." The counter-terror campaign does not distinguish fighters from little girls or, especially, men of fighting age. On December 24, two US drone strikes killed five suspected militants in al-Bayda and Hadramawt provinces. These have been more salvos in an ongoing battle of scores of bombardments by drone or fixed-wing aircraft since 2002, most in the past few years. Several high-profile al-Qaeda operatives, some nameless armed men, and assorted family members and innocent civilians have been blown to smithereens by Hellfire missiles. In the last days of 2009 Obama authorized a strike that left at least 20 children and a dozen women dead in the southern town of al-Majala, along with one militant. Later the US-born Anwar Nasir al-Awlaqi, a preacher suspected of inspiring the perpetrator of the Fort Hood shootings and the failed "crotch bombing" aboard a Detroit-bound commercial airliner at Christmas 2009, was killed; weeks later, so was his teenage son. Even American citizens are not due trial before execution, evidently.

Most of the more than 50 recorded air attacks inside Yemen in 2012 are known or supposed to have been launched by Americans. Most dramatically, a September 2 airstrike near Rada', a historically important but now godforsaken, flyblown town in al-Bayda province where al-Qaeda militants had encamped, exterminated three children and nine other civilians. Around Rada' and many other towns, the maddening overhead buzz of drones is a persistent token of American surveillance. The Obama administration's remote-controlled "signature strikes" directive posthumously deems any able-bodied men in the line of fire legitimate targets in the war on terror. This is the shoot-first-ask-questions-later opposite of the strategy depicted in *Rules of Engagement.*

Despite its intensifying involvement in Yemen, the United States has not formulated a Yemen policy or even a genuinely diplomatic mission there. Instead it has a policy of keeping the Saudi monarchy secure and happy—and a related counter-terrorism policy that is an extension of the post–September 11 "Af-Pak" strategy. Washington regards Yemen as a theater of counter-terrorism in Saudi Arabia's backyard. It's as if it isn't a real place where real people demand decent governance or respect for human rights. The Obama administration has wasted scant breath supporting Yemen's demonstrators for democracy and social justice. US ambassador Gerald Feierstein was tapped for his counter-terrorism credentials as well as his diplomatic experience. He works closely with intelligence and military officers. During the protracted negotiations under the Saudi-led initiative of the Gulf Cooperation Council to facilitate a transition from the rule of Salih to the presidency of his deputy 'Abd Rabbu Mansour Hadi, Washington's envoy was a spy agency operative, John Brennan, not someone with a State Department pedigree or Hillary Clinton's ear. The American reaction to Yemen's prolonged pro-democracy uprising in 2011–12 was not to provide moral support to activists clamoring for social justice, much less to call for free elections or women's rights. Rather, Obama, Clinton, Brennan and Feierstein sought to placate Riyadh by battling an enemy called AQAP.

Best known in the United States for a pathetic dildo bomb planted on a Yemeni-trained Nigerian bound by air for Detroit, AQAP is often said to constitute a grave threat to the American homeland. Local commanders and spokespersons reveled in the publicity, a boon for recruitment of jihadi wannabes from inside and outside Yemen, whose numbers swelled from a couple hundred to perhaps a couple thousand.

"AQAP" is an unconventionally bilingual neologism, neither English fish nor Arabic fowl. "AQ" stands for the Arabic-language al-Qaeda, giving extraordinary grammatical weight to the definite article "al-." "AP" stands, in English, for the Arabian Peninsula. The Pentagon-speak acronym AQAP, adopted as if it were a proper noun by the US-based punditocracy and security wonks, evokes an image of formidable military prowess, perhaps rivaling the former USSR. The Anglophone term both does and does not convey the meaning in the Arabic phrase *al-Qaeda fi al-Jazira al-'Arabiyya*, which suggests a rebellion in the whole Peninsula, stretching beyond Yemen to Saudi Arabia and the other Gulf princedoms. Whereas the Arabic phrase signifies struggle against local despots, the English acronym is coded as a terrorist menace to the United States. As such, "targeted strikes" against "AQAP" suspects can be portrayed not as intervention but as self-defense—operations to preempt another September 11.

The United States is now fully yet incompletely engaged in South Arabia. In addition to surveillance and frequent bombardments, American measures to "stabilize" Yemen now include provision of light aircraft, armed vehicles, gadgetry and training; direct military cooperation with and command-and-control backing for Yemeni forces; cheerleading for Hadi's restructuring of Yemen's military command; some humanitarian assistance and token support for civil society initiatives; protection for the "Green Zone" comprised of the embassy and the Sheraton Hotel (fully rented for American military and civilian personnel); and extra coordination with Saudi security institutions to make sure that Yemen's multiple conflicts do not spill across the border. Efforts to engage pro-democracy activists, Houthi rebels and/or Southern separatists are marginal compared to the escalating drone war.

Secret US Bases?

Sheila Carapico • Originally published as
"The Laryngitic Dog," *MERO*, Feb. 14, 2013

Senate hearings to confirm John Brennan as the Obama administration's appointment to be director of the CIA brought to light a heretofore clandestine American military facility in Saudi Arabia near the Kingdom's border with Yemen. While journalistic and public attention rightly focused on extrajudicial executions of Yemenis and even American citizens, the new revelations suggest a larger covert Saudi-American war against Yemen. There's almost certainly more to this story than what Saudi Arabia fails to confirm.

Information about the base was long withheld from the public by both the government and the media. NBC News, the *New York Times* and the *Washington Post* reported on February 5 and 6 that the United States built a secret airfield in Saudi Arabia over two years ago, primarily as a staging

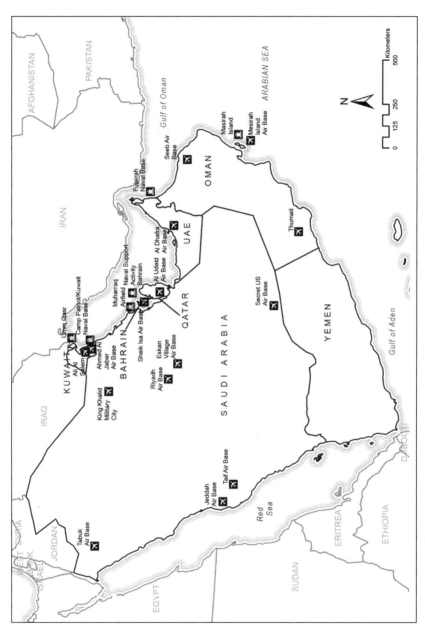

Map 4: US Military Installations and Shared Local Facilities in the Arabian Peninsula and Coastal Waters Produced by the Spatial Analysis Lab, University of Richmond

ground for strikes in Yemen. Both flagship newspapers acknowledged keeping this fact under wraps in deference to the Obama administration's request for secrecy on national security grounds. Reportedly, the first operation conducted from the base was the one that killed the Yemeni-American preacher Anwar Nasir al-Awlaqi.

Microsoft Bing aerial photographs from 2012 appear to show a facility in southeast Saudi Arabia, north of the Yemeni border and west of the Omani frontier, in the remote expanse of sand dunes called the Empty Quarter.

There also seem to be launching pads for unmanned Predator drones and/or Hellfire missiles at al-Anad Airbase near Aden. Al-Anad is an established installation on Yemen's southern coast near the Bab al-Mandab, a crucial waterway connecting the Red Sea to the Indian Ocean. Now evidence has surfaced of yet another US base in the Hadramawt, in eastern Yemen, not far from the base in Saudi Arabia.

As more sleuths inspect more maps, we could learn of more military construction in the Peninsula, and of more Saudi engagement than has been acknowledged.

A reporter for the *Guardian* quoted journalism professor Jack Lule of Lehigh University, who called the media's complicity in secrecy about the drone program "shameful." Lule added, "I think the real reason was that the administration did not want to embarrass the Saudis—and for the US news media to be complicit in that is craven."

Why would the Saudis be embarrassed? US-Saudi security cooperation has a history dating to the 1950s. Saudi Arabia offered facilities for the US-led Desert Storm campaign to restore Kuwaiti sovereignty after Saddam Hussein's 1990 invasion. Yet the massive positioning of foreign forces in the land of the Islamic holy places, Mecca and Medina, later stirred controversy. When Osama bin Laden and his jihadi followers decried the presence of "infidel" armies on sacred territory, and used these boots on the ground as a pretext for the September 11 attacks on the United States, the Saudi defense minister ruled that bases inside the Kingdom could not be used for attacks on Afghanistan's Taliban or other Muslim targets. Accordingly, American installations, including the King Sultan airbase in Khobar province, were relocated to other Gulf spots such as Qatar.

There's more, perhaps lots more. There have been many targeted attacks purportedly conducted by the US military or the CIA against suspected militants in Yemen in the past two or three years. There have also been signature strikes. These are not aimed at persons who intelligence agencies have identified as enemies of the US. Instead, signature strikes are robotic attacks triggered by evidence of "suspicious activities" or "patterns of movement" observed, by drones, from the air, such as the loading of rifles onto pickup trucks. Although lethal targeted attacks, especially against al-Awlaqi, his teenage son, and at least two other American citizens have attracted the most attention of late, the signature attacks are even scarier. Yemenis are extraordinarily well armed, ranking alongside the US in number of firearms per capita. And gun-toting Yemenis almost certainly pack more firepower than their American counterparts: Markets in the northern part of the country sell bazookas and rocket-propelled grenade launchers. Further, Toyota pickups are ubiquitous in Yemen; four-wheel drive vehicles are a logical choice for navigating the country's unpaved mountain roads. Grenade launchers in Yemen pose no credible threat to the American homeland. But they might, conceivably, be a menace to Saudi Arabia.

Exactly whose forces launched which attacks remains an unsolved mystery. Washington neglects to release accurate data on its forays into Yemen, while the Yemeni regime wishes to convey the impression of Sanaʻa's own prowess in counter-terror operations, and so keeps quiet about its foreign co-combatants.

There's a third possibility. The *Guardian* recently suggested that some deadly bombings in Yemen were carried out not by American drones, or Yemeni counterparts, as often presumed, but rather "outsourced" to the Saudi air force. Saudi foreign minister Prince Saud al-Faisal flatly denied these reports. But there were other reports that the first US drone strike in Yemen in 2013 was assisted by Saudi fighter jets.

Saudi weapons purchases are the lifeblood of Western arms manufacturers. In 2010, the Pentagon notified Congress of $60 billion in arms sales to the Kingdom over the next five to ten years. If all goes well for the American weapons makers, this transfer will be the largest single package for any foreign country in US history. In the short term, however, according to the German magazine *Der Spiegel*, European nations are topping their Yankee competitors: France comes in first with 2.17 billion euros in sales, followed by Italy with 435.3 million euros and Great Britain with 328.8 million, contributing to total European sales of 3.3 billion euros or $4.4 billion. It makes sense that these armaments would be used, not merely stockpiled. True, documentation is thin. In 2010, Amnesty International said it was "extremely likely"—though difficult to verify—that Tornado fighter-bombers supplied by Britain to Saudi Arabia were used in indiscriminate attacks against Houthi rebels in northern Yemen that killed Yemeni civilians as well as militants.

The fact that America's most prominent news organizations have not yet implicated Riyadh in the Obama administration's war in Yemen is hardly evidence that Saudi interests and forces are not involved. The *Times* and the *Post* bury news of the Kingdom's military affairs beneath titillating tales about women drivers, athletes and lingerie sales. Scoops about clandestine bases, collateral murder and counterrevolutionary meddling are left to intrepid investigators, bloggers and British reporters. If Saudis aren't worried about the reports of secret bases, the story goes, then why should anyone else care?

Of Dangling Bodies

Al Miskin • Originally published as
"Of Bodies and Blank Notebooks," *MERO*, Jun. 28, 2013

Five corpses dangle from a bar slung between two construction cranes in Jizan in the southwest corner of the Kingdom near the Yemeni border. In several videos posted on YouTube in May 2013, the severed heads appear to be in plastic bags tied to the bodies. The sun is blazing. It looks like a busy intersection, with both vehicular and pedestrian traffic. Boys gather to gawk. Their elders either avert their eyes or snap their cell phone cameras to record the scene. According to Reuters, Al Jazeera, BBC and Amnesty International, the dead are five Yemeni gang members "beheaded by the sword" for killing a Saudi Arabian national and committing several robberies. The "crucifixion" (as it was called) was evidently imposed as additional punishment, post-execution and pre-burial.

Why did authorities arrange the macabre display? A court in Jizan must have deemed it *shari'a*-based justice. But maybe there was a purpose beyond giving these murdering thieves their proper deserts. Maybe stringing their bodies 25 feet off the ground was meant to send a message to others as well. Was it supposed to deter potential criminals who happened to be passing by? The Kingdom is in the process of expelling tens of thousands of Yemeni migrant workers—were authorities signaling to other Yemenis to go back south over the border where they belong?

Or—wait—are the intended audience the eyewitnesses visible in the surreptitious photographs? If so, what would be the message to apparently normal, law-abiding citizens crossing the street or driving down the road? What can they be thinking their government is telling them about the power of the state and the force of law?

Stuck (or Not) in a "Special Relationship"

Toby Jones • *MERO*, Mar. 27, 2014

What to make of the anxieties surfacing in the press in advance of President Barack Obama's stopover in Saudi Arabia? Is the US-Saudi "special relationship" really in trouble?

Officials say no, of course. But beneath the surface, the relationship is indeed marked by uncertainty. The rulers in Riyadh have come to question Washington's commitment to the Kingdom's security, to Saudi primacy in the Gulf and to what has been one of the region's most durable (and profitable) alliances.

Saudi trepidation is not entirely unfounded. Over the last three years, the two states have at least appeared to be at odds, with regard to the Arab uprisings and the resulting popular empowerment, intervention in Syria and the proper level of aggressiveness for cracking down on Islamists, especially the Society of Muslim Brothers. Given the Saudis' thin base of support at home and their need to oppress their way to survival, it is hardly surprising that Riyadh that has led the counterrevolutionary charge in the Arab world since 2011.

Most importantly, the Saudis fear that the United States, in negotiating with Iran over the future of its nuclear research program, is cozying up to their most powerful regional rival. For years, Saudi Arabia has made

Iran the target of the worst kind of sectarian opprobrium, treating the Islamic Republic as a bogeyman to be exploited in the interest of keeping American leaders sympathetic. It has not hurt the Saudi case that its most devoted supporters in the US are also closest to Israel, which shares a venomous view of Tehran. While it is unclear whether US-Iranian negotiations will yield anything meaningful, that the two are talking at all has shaken the Kingdom.

Quietly, US officials have begun to wonder about the same things. Is the US-Saudi relationship one that should remain unchanged? These Americans understand that the Saudis have set a dangerous regional course, one that has bought only temporary favor for a military regime in Cairo, won precarious "victories" in Bahrain and Yemen, and left a trail of human rights abuses and political malfeasance. There is a belief in Washington that Saudi Arabia remains at least somewhat cooperative in matters of counter-terrorism. But Saudi Arabia's aggressive expansion of the politics of *irhab*, or terrorism, and its sudden acceleration of attacks on the Muslim Brothers is understood as double-edged—likely to deliver positive results in the short term but with catastrophic potential over time. After all, Saudi Arabia has been here before.

While American leaders ponder the reimagination of the "special relationship" in the distant future, the White House's default position is to double down on the status quo, reassuring Riyadh that nothing has changed and supporting the regime by standard means—looking the other way while the regime terrorizes Saudi Arabian citizens, backs reactionary forces in Egypt and Bahrain, and abets violence in Syria. And, of course, avaricious arms merchants, with support from the Pentagon, continue to sell Riyadh billions of dollars in weapons.

Outside the circles of hawks and realists who are untroubled by Saudi Arabia's bad behavior, more reasonable officials run up against a political inertia that claims the Kingdom is the least bad Gulf partner in challenging times, and that even while Iran sits at the negotiating table, the Islamic Republic is doing more harm than good.

Meanwhile, US and Saudi leaders have long shared antagonism toward, or at least skepticism about, the democratic potential of Saudi Arabia itself. James Schlesinger, a secretary of defense under Presidents Richard Nixon and Gerald Ford who passed away today, put it this way: "Do we seriously want to change the institutions of Saudi Arabia? The brief answer is no; over the years we have sought to preserve these institutions, sometimes in preference to more democratic forces coursing throughout the region. [The former] King Fahd [of Saudi Arabia] has stated quite unequivocally that democratic institutions are not appropriate for this society. What is interesting is that we do not seem to disagree." While US officials are likely more open to the possibility today, there is so far little political will to encourage change in any meaningful way, and certainly not in public. The desire for autocratic stability in Arabia, embraced by old hands like Dennis Ross, has been replaced by the inertia mentioned above. Today, however, the stakes are higher, as a simultaneously emboldened and embattled Riyadh seeks to mold reactionary outcomes across the region, helping to push countries like Syria and Bahrain in terrible directions. While many observers would argue that supporting tyranny was never politically prudent for citizens in Arabia or for America, it is even more clearly the case today that the Saudis are the worst of the worst.

Among the cool heads in Washington, the prevailing view is that the United States is stuck, bound by President Obama's minimalist approach to the region and the practical limits of American power. This is all true, of course. But these facts do not and should not mean that the United States has to remain dedicated to its historical alliance with Riyadh, particularly as the Saudis and their proxies continue to poison regional politics.

Romancing the Throne

Sheila Carapico • *MERO*, Mar. 27, 2014

President Barack Obama plans an overnight stay in the Kingdom of Saudi Arabia on March 28–29 for a rendezvous with King Abdallah. The enduring but always strange bedfellows have been quarreling of late over Saudi Arabia's belligerent relations with neighbors Iran and Syria. Both sides hope during this visit to kiss and make up.

It's a titillating occasion for the Saudi lobby, including the Saudi-US Information Service that churns out good news from the happy kingdom. The Service's website filled a "special section" with feel-good links for the occasion. Johann Schmonsees, spokesman for the US Embassy in Riyadh, likewise trilled that the presidential visit "will be an opportunity to reinforce one of our closest relationships in the region and build on the strong US-Saudi military, security and economic ties that have been a hallmark of our bilateral relationship." And erstwhile Israel-Palestine negotiator and diplomat extraordinaire Dennis Ross weighed in with an op-ed entitled "Soothing the Saudis," advising the president to appreciate the fragile feelings and physical vulnerabilities of the royal family.

Following in the steps of predecessors from Franklin Delano Roosevelt to Jimmy Carter to George W. Bush, President Obama will ceremoniously re-consummate Uncle Sam's semi-clandestine bilateral romance with one of the most intolerant, sadistic partners on the planet. As Anthony Cordesman of the Center for Strategic and International Studies recently observed in his essay "The Need for a New 'Realism' in the US-Saudi Alliance," it is a liaison based on some common angst but few shared values. It's an illicit affair conducted mostly behind closed doors.

As Schmonsees, Cordesman, Ross and others see it, American and Saudi concerns converge in worries about the terrorist threat to their conjoint military entanglements. The long backstory to this cooperation ranges from Saudi support for the anti-Soviet mujahidin in Afghanistan (Ronald Reagan's "freedom fighters") that spawned al-Qaeda to the prominent roles of Saudi Arabian citizens, including Osama bin Laden, in the September 11, 2001, attacks to ongoing real-time joint operations in Yemen.

Whether for internal political reasons or in anticipation of the Obama visit, in the past couple of months Saudi Arabia has expanded its definition of *irhab* beyond the post–September 11 hysteria in the American press encouraged by the Bush administration, beyond the Egyptian criminalization of the Society of Muslim Brothers under Nasser, Sadat, Mubarak and al-Sisi, and beyond even Riyadh's own past crackdowns on dissident liberals and Islamists.

How has the Kingdom tightened the vise? *Umm al-Qura*, the official Saudi gazette, published a new Penal Law for Crimes of Terrorism and Its Financing on January 31, 2014, effective as of the following day. *Irhab* is now a sweeping term that covers not only violent attacks but also "any act" that would "insult" the reputation of the state, "harm public order," espouse "atheism," shake the "stability of society" or advocate any form of dissent, according to Human Rights Watch.

Going further, on March 7, the Interior Ministry issued a list of "terrorist organizations." The criminalization of association with the Muslim Brothers rightly attracted the most attention because the Brothers are a legitimate (though illegal) political party in Egypt, and operate under other different names in other Arab countries, and because the Saudi ban on the Brothers features in the Kingdom's spat with the spunky micro-petrokingdom of Qatar and its media arm Al Jazeera, both accused of favoring the Egyptian branch of the Brothers.

But the Interior Ministry named not only the Society of Muslim Brothers, which is not as such an armed group, but also other guerrilla groups, some of them already on the US terrorist list, and two heretofore undesignated Yemeni entities. Several militant groups outlawed (in some cases not for the first time) were predictable enough, namely al-Qaeda and its eponymous offshoots in the Arabian Peninsula and Iraq. Two radical paramilitaries fighting in Syria, Da'ish (also known in English as the Islamic State of Iraq and Sham, or ISIS) and Jabhat al-Nusra, which not long ago looked like Saudi proxies, were also designated. All of these are Islamist militias of a Sunni *salafi* persuasion. Ideologically, they are distinguishable from the ruling Wahhabi doctrine in Saudi Arabia mainly by their opposition to dynastic rule. A little-known entity presumably named after the Lebanese Shi'i militia called Hizballah in the Hijaz was also declared to be a terrorist organization.

Finally, the new Saudi list named two Yemeni groups that have been engaged in mortal combat with one another for several years. *Shabab al-mu'minin* (Believing Youth) is a Zaydi Shi'i revivalist movement with a militant wing known as the Houthis who have held their own against Saudi forces, Wahhabi *salafi* evangelists and the Yemeni army along the Saudi-Yemeni frontier for the past decade. The Believing Youth's nemesis, the Reform Congregation (known as Islah), is a right-wing political alliance of Sunni *salafis*, Muslim Brothers, tribal leaders (especially from the preeminent family of the Hashid confederation, Bayt al-Ahmar) and a segment of the Yemeni business community that for two decades received financial and moral support from Riyadh. Many Yemenis were surprised to see Islah, a legal political party represented in the Yemeni parliament, on the list. [Note: Islah was later dropped from the list.]

The broad set of criminalized activities under the Saudi Interior Ministry's new rules include but are not limited to membership in, meetings or correspondence with, sympathy for, or the circulation of the slogans or symbols of any of these groups.

Obama's conversations with King Abdallah and ruling family scions will not address human rights, women's rights, democratization or social justice. The American embrace of Saudi Arabia is carnal and/or crassly materialist, not principled. Don't expect a replay of Obama's supposedly inspirational 2009 speech to Muslims and Arabs in Cairo, or an adversarial press conference. The White House would rather not draw attention to its dalliance with the misogynist Saudi gerontocracy. Press coverage of the visit is likely to be scant.

The two leaders are likely to discuss arms sales, the linchpin of the bilateral relationship. Ambassador-designate Joseph Westphal reiterated this realist perspective in his Senate hearing statement on March 24 about a mutually fulfilling relationship servicing both Saudi survival instincts and the American military-industrial complex. "We also have a critical security partnership," he said. "Saudi Arabia is our largest Foreign Military Sales customer, with 338 active and open cases valued at $96.8 billion, all supporting American skilled manufacturing jobs, while increasing inter-operability between our forces for training and any potential operations."

In addition, Obama and Abdallah will almost certainly affirm American and/or joint operations against al-Qaeda in the Arabian Peninsula, operations which continued in a series of deadly drone strikes against targets in Yemen in early March. The king may be upset that the United States has not taken military action in Syria or Iran, but he will almost certainly take comfort from American promises to defend the House of Saud against the most proximate threat to its security and well-being.

What About 'Abd al-Rahman al-Awlaqi?

Lisa Hajjar • *MERO*, Jun. 29, 2014

The US government wanted to kill Anwar al-Awlaqi long before a CIA-led drone strike actually succeeded in doing so on September 30, 2011. Before and after that deadly strike, al-Awlaqi's kill-ability was and remains a bone of contention because he was a US citizen. The cleric, who had become radicalized as the "war on terror" wore on, moved to Yemen, his ancestral homeland, in late 2004. There, he became a prolific jihadi propagandist on the Internet.

On January 27, 2010, the *Washington Post* reported that he and at least two other citizens had been designated for extrajudicial execution. The listing of al-Awlaqi came on the heels of two incidents to which he was reportedly linked: the November 5, 2009, armed rampage by Maj. Nidal Malik Hasan at Fort Hood in Texas that killed 13 and wounded 29 people, and the December 25 attempt by a Nigerian, Umar Farouk Abdulmutallab, to detonate a bomb hidden in his underwear on a trans-atlantic flight bound for Detroit. Al-Awlaqi's alleged involvement in these crimes raises the question of why the government never indicted the cleric if it actually had information implicating him.

After the publication of the *Post* article reporting that al-Awlaqi had been put on the targeted killing list, the American Civil Liberties Union and the Center for Constitutional Rights filed a lawsuit in August 2010 on behalf of al-Awlaqi's father, Nasir, to challenge executive authorization for extrajudicial execution of a citizen (*Al-Aulaqi v. Obama*). The case was dismissed that December when the court ruled that Nasir al-Awlaqi lacked standing, since the government had no intention of killing him, just his son.

Meanwhile, on July 16, 2010, the Justice Department's Office of Legal Counsel (OLC), which functions as the "government's lawyer," produced a memorandum laying out the legal rationales for the killing of al-Awlaqi. That memo remained a closely guarded secret until last week, when the government finally released it in heavily redacted form. Among the redacted portions is the first 11 pages laying out the factual basis for determining that al-Awlaqi had gone from inspirational to operational and become an "enemy combatant" and leader of AQAP, which is at war with the United States.

Leaving aside the quality of the OLC memo's legal arguments, the underlying premise that killing al-Awlaqi in a military operation was a legal option depended on information provided by unnamed "high government officials" who "have concluded, on the basis of al-Aulaqi's activities in Yemen, that al-Aulaqi is a leader of AQAP whose activities in Yemen pose a 'continued and imminent threat' of violence to United States persons and interests."

The phrase "have concluded" sounds so authoritative. The secrecy that guards such intelligence makes its veracity literally unarguable. But what about the "intelligence" and the "legal logic" for the October 14, 2011, drone strike that killed al-Awlaqi's 16-year-old son 'Abd al-Rahman, as well as his 17-year-old cousin and five others while they were dining in an open-air restaurant? In the immediate aftermath of that attack, officials claimed that 'Abd al-Rahman was a 21-year-old militant. After his grandfather produced the boy's birth certificate proving the lie, the administration reverted to its default position of asserting that CIA operations are classified and cannot be commented upon. Indeed, the Obama administration has never produced an official justification or explanation about the killing of 'Abd al-Rahman (who, by the way, was also a US citizen).

The OLC memo offers nothing in the way of understanding intelligence mistakes, which are numerous, as reflected in the large number of

civilians who have been killed in drone strikes. 'Abd al-Rahman's killing is a particularly salient example of why it behooves us to be skepti-
cal about the assurances of "high officials" who "have concluded" that
death-causing intelligence is valid.

So far, federal courts are no help. On April 4 of this year, Nasir
al-Awlaqi lost a second lawsuit, *Al-Aulaqi v. Panetta*, challenging the
government's constitutional right to kill US citizens without trial (and,
in the case of his grandson, for no stated reason). As one of his lawyers,
Maria LaHood, said after hearing of the judge's dismissal of the case: "It
seems there's no remedy if the government intended to kill you, and no
remedy if it didn't."

Obama's Firing Range in Arabia

Chris Toensing • Originally published as
"From the Editor," in *MER* 273, Winter 2014

Midway through Barack Obama's second term as president, there are two
Establishment-approved metanarratives about his foreign policy. One,
emanating mainly from the right, but resonating with several liberal in-
ternationalists, holds that Obama is unequal to the task of running an empire. The president, pundits repeat, is a "reluctant warrior" who declines to
intervene abroad with the alacrity becoming his station. The other, quieter
line of argument posits that Obama is the consummate realist, a man who
avoids foreign entanglements unless or until they impinge directly upon
vital US interests.

As usual, the mainstream assessments are more interesting for their
unspoken assumptions than their truth value. In both takes, the president
of the United States is appointed ipso facto as a world policeman whose job
performance is rated almost solely on the basis of how often he orders the
Pentagon into action. But the dominant evaluations of Obama are incorrect as well. And, at least in the Middle East, there is no better illustration
than Yemen, the terribly impoverished and perennially misunderstood
country in the southwestern corner of the Arabian Peninsula.

Has Obama hesitated to use force? Not if the explosions in Yemen are
any indication.

Until the fall of 2014, Yemen was the primary Arab battleground of the
Obama administration's war on terror—but a firing range rather than a
front. According to the London-based Bureau of Investigative Journalism,

United States and Saudi Arabia at poker game seem to have discarded Hadi. (March 3, 2015)
By Samer Mohammed al-Shameeri

there have been no fewer than 71 US drone strikes in Yemen since 2002, with hundreds of fatalities, including a minimum of 64 civilians. The New America Foundation estimates that US drones and warships have fired 116 missiles at Yemeni territory in the same time period, killing no fewer than 811 people, at least 81 of them non-combatants.

The actual numbers of attacks and casualties are almost certainly higher: Both of these studies rely on methodologies of cross-referencing press reports, and many of the drone strikes occur in remote locales where journalists are few and far between. And the start date of 2002 is misleading. Except for the assassination of alleged al-Qaeda figure Abu 'Ali al-Harithi in December of that year, all of the strikes have been launched under President Obama.

The White House, indeed, views Yemen as a showcase of its approach toward al-Qaeda and sundry radical armed Islamist groups. "This strategy of taking out terrorists who threaten us, while supporting partners on the front lines, is one that we have successfully pursued in Yemen and Somalia for years," Obama said in his September 10 speech extending the war on terror once more to Iraq and Syria. There were querulous rumbles on left and right at the notion that the statistics above constitute "success," but from the Obama administration's perspective, the claim is self-evident. The war in Afghanistan occasionally makes headlines, when American soldiers are killed or when the failure of US efforts to build a stable Afghan client state is further exposed. The war in Yemen is prosecuted entirely from the sky, with the odd, top-secret drop-in visit from Special Forces, so the dead bodies are all faceless and foreign and the story stays buried in the back pages.

Perception management aside, Obama's boosters might argue that airstrikes on al-Qaeda in the Arabian Peninsula (AQAP) are precisely the judicious, low-cost (to Americans) uses of force that a narrow interpretation of the national interest recommends. But this militia poses no serious danger to the continental United States. It has disavowed the so-called Islamic State, or Da'ish, that declared a caliphate in Iraq and Syria, and it has tenuous connections at best with al-Qaeda franchises elsewhere.

The immediate interest that is served with the Obama administration's aerial campaign in Yemen is that of the "partners on the front lines," the would-be central government in Sana'a and its main regional sponsor, Saudi Arabia. These are the parties threatened by AQAP's implied aspiration to ignite jihadi revolt "in the Arabian Peninsula." In one sense, therefore, the war against AQAP is a local fight in global camouflage—like so much of the war on terror elsewhere. In a broader sense, however, the airstrikes are part and parcel of the same expansive construction of the national interest that has guided administrations of all ideological persuasions since the 1940s. The United States defers to the Saudi monarchy and its Yemeni allies in the name of "stability" in the landmass atop the world's largest known reserves of oil and natural gas. In return, the United States gets a proving ground for its formidable firepower and an open-ended justification for its military hegemony in the Persian Gulf and beyond.

Whether this arrangement delivers "stability" to the region is another question entirely. The escalation of the drone war in Yemen has coincided with deepening political and economic turmoil. The regime in Sana'a was already facing pesky rebellion in the northern highlands and increasingly militant mass demonstrations in the southern provinces that made up an independent country from 1967 to 1990. Then came the 2011 popular uprising against the three-decade rule of President 'Ali 'Abdallah Salih, culminating in his nominal removal as part of a "transition" brokered by Riyadh and blessed by Washington. The terms of the "transition"—immunity from prosecution for Salih, transfer of the presidency to his long-time deputy, division of ministries among Sana'a insiders—fell considerably beneath the expectations of the restive population. At press time, with the northern Houthi rebels controlling the capital and southerners demanding independence anew, the future of centralized control of Yemen is in doubt.

Underlying the unrest is the severe maldistribution of wealth. In 2012, according to UN data, Yemeni per capita income was under $1,330, less than $2 per day. For decades, Yemenis have sought more remunerative work abroad, particularly in the oil-rich monarchies of the Arabian Peninsula. But as the citizenry of those countries grows larger, relative poverty rises there, too, leading the regimes to tighten the screws on foreign labor. Over the course of 2013, Saudi Arabia expelled more than 550,000 Yemeni workers, along with tens of thousands of Somalis and other Africans. Yemen is a major transit point for Africans seeking employment in points north. The mix of desperate migrants, frustrated returnees, opportunistic traffickers and nervous, despotic governments is a human rights nightmare.

This gloomy picture suggests the real problem with Obama administration policy in Yemen, if not the Middle East and the rest of the world. Technocratic, tempted by top-down visions, tepid at best toward bottom-up change, the administration is content with the illusory "stability" created by constant crisis management. Absent structural improvements to the lot of the majority, the search for real stability is akin to a hunt for a unicorn.

8 Yemen's Implosions, 2014

Activists and intellectuals had greeted the National Dialogue Conference with a combination of optimism and skepticism. By 2014, however, the Dialogue, and behind it the GCC initiative, were foundering. Talks persisted inside the Mövenpick Hotel in the upscale Haddah suburb of Sana'a. However, elsewhere political, social, economic and environmental pressures were for the most part insufferable.

This chapter's opening selection, Katherine Hennessey's firsthand review of performances for a theatrical festival in Sana'a in May, is striking for two reasons. First, readers unfamiliar with cultural invention in the poverty-stricken, purportedly backward periphery of the Peninsula might be surprised that such a festival takes place at all. Secondly, in light of subsequent events the plays Hennessey reviews seem almost eerily prophetic of the dangers that lay ahead.

The other entries convey how complicated matters have become by this time. Susanne Dahlgren and Anne-Linda Amira Augustin, respectively, reflect the mood in Aden and the southern governorates where irredentist sentiments ran high in 2013–14. Tobias Thiel offers a map of the proposed "federal" boundaries and the reasons they were rejected by the Houthis (among others).

That autumn, as the GCC initiative and the National Dialogue Conference unraveled, Stacey Philbrick Yadav and I struggled to make sense of events: Houthi rebels marched beyond their home turf in Sa'dah, met resistance only in 'Amran, rather easily occupied Sana'a, and ventured into the Southern Uplands and the Tihama. Among the improbable twists was that after 10 years of warfare the Houthis joined forces with their old nemesis (the ostensibly deposed but still criminally proactive) 'Ali 'Abdallah Salih. The interim president Hadi (formerly Salih's handpicked vice president) fled Sana'a for Aden. The Houthi-Salih coalition followed him there, although it was abundantly clear that their fighters would face stiff, widespread popular resistance. Hadi left Yemen and sought refuge in Riyadh, Saudi Arabia (setting the stage for events in the final chapter of this book, the Saudi-led, US-backed military intervention).

Explosions and Ill Omens:
On the Stage at World Theater Day in Yemen

Katherine Hennessey • *MER* 273, Winter 2014

On October 9, 2014, a suicide bomber detonated himself in central Sanaʻa, killing dozens of innocent people. Upon reading the news coverage of this terrible event my thoughts leapt back to a series of plays that I had seen performed in Sanaʻa in the spring. Most of these performances took place under the aegis of the annual celebration of World Theater Day, known locally as the Festival of Yemeni Theater. Five months prior to the explosion in Sanaʻa, a surprising number of the festival's plays had made references to suicide bombing.

The festival's opening production, *Marzouq in the Role of the Terrorist*, directed by ʻUmar ʻAbdallah Salih and performed on March 30, is a play within a play. It features an inept actor named Marzouq who is assigned a role as a suicide bomber but struggles to comprehend the motivations of his character. At one point during the performance, Marzouq entered "in character," so far as he understands it: He is masked and carrying a rifle, which he points in the air, baffling his director. Marzouq explains that he is playing the kind of terrorist who attacks the power station and shoots at the power lines. The director responds furiously that Marzouq must follow the script: "The character wears a suicide belt. That's so you can blow yourself up, and everyone around you!"

The subsequent night's performance, *Wa al-Hall?* (What's the Solution?), written and directed by Salih al-Salih, portrayed a neighborhood of ordinary Yemenis—a bookseller, an egg and potato vendor, an owner of a tea and sandwich shop—all trying to eke out a living in an atmosphere of deteriorating economic conditions and fragmenting social relations. Consumed by their own quotidian problems, they fail to recognize the danger in their midst, in the person of a long-bearded youth who accuses them, one by one, of having strayed from the true path of the faith. Though his verbal attacks escalate and his behavior becomes increasingly erratic, the others dismiss him as histrionic but harmless. In the last few moments of the play, to the horror of the other characters, he reappears wearing a suicide vest, at which the stage lights go dark.

Al-Tawhan, directed by Muhammad al-Rakhm, followed a remarkably similar plot, with a group of Yemeni characters going about their daily affairs, oblivious to the dangers of extremism until it is too late. A sinister, shadowy figure who lurks at the margins of the neighborhood eventually turns out to be a suicide bomber who has been biding his time so as to inflict the maximum possible damage with his lethal act.

Still another performance, *Irhab ya Nas!* (It's Terrorism, People!), depicted a suicide bombing as one incident in a destructive chain of extremist violence that wreaks havoc on social relations. Here the central group of characters—once again, a set of "average" Yemenis, though this time predominantly young people—are gradually dehumanized by the fear and loss that mount inexorably with every explosion, every slaughter. In a stark departure from the social realism of the two aforementioned plays, this performance experimented with tableau scenes and stylized, symbolic action. At one point, the characters descended into animalistic fury, shrieking wordlessly at each other like monkeys, then snarling and snapping like a pack of stray dogs.

In May, as I watched the festival unfold on the stage of the Cultural Center night after night, the repeated focus on the issue of suicide bombing struck me as odd. Yemeni theater has not shied away from grappling with the issue of terrorism in the past. There are numerous Yemeni plays that show, for example, the aftermath of an explosion, or an act of mass violence, just as there is a subset of Yemeni plays that portray war and revolution. But contemporary theater in Yemen treats a remarkably diverse range of social issues. That four plays in a series of 13 at the Cultural Center would select the selfsame issue as a central theme was surprising, especially given the sadly broad range of threats and challenges facing Yemeni society.

More startling, though, was the repeated implication that suicide bombing was a serious threat facing the average Yemeni in Sanaʻa. Certainly, the capital had seen its share of violence during the 2011 uprising, and had grown increasingly unstable in the subsequent years. Politicians and military figures ran the risk of assassination; the frequency of extrajudicial executions carried out by teams of two men on motorbikes, a driver and a gunman, even led to a ban on civilian motorbike traffic in the capital in September 2013. Indeed, as the festival ran its course this type of violence continued, most dramatically on May 5, when a French security guard was shot and killed in his car in broad daylight at a busy intersection in the heart of the capital. Yet this murderous violence, by and large, targeted particular individuals, and in that respect differed from a bomber detonating his belt in a crowded public square.

Residents of Sanaʻa would of course have known about the gruesome violence of suicide bombing in other Yemeni cities, like the attack on

South Korean tourists in Shibam in 2009. But this type of violence had rarely occurred in Sanaʿa: One of the attackers killed in the 2008 attack on the US Embassy apparently wore an explosive vest; another in 2009 targeted the South Korean convoy that had come to repatriate the victims of the Shibam attacks, but that time the bomber killed only himself. In May 2012 the deadliest suicide attack in Yemen to date killed nearly 100 Yemeni soldiers as they rehearsed a parade for the annual celebration of Yemeni unification. Yet as frightening as that event was, many Yemenis continued to think of suicide bombing as being directed at particular targets—foreigners, the US Embassy, the military—rather than Yemeni society or the Yemeni everyman.

Clearly, Yemeni theater practitioners viewed the issue in a different light. Despite the fact that various other types of terrorist violence were making headlines and could conceivably have served as material for a play, all four of the plays described above focused on the issue of suicide bombing, as a clear and present danger to all citizens, about which residents of Sanaʿa needed to be warned.

Monsters, Murders and Mayhem

Yemeni actors and directors often describe themselves as educators. In Yemen, theater imparts essential information to a populace that still struggles with basic literacy; it strives to fill in some of the massive gaps left by a failed educational system. Theater is also both a means of and a forum for free and creative expression and for public debate about the myriad challenges facing the nation. To attend a theatrical performance in Yemen is, almost invariably, to witness a particular issue or perspective held up to public scrutiny on stage, embodied with careful consideration and in rich detail, with the aim of provoking social change—political reform, for example, or greater rights for women, or improvements to health care and education.

To attend the annual Festival of Yemeni Theater, then, with 10 or 12 plays staged in the course of a fortnight, is akin to peering at a cross-section of the social problems that Yemenis judge so pressing as to warrant the time and intellectual energy required to write, rehearse and stage a play. Suicide bombing was strikingly prominent as a theme, but the 2014 theater festival also provided audiences with a further assortment of thought-provoking topics running the gamut from human trafficking to preventive medicine.

Yet where in previous years the festival brought an exhilarating range of comedy, tragedy, farce, satire and melodrama to the stage, the 2014 festival instead struck a series of darkly pessimistic notes. Rather than enthusiastic calls to action, the 2014 performances repeatedly staged corruption and stagnation, violence and destruction. And where in the past the Yemeni stage tended toward utopian, wish-fulfilling conclusions in which the honest but downtrodden hero or heroine eventually triumphs and the evildoer is unmasked and punished, the 2014 plays predominantly portrayed villains who escape justice and suffering protagonists powerless to change their fate.

One of the festival's first performances, *Al-Tifl* (The Child) directed by Ha'il al-Salwi, reads very clearly as a parable about the imminent dangers that violence poses to the innocent. The performance culminates in a chilling scene in which a frantic father grabs a rifle and shoots at the ruffian who has been ordered to spirit away his only son—but the bullet strikes and kills the infant instead of the thug. I had attended several rehearsals of the play in the weeks before the festival, but found myself unprepared for the disconcerting experience of watching the portrayal of the shooting death of an infant in a theater filled with Yemeni families and small children (parents may well have assumed from the title that the play was meant for children).

Al-Tifl was not the only festival play that startled its audience with its subject matter. *Barakash wa al-Kash* (Barakash and the Cash), written and directed by Luna Yafa'i, took up the issue of human trafficking in Sa'dah, a northwestern province on the Saudi Arabian border, as perpetrated by the greedy and utterly unscrupulous Barakash, who at one point in the play promises a prospective client "whatever you want, a Somali, an Ethiopian, a Djibouti." Barakash targets the isolated and marginalized, kidnapping a young Yemeni woman, orphaned and with no adult male relatives, as she travels without a chaperone to take up a job to support her brood of small siblings. Barakash and his assistant repeatedly comment on the young woman's beauty, implying that the captive is not merely a commodity for sale but also a potential sex slave.

Even more controversial was Yafa'i's decision to portray Barakash and his cronies as members of the Yemeni armed forces stationed in Sa'dah. The portrayal of the army is somewhat redeemed by the play's ending, in which an officer shocked by Barakash's excesses blows the whistle, and a crack commando unit—whose captain is female—storms in and arrests Barakash's henchmen. But the title character himself gleefully escapes, dressed Saudi-style in a *thawb*, a red-and-white *kaffiyya* and sunglasses, and carrying a briefcase stuffed with the profits of his trade. This conclusion seemed to sit poorly with certain members of the audience, particularly the armed, camouflage-uniformed guards who entered the theater during the final act to break up a scuffle between two rowdy groups of teenagers in the audience, and who remained stationed in the aisles, stone-faced, until the play's conclusion. Yafaʿi has since complained that the administration of the Cultural Center refuses to provide her with a copy of its video footage of the production, which they allege insults the armed forces.

Yafaʿi was one of three female directors slated to produce their work at the 2014 festival. Unfortunately, one of the other female directors, Nargis ʿAbbad, withdrew *Dabʿ al-Maydan* (The Hyena in the Square), her creative adaptation of Bertolt Brecht's *Mother Courage and Her Children*, after eleventh-hour cuts to the budgets that the Ministry of Culture had offered the directors threw the festival into turmoil. It was a real loss for the audience: ʿAbbad had a grand, ambitious vision for her production, which meditated on the history of South Yemen and its fragile union with the north.

The festival's other female director, Insaf ʿAlawi, struggled with her production, *Al-ʿUshaq Yamutun Kull Yawm* (The Passionate Die Every Day). ʿAlawi intended the performance of this classic Yemeni play as a tribute to its author, the well-loved and recently deceased poet and playwright Muhammad al-Sharafi, and it began well: The opening scene shows the audience the head of a morgue, who must decide whether the bodies of those killed in a recent conflict deserve the honor of interment in the Martyrs' Cemetery, after their souls appear before him to plead their cases. Yemeni actor Muhammad al-Daybani gave a particularly powerful performance as a paraplegic in a wheelchair who recounts a tale of unjust suffering, including having his hand cut off as punishment for a theft that he did not commit. He cackles eerily at the end of his monologue that he should not be interred in any cemetery, since he is "the living dead."

After this promising start, however, the production careened downhill. ʿAlawi inexplicably elected to replace the remainder of al-Sharafi's script with an acrobatic performance followed by a video montage that included a filmed scene of various characters rising from their graves to perform a musical number and a series of images of world landmarks, and finally, a patriotic salute to a photo of al-Sharafi projected onto the back wall of the stage. All were perplexing choices, and most were executed in such deplorably amateurish fashion that one of the actors took to the stage afterwards to apologize for the faults in the production. The general consensus from stunned audience members was that the performance was a travesty of al-Sharafi's script.

From teetering on the edge of disaster, the festival came storming back the following night with *Man Anta?* (Who Are You?), written and directed by 'Abdallah Yahya Ibrahim. Its opening featured a laser light show set to thunderous techno music, and an actor in a monster mask skillfully breakdancing through a mist of dry ice, against a backdrop of black cloth, with irregular holes backlit in green, blue and purple, all of which was carried out with an unexpected degree of technical precision. It riveted the children and enthralled the teenagers in the audience—a crucial achievement, since the play revolves around a mystery and must hold viewers' attention, no easy feat in the chaotic atmosphere of a Yemeni playhouse.

The plot features a monster that terrorizes a Yemeni neighborhood, kidnapping victims and dragging them off to his lair. An old man who escapes recounts that the monster's hideout is filled with piteous crowds of captives—men and women, children and the elderly, Yemenis of every social status and description. The frightening scenes are interspersed with slapstick hilarity: Two chain-smoking, card-playing neighborhood youths keep up a rapid-fire series of jokes at the other characters' expense, and the monster deftly inserts himself into two very funny dance numbers. The characters repeatedly but fruitlessly speculate about the monster's identity, and eventually a courageous father vows to kill the monster and free his son from the dungeon.

After a thrilling fight scene the father stabs the monster with his *jambiya*, the curved dagger worn by many Yemeni men. The monster slumps to the ground—only to rise again, horror-movie fashion, startling the other characters (and some members of the audience). At this point a fearful character calls out, "Who are you?" The monster picks up a placard from a table on the set and brandishes it at the audience. On it is written a single word: *al-saratan*, Arabic for cancer.

The point of this production, as it turned out, was to educate Yemeni audiences about the disease and about the benefits of screening and early detection. At the conclusion of the play the actors addressed the audience from the stage, explaining that like the monster, cancer is a disease that can afflict Yemenis of all ages and classes. Volunteers passed out pamphlets including lists of risk factors and symptoms, as well as contact information for local clinics equipped to screen patients for various forms of cancer. In addition to its utility as a public service announcement, *Man Anta?* was technically sophisticated, visually appealing and cleverly written; it was an excellent piece of theater, the best in the 2014 festival. Moreover, despite the sobering material it was one of the few festival plays to pinpoint both a problem and a potential solution—a "call to action" in the typical tradition of Yemeni theater.

In contrast, *Al-Hafila* (The Bus), which depicts the struggles, fears and petty quarrels of a group of passengers who are stranded in a wasteland when their bus breaks down, seemed like its characters lack direction and purpose. Written and directed by Yahya Suhayl, it provided some colorful moments—the opening scene, for example, featured a wedding procession with both male and female characters in full regalia, accompanied by a group of musicians playing at earsplitting volume, no doubt titillating spectators accustomed to gender-segregated celebrations—but offered little of deeper significance.

Hikayat Amal (Amal's Tale), written by 'Adil al-'Amri and directed by Nabhan al-Shami, achieved a more sophisticated level of character development than Suhayl's play, then squandered it on a pat ending. The play dramatizes a piece of Yemeni folklore about the *wahsh al-jabal*, the mountain monster, whose lascivious attempts to prey on a young woman are thwarted when her friends and her teacher (all female) and their bus driver (male) band together to save her. They encircle the monster, accusing him of embodying all the social ills that they have endured in their lives ("You are corruption! Fear! Unemployment! Backwardness!"), then beat and execute him. A salutary message of strength in unity, certainly—if only "kill the monster" were a viable step toward a more stable and prosperous Yemen.

Mukafahat Nihayat Khidma (End-of-Service Payment), a one-woman show written by Munir Talal and capably acted by Amani al-Dhamari, searchingly explored the struggles of single women in Yemeni society—the pressure to accede to early or arranged marriages, the difficulties of pursuing higher education, the oft-frustrated desire to participate in society beyond the protective walls of the domestic sphere. The protagonist harbors hidden artistic talent, which she expresses by sculpting with her fingers a series of images in a thin layer of sand, constantly rearranging the grains on her makeshift canvas to create new forms out of the previous ones—each as beautiful, fragile and ephemeral as her hopes for happiness.

The festival's final play, *Al-Masir al-Ghamid* (Destination Unknown), written and directed by Adam Sayf, was widely expected to be a rollicking musical comedy, the genre for which Sayf is best known. Yet rather than for the dances and the elaborate jokes, audiences will remember this performance for the moment that Sayf, in the midst of dialogue with another actor, turned to the minister of culture in his front-row VIP seat, and proceeded to mock the Ministry for the funding debacle that had thrown the festival into chaos.

The jokes were arch rather than devastating, and delivered with the sort of teasing tone one might take when ribbing a long-time friend. Nevertheless, it was clearly a moment in which a Yemeni artist had chosen to take his government to task—and the audience joined in, gleefully applauding Sayf's every line. The lighting technicians even brought up the house lights, allowing the crowd to see plainly that the minister had been caught completely off guard at becoming a part of the play. While amusing, this interlude was also rather disquieting for those concerned about Yemeni government officials' ability to respond adroitly to the unexpected.

Thus, even in its most bracing and memorable moments, the festival presented a grave, sobering assessment of the state of Yemeni society, and precious little hope for its future. Some of this pessimism no doubt stemmed from the shambolic administration of the festival. Disenchantment with the transitional government and the National Dialogue may have also contributed to the atmosphere of sardonic depression. Yet in hindsight, and in the wake of the Houthi takeover of Sana'a in September and the suicide bombing in the capital in October, the performances also seem strangely prescient, as though, rather than portrayals of the current state of Yemeni society, they were in fact portents of its impending disintegration.

Southern Yemeni Activists Prepare for Nationwide Rally

Susanne Dahlgren • *MERO*, Apr. 24, 2014

For the first time, a Million-Person Rally or *milyuniyya* will be held in Yemen's oil-rich eastern province of Hadramawt. It is being called *milyuniyyat al-huwiya al-junubiyya* or the Million-Strong Rally for Southern Identity.

The mass demonstration aims to unify all of the southern Yemeni protests against the Sana'a regime. For two years now, *milyuniyya* rallies have been held in Aden, the hub of southern Yemeni revolution, gathering large crowds of men from all over the southern provinces and women from less far-flung areas to give voice to the concerns of southerners before the world. The object of the April 27 rally is to commemorate the 1994 "war against the south" that led to the downfall of the southern army and the solidification of 'Ali 'Abdallah Salih's rule, understood by many southerners as a northern occupation. The choice of Mukalla, Hadramawt's main port, as the site for the demonstration is significant: only months earlier tribes gathered to form the Hadramawt Tribes Confederacy in order to resist what is considered a systematic looting of the fruits of the land by the regime, which is distributing business deals to its cronies while marginalizing locals. The tipping point was the murder of a notable tribal sheikh at an army post, which sparked a full-blown popular uprising.

The uprising has halted oil production in this province where about 80 percent of Yemen's oil reserves are located. The Council of Peaceful Revolution for Freedom and Independence in Hadramawt has declared each Thursday a day of civil disobedience in a manner copied from other southern provinces and attracting an astonishing unanimity of popular participation. Hadramawt's involvement in the all-southern uprising was further strengthened by the agreement declared in February from Beirut between the former southern leaders 'Ali Salim al-Bayd and Hasan Ba'um, two rival leaders of the uprising. The slogans for Mukalla are strongly worded, to say the least: One reads, "I am a Southerner, oh nation! No Yemenization after today."

Still, many people in Aden are hesitant to make the 310-mile trip to Mukalla for fear of an army crackdown after the entry of forces into the area earlier this week. For those who are not willing to make the dangerous trip, another million-strong rally is planned for downtown Aden. Still, for others, like the young activist and poet Huda al-'Attas, the question remains: Will such gatherings solve the problem of world indifference to southerners' rightful demands?

The Yemeni regime in Sana'a could take this opportunity to show that the transition process agreed upon under the patronage of the GCC countries, the United States and European states, and the National Dialogue Conference it set in motion, are indeed peaceful and inclusive. The entry of tanks into downtown Mukalla, violence against activists in Lahij and Aden and the crackdown on the revolutionary square in Mansoura, where two activists remain "disappeared," all suggest otherwise.

Chanting for Southern Independence

Anne-Linda Amira Augustin • *MER* 273, Winter 2014

"Our revolution is the South Arabian revolution," shouted five or six men at a march in Crater, a district of Aden, on March 20, 2014. The mass of demonstrators answered in unison: "Get out, get out, oh colonial power!" The call-and-response pattern continued: "Our revolution is the South Arabian revolution." "Against the power of the tyrants." The stanza concluded with the chant leaders prompting, "No unity, no federalism," and the crowd again thundering, "Get out, get out, oh colonial power!"

It was a protest mounted by the Southern Movement, or the Hirak, whose activists hail from the full spectrum of southern Yemeni society. In 2007, former soldiers, students, state employees and unemployed youth took to the streets of Aden and other towns to demand an end to the marginalization of the south at the hands of the central government in Sana'a since unification of the north and south in 1990. The "southern cause" (*al-qadiya al-janubiyya*), as southerners call their collective grievances, came to be felt keenly after the war between north and south in 1994, when southern factories were looted, land was stolen and southerners were forcibly retired from the civil service and the army. After the government's security forces beat back the first protests, the Hirak began to sharpen and harden its objectives. It now calls for the complete independence of the territory of the former People's Democratic Republic of Yemen (PDRY) from Sana'a. The "southern cause" has become the "South Arabian revolution."

Slogans are mirrors of a movement's values and claims. In the Southern Movement's rhetoric, the territory of the former PDRY is "occupied" by (northern) Yemenis. The term "colonial power" (*isti'mar*) refers to southerners' perception of northern domination, prompts a comparison of Sana'a's control to British rule and evokes the independence struggle of the 1960s.

Moreover, the denunciations of colonial power reflect southerners' rejection of the shape of the political transition in Yemen that began at the close of 2011. Facing popular uprisings and armed rebellions, former long-term president 'Ali 'Abdallah Salih was compelled to resign from office as a result of an initiative by the Gulf Cooperation Council, made up of Saudi Arabia and the other monarchies in the Arabian Peninsula. One key outcome of the National Dialogue Conference that followed Salih's resignation was the decision to reorganize Yemen into six federal regions, two of which are to divide the south. The Hiraki leadership refused to participate in the Conference because the Sana'a elites and their international partners did not recognize the right to self-determination for the south.

On the afternoon of May 21, two months after the rally in Crater, the Adeni quarter of Mu'alla was the scene of a mass demonstration (*milyuniyya*) whose discourse was also revealing of the Hirak's determination to achieve independence. Mass demonstrations in the south normally take place on two consecutive days and bring together groups from inside and outside Aden. The occasion this time was the twentieth anniversary of the announcement of southern disengagement from the north before the 1994 war by 'Ali Salim al-Bayd, the Socialist Party head under the PDRY who briefly served as vice president of unified Yemen. An intrinsic part of every rally is the *fa'aliyya*, a celebration during which everyone in attendance has the opportunity to perform a song, recite a poem or deliver a speech from the stage. Demonstrators fill the short breaks between the different acts with chants.

Journalist Radfan al-Dabis of the Aden Live satellite channel headlined the May 21 event. "We swore by God," he incanted into his microphone, "we swore." The crowd of thousands of southerners gathered in Madram Street roared in response, "Sana'a cannot govern us!" The slogan makes explicit that the Hirak considers Aden, the former capital of the PDRY, to be the center of legitimate power.

Next came a song whose refrain the protesters repeated over and over: "My country, my country is South Arabia / And the capital of the republic is Aden." It was an old Yemeni anthem composed by Ayyoub Tarish but with a Hiraki twist. The original chorus goes: "My country, my country is Yemen / I greet you, my homeland, in the course of time." The rephrasing ties today's movement to the southern Yemeni past. Before 1967, the year the PDRY gained its independence, the territory was governed as the Federation of South Arabia (Aden and its hinterland) and the Protectorate of South Arabia (eastern part of southern Yemen) by the British and local sultans and sheikhs, respectively. The revised refrain refers simply to "the south" (*al-janub*), the popular abbreviation for *al-janub al-'arabi*, or South Arabia. Any reference to Yemen is pointedly omitted.

After a woman gave a speech, the May 21 protesters launched into another set of rhyming slogans: "State of South Arabia / Free it, oh struggler / I want our territory / And nothing nugatory (*dawlat al-janub / harrarha ya munadil / bafani ardna / ma bafani shay' batil*)." "Territory" or "land" is a central theme in the Southern Movement's rhetoric and in local newspapers. After unification in 1990, the command economy of the avowedly Marxist PDRY was liberalized. An investment law opened the country to foreign capital, and the September Directive of 1991 enabled the sale of land that had been nationalized in the PDRY's early days. In the ensuing decade, there was a rush on the former state land. Functionaries in the state bureaucracy and army officers took immense kickbacks from the sales and expropriated some of the estates themselves. Southern feelings about the land grab are still raw.

The protesters on May 21 went on to applaud a pro-independence pop song, and then a brass band in PDRY marine uniform provided the soundtrack for a march of women up and down Madram Street. Again, the women sang, "My country, my country is South Arabia / And the capital of the republic is Aden." After several repetitions, the crowd chanted in rhythm, "Get out (irhal), get out, get out of Aden, get out of Aden." The target of their ire was clear—northern Yemenis who work in trade or study at the university. Many southerners see it as an affront that they have to compete with northerners for places at the institution of higher education or in the civil service—a competition in which they often lose out.

To the accompaniment of the brass band, young men cried out, "With spirit and blood, we devote ourselves to you, oh South Arabia." It was another resonance with the past—or, more precisely, today's reinterpretation of the past. In the days of the PDRY, southern children chanted this classic Arab political slogan in school, but to dedicate themselves to Yemen, not the south. The refashioned slogan draws a clear distinction between southerners and northern Yemenis. The "South Arabian identity" is constructed from remembered experiences of life under the PDRY. In the memories of the older generations, and the nostalgia they pass down to the young, southern identity stands for modernity and cosmopolitanism, whereas "Yemeni identity" is seen as backward, tribal and corrupt. Many southerners think of the PDRY as a secure, well-functioning civil state that supplied jobs, education and health care to all. They believe that northerners, by contrast, are unable to build a civil state—hence the failure of the National Dialogue.

At first, the women who had been marching urged on the male youths: "Advance, oh men, advance, advance, advance." After a while, though, the women joined in the men's devotion of themselves "to you, oh South Arabia."

The next chant on the agenda again rebuked the government in Sana'a. "O South Arabian, raise your voice! Independence or death!" The protesters here expressed the depth of southern distaste for northern rule. They also played on a saying of 'Ali 'Abdallah Salih, "Unity or death," which he had inserted in speeches and emblazoned on placards in Aden's streets to convey to southerners that any attempt at independence would fail. As this chant resounded, the marching women returned to their seats.

The May 21 *milyuniyya* finished with another sequence of call and response. "Raise your head," television anchor al-Dabis exhorted the throngs of southerners, who answered him, "You are a free South Arabian." This Hiraki adaptation of an iconic holler from the Egyptian uprising of 2011— "Raise your head, you are Egyptian"—can also be found scrawled on walls all over Aden.

The rallies of the Hirak have the dual function of displaying the breadth of dissent to the regime in Sana'a and informing the outside world about the "southern cause." The anti-northern stance is obvious. But the protests also have a large impact internal to the Southern Movement, particularly via the PDRY slogans that have been reinterpreted for the exigencies of today. The slogans contribute to the formation of identity and collective memory among Hirak activists—and can even constitute instruments of collective power.

The protesters in Aden's streets are mostly underprivileged—aging southerners who lost their jobs after 1994 or youths who have never been able to find a job at all. Many of the activists lead individual lives of quiet frustration, even desperation, but chanting and marching to music they turn their airing of grievances into a loud, whooping celebration. Together, they can be heard from afar.

A Poor People's Revolution: The Southern Movement Heads toward Independence from Yemen

Susanne Dahlgren • *MER* 273, Winter 2014

"This is no longer a movement," said the young man whose Facebook name is Khaled Aden. "This is a revolution."

Khaled, whose real name is Khalid al-Junaydi, is a leading activist in the Hirak, or Southern Movement, which aims to restore independence to southern Yemen. I met him on a Saturday morning in April 2013 at a street corner in Crater, the old part of Aden, located inside an ancient volcano. Here the liberation front fought some of their fiercest battles against the British colonial forces in the mid-1960s, and here the Hirak often confronts the security forces of the government in Sana'a.

The parallels between the two struggles are so striking that Aden Live, a Hiraki satellite channel based in Beirut, regularly airs a clip splicing images from the 1960s together with footage from today's confrontations.

[...]

Khaled Aden, as he likes to be called, lives in the same area that I did and is one of the few wealthy enough to have a car. He is an engineer and runs his own small business, the only way for graduates here to get a job, as public-sector positions are distributed from Sana'a. While driving through the narrow streets of colonial-era neighborhoods, Khaled told me that the gas I inhaled is meant for exterminating animals and not for crowd control. It causes rashes and severe breathing problems. But the gas was not the only reason why he was there every Saturday and Wednesday morning. Demonstrators were being hit by live ammunition every week, and his car was needed to take the injured to the clinic.

When we arrived at the clinic, the owner was himself receiving medical attention—he had been attacked by government troops in a nearby street. Clinics and hospitals in southern Yemen were once functioning parts of the World Health Organization system, but no longer. This private clinic is one of many in town that provides decent care—to those who can afford it. The owner is a supporter of the Hirak; the activists said he has guaranteed free treatment to demonstrators who have been hurt.

On one occasion, the activists brought an injured plainclothes member of the security forces to the clinic. People in the street had set upon the security man with fists and handbags after he was identified as the killer of an unarmed activist, based on a video clip. Young boys call him the Blue Ghost, for his blue eyes, a rarity in Yemen. He has a reputation for utter mercilessness, and Khaled told of being criticized by comrades for staging the rescue. Government troops recovered the Blue Ghost from the clinic, and the authorities never investigated the allegations against him.

The following Wednesday morning, the situation was even more serious near my house. There were more gunshots as troops ran into Crater. They had come to trash one of the squares where the Hirak holds its gatherings. Older men shouted at the troops as one of their number was struck by a soldier's rifle butt. The troops returned later to finish the job. Two middle-aged women yelled at them, but the confused soldiers left them alone. After the troops left Crater, I heard that two teenaged boys had been shot, one of them fatally. In the square, the photos of previous martyrs were torn down and the modest platform that activists had built totally destroyed.

The next day some 60 residents gathered in the square, men and women, of all ages, mostly very poor. Overnight someone had printed photos of the dead boy, Ahmad Darwish, 17, on posters and distributed them. Ahmad's mother and grandmother were there to vent their anger amid their grief. The grandmother, dressed in a worn-out overcoat, asked the emotionally charged questions on everyone's lips: "Where is the United Nations? Where are our human rights?"

On the Saturday following these dramatic events, older people came into the streets to protect the young boys. Troops arrived in tanks and fired tear gas. But this time there were no casualties—perhaps because of the presence of women in the streets. While women have lost their lives, too, their challenges to "the occupying forces," as government troops are called here, are somewhat protected by the culture of men showing respect for women.

For all the similarities to the mid-1960s, there is one clear difference—today's "anti-colonial" movement insists on unarmed resistance. In the birthplace of the struggle against the British, the Lahij governorate, the fighting has been bloody for years. But in Aden, once the cosmopolitan hub of the Arabian Peninsula, resistance means civil disobedience, strikes, meetings to educate the younger generation in history and the strong presence of women.

The more well-to-do activists say they aim to restore a civil state—one free of domination by the tribal, religious and military elites who rule in Sanaʻa. They want a multiparty system and a strong focus on services for the poor. For the less well-off, though, the Hirak is a revolution for a decent life. Women's rights is also a key political goal. As a young woman explained, women want to reemerge from the shadows where they have been since the 1990 unification. At the various gatherings, however crowded, the only seats available are reserved for women and there is no harassment. Men lament the increased prominence of the *niqab*, the full-face veil. There is a general will to restore women to their place "alongside men in building society," as per the rhetoric of the Yemeni Socialist Party that governed the People's Democratic Republic from 1967 to 1990. Intellectuals and schoolteachers complain about the distortion of southern history by the regime in Sanaʻa. According to the regime narrative, before unification the south was barely developed and Aden was merely a village. Southerners are now more or less unanimous that they will not regain their dignity as long as they are together with the north. Still, while men in the street use harsh words about northerners, the Hirak leadership tries to downplay the idea that the movement is against northerners as people. Such an idea would be racist, one Hirak leader told me.

[...]

Though the entirety of southern society supports the cause, it is the poor who confront the troops sent by Sana'a. The revolutionaries who brave the bullets are primarily young boys with no shoes. In many squares, meanwhile, it is poor women of all ages who play the most vocal part with their demands for a normal, decent life. It is the poor who organize the demonstrations and attend the lectures in the squares. These places of street-level organizing can be found in almost every district of Aden. The uneducated learn about the city's history, and the young learn about life before unification, when there were no water and power cuts and every graduate got a job. Occasionally, a preacher is invited, and numerous men of religion have joined the movement, but overall the movement is clear that southerners will not be subordinated with appeals to faith. One of the key demands of the Hirak is an apology for the fatwas that reactionary northern clerics have issued against "unbelievers" in the south.

On October 14, the Hirak convened in Aden to commemorate the fifty-first anniversary of the uprising against the British. At the march the movement issued a hasty plan: The Yemeni administration and army is to withdraw from the entirety of southern territory by November 30, the date of southern independence in 1967. While the streets are ready for independence, Adeni intellectuals fear that the movement is not. The intellectuals fear a repeat of 1967 when the sudden British exit left behind a new country with almost no resources. Amid the frenzy the Houthi take-over of Sana'a has created in the south, an Adeni activist commented wisely on his Facebook wall: Southerners did not realize it until weeks later, but the date of separation of north and south was actually September 21, the day the Houthis rolled into the Yemeni capital.

And Khaled Aden, the engineer who ferries the wounded in clashes with government troops to the clinic? According to Amnesty International, he was arrested and held without charge in Aden's al-Sulban prison, twice in 2011 and again in November 2013. He was kept in a small cell without ventilation, lights or a toilet. On August 31, 2014, Khaled Aden disappeared again. He was held incommunicado for nearly three months. Upon his November 14 release, he received a hero's welcome in Aden's protest square.

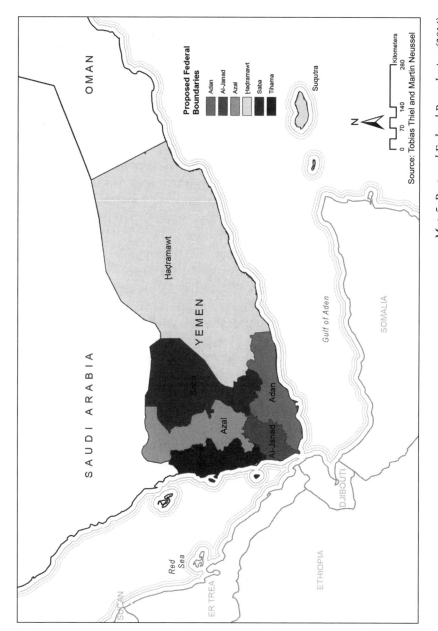

Map 5: *Proposed Federal Boundaries. (2014)*
Produced by the Spatial Analysis Lab, University of Richmond

Yemen's (Super-)Imposed Federal Boundaries

Tobias Thiel • *MERO*, Jul. 20, 2015

With the war in Yemen well past its hundredth day, confusion persists as to the underlying causes of the conflict. Far from a sectarian proxy war between Shafi'is under the patronage of Saudi Arabia and Zaydis backed by Iran, as the mainstream media would have it, the hostilities are rooted in local quarrels over power sharing, resources and subnational identities. These wrangles, in turn, are part of a broader negotiation process among domestic forces over a new social contract after the 2011 removal of the long-time president, 'Ali 'Abdallah Salih. At the core of this struggle lies a dispute about the future state structure, which provided the catalyst for the breakdown of the post-Salih transition road map sponsored by the Gulf Cooperation Council and the ensuing escalation to full-blown inter-state war.

The continuing failure to bring the adversaries to the table recalls the civil war in North Yemen in the 1960s, when rivalries for regional hegemony between Egypt, Saudi Arabia and Britain prevented a local settlement between Yemeni royalists and republicans. Much to the same effect, today's international support for President 'Abd Rabbu Mansour Hadi fuels the adamant insistence of his locally untenable government-in-exile on the implementation of the lopsided UN Security Council Resolution 2216, which calls for the unilateral withdrawal of Houthi fighters from captured territory and the resuscitation of the GCC initiative as preconditions for, rather than objectives of, talks. In order to break the deadlock, it is crucial to reopen a dialogue about the six-region federal division, which was rammed through, over the objections of the Houthis and others, at the National Dialogue Conference (NDC) that was intended to be the showpiece of the post-Salih transition.

Though hailed as a forum for averting Syrian-style civil war in Yemen, the NDC did not live up to expectations. As a Yemeni friend of mine sarcastically remarked after its conclusion in early 2014, "the NDC resolved all of Yemen's problems—except for the secessionist strife in the south, the Sa'da conflict in the north, national reconciliation, transitional justice and state building." In other words, it failed to overcome every major stumbling block on its agenda.

The lack of genuine consensus on a new state structure proved the most salient shortcoming. As the NDC approached its original closing date in September 2013 with no agreement in sight, a subcommittee with eight representatives from each side, north and south—known as the 8+8 Committee—was charged with finding a solution to the southern question. In its Agreement on a Just Solution, the working group, which included one Houthi delegate, unanimously affirmed that the Republic of Yemen—a unitary state with 21 governorates—should become a federal entity. This agreement was never revisited or approved by the NDC's 565-member plenary, but simply accepted as a *fait accompli*.

Though united behind the principle of federalism, the 8+8 Committee failed to settle on the number of new federal regions (two, five or six) or their boundaries. Instead, the committee outsourced these decisions to another fairly unrepresentative committee, handpicked and chaired by President Hadi, which was to study the parameters of a federal order. Established shortly after the release of the NDC's final communiqué, this 22-member Committee of Regions took less than two weeks to delineate six new federal regions—Azal, Saba', al-Janad, Tihama, Aden and Hadramawt. The process violated NDC rules, lacked broad consultation and was too short for the detailed studies that should have been commissioned. Nevertheless, its conclusions were referred to the Constitution Drafting Committee.

Even though all but the Houthi representative had signed off on the new map, most major political movements, including the Yemeni Socialist Party, the *salafi* Rashad Union and the southern Hirak, as well as the Houthis, publicly rejected or expressed reservations about the six-region federal division. The Houthis argued that the plan distributed natural wealth unevenly. It deprived the Azal region, in which the Houthis' historical homeland of Sa'dah is situated, of significant resources and access to the sea. Here the Houthis were referring, respectively, to the hydrocarbon-rich governorate of al-Jawf and the Red Sea province of Hajjah, both of which the movement has traditionally considered within its sphere of influence.

Riding a wave of popular discontent with the transition, the Houthis radically altered the political landscape when they took control of the capital Sana'a in September 2014. The conquest fell just short of a coup, as the Houthis signed the Peace and National Partnership Agreement (PNPA) with President Hadi and others to relieve tensions. Articles 8, 9 and 10 of this agreement called on Hadi to reconstitute the National Body for the Implementation of NDC Outcomes, which was to revisit the state structure to align it with the agreements made by the NDC rather than those by the Regions Committee.

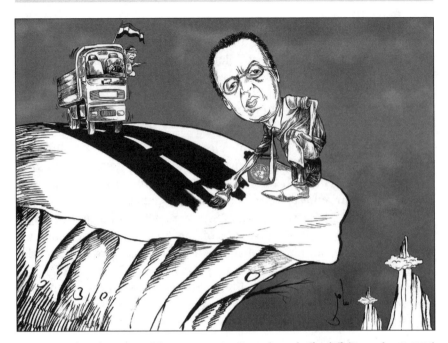

UN Special Mediator Jamal Benomar paving Yemen's road off a cliff. (December 2, 2013)
By Samer Mohammed al-Shameeri

Even before the draft constitution was released in January 2015, the Houthis reiterated their rejection of the six-region federal structure contained in the document. When Hadi nevertheless attempted to move forward the constitutional process by circumventing the PNPA, tempers flared. On January 17, the president sent his office director Ahmad bin Mubarak to deliver the draft document to the National Body, which had not been reconstituted. Enraged by this political intrigue, the Houthis flatout kidnapped Mubarak to thwart the six-region federal order. The move set in motion a chain of provocations that culminated in the overthrow of the Hadi government, his escape into exile and the Saudi-led bombing campaign.

A crucial, albeit frequently overlooked fact is that the Houthis have repeatedly stated their acquiescence to a federal system—be it jointly with the Hirak, in the form of a two-region federation, or in the form of a six-region division based on a sound political process. Rather than a rejection of federalism per se, the Houthis' refusal of the six-region division is as much grounded in the lack of a genuinely inclusive decision-making process as in the specific parameters that undermine their interests. While none of this background serves to justify the Houthis' recourse to arms, it does highlight the need for a new transition process based on equitable power sharing and sincere ownership across Yemen's diverse political and geographic landscape as the only way out of the crisis.

The Breakdown of the GCC Initiative

Stacey Philbrick Yadav and
Sheila Carapico • *MER* 273, Winter 2014

On September 21, 2014, fighters of Ansar Allah, the military wing of the Houthi movement, conquered Yemen's capital. Soon some militants occupied the home of 2011 Nobel Peace Prize winner Tawakkul Karman, a leader of the 2011 uprising against the regime of President 'Ali 'Abdallah Salih and a member of the Islamist party Islah. When the young men tweeted photos of themselves sprawling on her flowery bedspread with automatic weapons and bags of qat littered around them, the Houthi fighters conveyed a triumphal logic of coercive power, here sexualized for maximum impact. They later apologized, saying that the intent was to "guard" the Nobel laureate's home. But the takeover of Karman's house fell into a pattern of attacks on the homes of Islahi leaders, including the villa of the infamous Gen. 'Ali Muhsin, commander in Salih's wars against Ansar Allah. Many outside observers reported the advance of a ragtag militia into Sana'a and beyond as a struggle between the "Shi'i" Houthis and assorted "Sunnis," among them Islah. More than sectarian animus, though, the autumn turn of events demonstrated the political appeal of some Houthi positions, including critique of the excesses of Yemen's established elite and rejection of the transitional mechanism advanced by the Gulf Cooperation Council and Western enthusiasts. It was, as journalist and youth activist Farea al-Muslimi observed, "a breakdown of the Saudi-backed order."

Mainstream Malapropisms

Most English-speaking journalists and policy analysts have advanced one of two main speculations about the Houthi advance. The first dominant trope emphasizes the Zaydi roots of the Houthi movement, ahistorically framed as an "Iranian-backed Shi'i militia." In assuming an all-purpose Shi'i vs. Sunni simplification, transposed from Iraq and

Lebanon onto Yemen, this storyline deductively misidentifies all of the Houthis' adversaries—from the government to the tribes surrounding Sanaʿa—as "Sunni."

This notion is flat-out wrong. Zaydism is related to the dominant Twelver form of Shiʿi Islam institutionalized in Iran in the same way that, say, Greek Orthodoxy is an offshoot of Catholicism—the statement makes sense, maybe, in schismatic terms, but in terms of doctrine, practice, politics and even religious holidays Zaydism and Twelver Shiʿism are quite distinct. Moreover, historically, the city of Sanaʿa and all points north were the Zaydi heartland. Resistance to the Houthi advance did not come from "Sunni tribesmen," as so many reporters suggest, but from sons of Zaydi tribesmen who, when they joined the neo-conservative Islah, adopted or converted to a "Sunni" identity inspired by Saudi Wahhabism and/or the Egyptian Society of Muslim Brothers. The al-Ahmar clan, paramount sheikhs of the historically Zaydi Hashid tribal confederation clustered between Saʿdah and Sanaʿa, and who detest the Houthis, are Zaydi by parentage and Sunni by denominational conversion via partisan affiliation with Islah. On the other side, the majority denomination in the coastal and southern midlands provinces are the Shafiʿis, who are Sunni (in the same way that Lutherans or Methodists are Protestant) but rarely identify themselves as such—even if historically they distinguished themselves from the Zaydi regimes in Sanaʿa. Instead, to the limited extent that this conflict is "sectarian," it is also institutional: It began with a rivalry between Houthi summer camps and the Saudi-financed Salafi institute in the small, historically Zaydi town of Dammaj, which is a story rather more precise and interlaced with contemporary state power than the implied frame of an "age-old" dispute between the two main branches of Islam allows.

[...]

The second prevalent narrative places great faith in the will and capacity of foreign donors and consultants to broker a gradual, peaceful transition from authoritarianism. It goes something like this: Yemen is yet again "on the brink" of self-destruction, but the GCC monarchies and Western advisers can save it from itself.

These two angles have converged in a cockeyed view of the impact of regional and international forces. Iran is often said to be the bugaboo behind the Houthi militia, seen as a wannabe counterpart to Hizballah in Lebanon. Yet Saudi patronage of *salafi* elements within Islah and long-standing Saudi backing of the Salih regime have been bracketed off

Houthi forces march into the South Yemeni quicksands. (March 2015)
By Samer Mohammed al-Shameeri

from explanations of what are purported to be purely domestic machinations. Furthermore, journalistic and think-tank reporting has tended to overlook the deleterious effects of US counter-terror airstrikes against al-Qaeda targets on state sovereignty and regime legitimacy.

In focusing on sectarian divisions and/or the Yemeni state's (in)capacity to monopolize the legitimate use of force, the mainstream accounts distract attention from fundamental renegotiations of the nature of the state and the regime. The dominant narratives also misstate the threats to Yemeni sovereignty, which abound, but are neither denominational nor purely endogenous.

Endogenous Dynamics and Exogenous Stasis

The Houthi militia's advance from their base near the Saudi Arabian frontier through Zaydi strongholds in 'Amran (seat of the Hashid confederation) into Sana'a—and onward into Shafi'i-majority provinces like Hudayda (on the Red Sea coast) and Ibb (in the mountainous midlands)—must be read as positioning, an intent to renegotiate Yemen's political regime. A regime is an intermediate stratum between the government (which makes day-to-day decisions and is easy to alter) and the state (which is a complex bureaucracy tasked with a range of coercive functions). As such, a regime is understood by political scientists as a system of rules and norms by which power is distributed across and through state institutions. Yemen's political regime is in the process of being rewritten. By engaging in armed conflict and political maneuvering around the composition of the new government and revolutionary populist appeals, the Houthis have attempted to influence Yemen's future regime on several fronts.

On another level, Yemen's convulsions can never be comprehended as separate from the power structures of the Arabian Peninsula, dominated by the Kingdom of Saudi Arabia and the other filthy rich petro-kingdoms of the GCC, which in turn are protected by the US military. With average per capita incomes not much higher than the poverty level in Saudi Arabia, Yemen absorbs both migrant laborers expelled from the Gulf and desperate refugees fleeing East Africa. Millions subsist on less than $2 per day. And things are getting worse.

In some ways the Houthis represented subaltern objections to the agreement initiated by the self-consciously Sunni petro-monarchies of the GCC, formalized by the United Nations and facilitated by international experts, that culminated in the National Dialogue Conference of March 2013–January 2014. The Houthis and other dissidents maintained that the GCC initiative sought to demobilize the mass 2011 revolutionary uprising by sanctifying an elite pact between members of the Salih regime and its formal, multiparty, cross-ideological "loyal" parliamentary opposition, the Joint Meeting Parties. The JMP, in turn, was dominated by a conservative northern alliance of Islah, the Sana'a old guard and the Hashid confederation. Given the GCC monarchies' interest in stability in the most restive quarter of the Arabian Peninsula, the agreement contained a number of provisions to undermine populist demands for a democratic transition.

These measures included legal immunity for former president Salih and his family; the uncontested election of his long-standing vice president, 'Abd Rabbu Mansour Hadi, as chief executive for the transitional period; exclusion of both the Houthis and the southern Hirak from the transitional governing coalition; and the division of cabinet portfolios equally between Salih's GPC and the JMP (mainly Islah). The Houthis' posture as "outsiders" let them present themselves as revolutionary challengers to the insufferable status quo ante. So the Houthis walked into Sana'a largely unopposed, mainly because people were fed up with the GCC's repackaging of the ancien régime, and secondarily for primordial reasons (because Sana'a remains a largely Zaydi city where historically prominent local families are, like the Houthis' leaders, *sayyids*, or direct descendants of the Prophet). Rather than a sectarian appeal, the speech given by the movement's leader, 'Abd al-Malik al-Houthi, to mark Ansar Allah's occupation of the capital was full of stirring populist, nationalist rhetoric and widespread complaints about corruption intended to appeal to southerners, other Shafi'is and most Yemenis.

Domestic Power Politics

Surely control of state institutions is crucial. There was credible speculation that President Hadi decided against resisting the Houthi advance into the capital; although counter-intuitive given his past wars against them, it also became clear that Salih was encouraging Ansar Allah in order to disrupt the transition. As vice president, Hadi had witnessed firsthand the perpetual triangulation that helped to sustain his predecessor's power. In the 1990s, the GPC and Islah, both based in what had been North Yemen, ganged up against the Yemeni Socialist Party. After vanquishing the south and diminishing the Socialists in 1994, Salih turned on his right-wing challengers and erstwhile allies in Islah. In response, Socialists joined centrist elements in Islah and several smaller parties in the JMP to forge a unified counterweight to one-man military-based rule. Throughout the 2000s, Salih worked to neuter this parliamentary alliance by chipping away at Islah's *salafi* edge and pitting it against the moderate opposition center. Never fully successful, this strategy strained the alliance and preoccupied its leadership at the expense of its grassroots. Salih's triangulation helps to explain why, on the eve of the 2011 uprising, and during "youth" encampments spanning over a year, the loyal opposition enjoyed so little credibility. Its formal condemnation of human rights abuses had fallen by the wayside.

Meanwhile the Houthis had a history of conflict with Islahis and associated *salafis* in far northern Sa'dah. When the GPC needed Islah, Salih's party protected its religious schools, which were recruiting converts in the Zaydi heartland. When the Houthis protested—and eventually took up arms—some Islahi leaders supported Gen. 'Ali Muhsin's scorched-earth campaigns.

In 2011, centrist Islahis like Karman seemed to find common ground with Houthi partisans while camped out in protest squares for months on end to bring down Salih. As the GCC agreement became a reality, however, conservatives in Islah, burnishing a "Sunni" philosophy favored by the Gulf monarchies, were rewarded by the transitional terms.

Once in power, Hadi returned to Salih's playbook to cut Islah down to size. As the largest and most influential member of the Opposition Coalition, and as a party willing to buy into the GCC initiative, Islah benefited disproportionately from the deal. It was the best organized of the member parties, with the largest popular base and share of parliamentary seats (however moribund the parliament, elected in 2003, may have been) and the strongest backing from nearby petro-monarchies. Fighting broke out between militias affiliated with Ansar Allah and tribal forces identified with Islah and/or backed by neighboring "Sunni" monarchies, first in al-Jawf and eventually during the siege of the *salafi* school in the village of Dammaj near the frontier with Saudi Arabia, in the autumn of 2012.

Islah's reaction to the fall 2014 crisis showed its political experience relative to the Houthis, but also revealed its weaknesses. While condemning the Houthi aggression against its infrastructure and leaders, Islah nonetheless did not engage the Houthis militarily in Sana'a. Rather, leaders challenged the state to restore order. When instead Hadi allowed Houthi militants to overtake security and infrastructural institutions, he signaled his own desire to clip Islah's wings. Unable (or perhaps unwilling) to generate popular counter-mobilization, Islah quibbled over seats in the new government of Prime Minister Khaled Bahah on the basis of an outmoded parliamentary portfolio assembled in 2003.

The National Peace and Partnership Agreement signed by President Hadi, representatives of the Houthis and other political parties on September 21 called for a new, broadly inclusive and/or non-partisan technocratic government. To Islah's dismay, space was made for the Houthis and the southern Hirak, including some Socialists.

Debates over government portfolio allocations masked more serious issues related to the nature of the regime. While the privileging of Islah by transitional institutions fomented conflicts in Dammaj and al-Jawf and inflected the conflict with a neo-sectarian tenor, the Houthis' move into the capital coincided with mounting anxiety over the ongoing constitutional drafting process. The six new federal districts recommended by the National Dialogue Conference—two in the former south and four in the north—were avowedly designed to devolve some power to subnational units and also to stem the possibility of southern secession. In the abstract, or to outsiders, the federal proposal sounded appealing. Yet it was not anchored in local realities and reflected the advice of international consultants more than local constituencies. It seemed oblivious to the enormous technical, administrative and political difficulties to be faced in dismantling 22 existing provincial structures and creating new seats of authority. Pressure mounted on the Constitution Drafting Committee to reconcile the demands of the Houthis, the Hirak, entrenched political parties and external patrons.

Houthi speaking "in the name of the people." (February 8, 2015)
By Samer Mohammed al-Shameeri

As the Houthi military campaign pressed well beyond Sana'a, their fighters amassed heavy weapons in al-Bayda, north of the former inter-Yemeni border, site of numerous US drone strikes against al-Qaeda targets. There, Ansar Allah faced off against Ansar al-Shari'a, known in English as al-Qaeda in the Arabian Peninsula, or AQAP. Residents of al-Bayda and southern provinces sided variously with the Houthis, Ansar al-Shari'a or the Hirak based mainly on very local allegiances and grievances.

Of National, Regional and Global Power

When youths in Sana'a, Aden, Hudayda, Ibb, Ta'iz, al-Bayda and other parts of the country took to the streets in 2011 demanding "the downfall of the regime," they meant the status quo ante dominated by Salih, his family, the GPC, the Hashid tribal confederation, Islahi conservatives, the northern security apparatus and the entrenched corrupt bureaucracy—all rooted in the northern Zaydi heartland and all (nonetheless) backed by the Saudi kingdom, other GCC monarchies and, by extension, the United States. The GCC-brokered transition agreement kept this regime intact while politely inviting Salih to transfer the reins of power to Hadi (a native southerner and GPC member). American airstrikes against what recently seemed the main threat to both the Gulf monarchies and American hegemony in the Peninsula, the Sunni-identified Ansar al-Shari'a, continued or accelerated.

Ansar Allah's astounding military successes in, and then beyond, the northern Zaydi highlands confused matters—all the more so against the backdrop of the formidable sweep of the nihilist, radically anti-Shi'i neo-Sunni group in Syria and Iraq known variously as "the Islamic State," ISIS, ISIL or Da'ish, the Arabic acronym for ISIL. Within Yemen, Ansar Allah and Ansar al-Shari'a, both declared by the Saudi kingdom to be "terrorist" (read: anti-systemic) entities, have been presented as locked in mortal, antithetical, "sectarian" conflict. At about the same time, Washington called for sanctions against Salih and two Houthi leaders on the grounds that they were spoiling the GCC-sponsored transition plan. US policy in Yemen is, as ever, reactively aiming at a moving target, and strongly shaped by the US-Saudi alliance.

Like the strange selfies of Houthi home invaders luxuriating on Tawakkul Karman's bedspread, these events are nearly inscrutable to outsiders—or, indeed, to Yemenis, who are hardly of one mind amid the dizzying twists and turns. One commentator, Haykal Bafana, described the "jarring bipolarity" between de facto US support for the Houthis via drone attacks on rival AQAP targets in al-Bayda even as other organs of the Obama administration appealed to the UN for sanctions against Houthi militia leaders, considering this juxtaposition an "elegant summation" of dysfunctional and probably ineffectual American policy. Farea al-Muslimi noted with irony that the Houthis have given al-Qaeda even "more legitimacy than [US] drones did in the past." The Ansar al-Shari'a present themselves as a bulwark "against this new gorilla called the Houthis," he ventured, opposition to which "now sells" among the general public. Despite its origins in institutional conflicts and regime machinations, the "sectarian issue," al-Muslimi observed, now has provided "more political capital than AQAP ever dreamed of."

9 Saudi-Led, American-Backed Military Intervention, 2015

Directly or indirectly, almost every dispatch presented so far anticipates the grand finale, a brutal Saudi-led, American-backed military assault ostensibly to defeat the Houthis and reinstate Hadi as president of Yemen. As I wrote in an op-ed for *The Nation* magazine two weeks into the war, peace and social justice activists around the world should be mobilizing to protest this naked aggression—but not out of sympathy for the Houthi-Salih militias who also committed atrocities against civilians and are hardly progressives. In this chapter's entries, John Willis places the aerial bombardment in historical context. Marina de Regt calls attention to the plight of refugees fleeing to East Africa, and Jillian Schwedler and Stacey Philbrick Yadav ask Americans not to look away. I criticize the failure of the UN Security Council to call for so much as a humanitarian pause or even to mention the devastation caused by the Saudi-led intervention, and Gabriele vom Bruck explains one of several false Saudi overtures toward negotiations. Susanne Dahlgren and Amira Augustin follow up on their extensive reporting from the southern governorates, where the Houthi-Salih assault failed to pacify grassroots Popular Committees demanding southern independence. Finally, James Spencer analyzes the failure of the military campaign to achieve its stated objectives. Several caricatures by Samer Mohammed Al-Shameeri visually illustrate his view of these developments from Sanaʻa.

الشرعيه

*"Legitimacy": Saudi Arabia holding up 'Abd Rabbu Mansour Hadi amidst
the ruins of his country. (March 30, 2015)
By Samer Mohammed al-Shameeri*

Operation Decisive Storm and the
Expanding Counterrevolution

John M. Willis • *MERO*, Mar. 30, 2015

On the night of March 25 one hundred Saudi warplanes bombed strategic targets inside Yemen under the control of the Houthi rebels. A number of countries—the other Gulf Cooperation Council members minus
Oman, as well as Egypt, Jordan, Sudan, and Morocco—joined the effort
either directly or in support capacities. Although the Houthis have been
in control of the Yemeni capital Sana'a and the central government since
September 2014, it was the flight of President 'Abd Rabbu Mansour Hadi
to Aden and the subsequent Houthi attack on the southern city that constituted the breaking point for Saudi Arabia and the GCC. Thus began
what Riyadh has dubbed Operation Decisive Storm (*'Asifat al-Hazm*),
a military assault that has already caused considerable destruction in

Sana'a and elsewhere, and incurred dozens of casualties both military and civilian.

Saudi ambassador to the United States Adel al-Jubair described the air campaign as defending the legitimate Yemeni government led by Hadi, who replaced president 'Ali 'Abdallah Salih as part of a GCC-brokered political arrangement in 2011. Hadi's government, al-Jubair contended, "has agreed to a process that is supported by the international community, that is enshrined in several United Nations Security Council resolutions that call for all Yemeni parties to take a certain path that would lead them from where they were to a new state with a new constitution and elections and checks and balances and so forth." He referred to the Houthis as "spoilers" of this process, who refused to "become legitimate players in Yemeni politics," and who will not be allowed to take over the country. Al-Jubair's remarks on the legitimacy of the government were remarkable for several reasons, not least of which was the absence of any mention of the Yemeni people.

The Houthis' refusal to negotiate a political settlement in Riyadh has indeed disrupted the Kingdom's attempt to revive the original and problematic GCC initiative and National Dialogue Conference that was to resolve Yemen's deep political divisions. As Stacey Philbrick Yadav and Sheila Carapico have argued, "given the GCC monarchies' interest in stability in the most restive quarter of the Arabian Peninsula, the agreement contained a number of provisions to undermine populist demands for a democratic transition." It is no wonder then that the Houthis saw little possibility of addressing their concerns in a Saudi-sponsored conference that seemed to have as its goal the restoration of the political status quo.

Yet Operation Decisive Storm is not merely about Yemen's internal politics. It is emblematic of a broader political transformation—one that both has historical parallels and is strikingly new. For many, the assault raises the specter of a proxy war between Iran and Saudi Arabia, executed by a coalition of Sunni states and Iran's Shi'i proxies. Indeed, the forces aligned against the Houthis are Sunni-majority countries. As many analysts have noted, however, the narrative of sectarianism obfuscates the political context of the Yemeni crisis rather than clarifying it. For those with longer historical memories, this military campaign suggests a previous proxy war between Gamal Abdel Nasser's Egypt and Saudi Arabia, when both countries intervened in the Yemeni civil war (1962–67) to support the Yemeni republicans, on the one hand, and the Yemeni monarchy, on the other. In that conflict, the Saudis backed the deposed Zaydi imam while Egyptian troops fought on the side of the "free officers." Although the republican officers prevailed, Egypt suffered a kind of defeat, and Saudi Arabia ultimately extended its hegemony over what was then North Yemen.

A closer historical analogy might be the Iranian, Jordanian and British intervention in Oman against the rebellion of the Marxist Popular Front for the Liberation of Oman (PFLO) in the 1960s and 1970s. In that case an alliance of conservative monarchies joined forces to support the Omani sultanate against popular forces that had threatened to spread into the greater Persian Gulf. While the Houthis in no way resemble the leftist PFLO in ideology or revolutionary practice, the forces gathered against them have a great deal in common. Namely, they are all part of a counterrevolutionary front that has expanded beyond the GCC to include other authoritarian regimes. While not all these countries share the Saudi and GCC paranoia regarding Iran, they do, to varying degrees, fear the spread of ISIS or popular democratic forces. To these regimes, the Houthis represent one of many forces that threaten to undermine the regional order.

The coalition also shares a reliance on Saudi and GCC political and economic support. In Egypt, GCC member states Saudi Arabia, Kuwait and the UAE have supported the regime of 'Abd al-Fattah al-Sisi politically and financially since he formalized power in 2014. Collectively, they provided Egypt with an estimated $23 billion in grants, loans, petroleum products and investment in 2014 and a pledge for $12 billion more in 2015. Sudan's president, Omar al-Bashir, met with King Salman in October 2014 as part of a general rapprochement between the two countries that led to an unspecified aid package from Saudi Arabia. Both Jordan and Morocco were briefly in discussions to enter the GCC as part of a post-Arab uprising defense strategy intended to ensure dynastic stability in the face of increasing domestic opposition. Although they were ultimately not invited to join, the two monarchies still enjoy the financial support of GCC countries and share a similar commitment to combating the influence of ISIS.

The role of Pakistan is slightly more complex. Beyond the long history of military ties between the two countries, Prime Minister Nawaz Sharif owes his political life to Saudi intervention. The Kingdom gave him a comfortable exile in 2000 and again in 2007 (including financing his establishment of a steel mill in Jidda). Since Sharif's election in 2013, the Saudis have continued their support, most recently in April

Members of the anti-Yemen Decisive Storm coalition standing in line for the
Saudi cash machine. (March 31, 2015)
By Samer Mohammed al-Shameeri

2014 with an injection of $1.5 billion in loans into the Pakistani econo-
my to shore up its foreign reserves. In return, the Pakistani military has
actively supported the Gulf monarchies: The recruitment of Pakistani
mercenaries for Bahrain's security forces during the height of opposition
demonstrations in 2011 was organized by private security firms with
close ties to the Pakistani military.

Despite Saudi or even US assertions to the contrary, Operation
Decisive Storm has nothing to do with supporting the legitimacy of a political process in Yemen. Its goal is instead to maintain the continuity of
authoritarian governance in the region by actively repressing the forces
that threaten to undo the status quo. That this coalition has indiscriminately lumped together ISIS, Iran and the popular democratic movements
of the Arab uprisings of 2011 should indicate both its broader strategic
goals and, equally, the dangers to positive political and social change it
represents.

A Grim New Phase in Yemen's Migration History

Marina de Regt • *MERO*, Apr. 15, 2015

"Yemen's conflict is getting so bad that some Yemenis are fleeing to Somalia," read a recent headline at the *Vice News* website. The article mentions that 32 Yemenis, mainly women and children, made the trip to Berbera, a port town in Somaliland (and not Somalia). Hundreds of thousands of Somalis have crossed the Gulf of Aden since the outbreak of the Somali civil war in 1991. But now the tide seems to have turned. Yemen has become a war zone, as a coalition of Arab states led by Saudi Arabia bombs the country in an attempt to stop the Houthis, an insurgent movement opposed to the government, from gaining control over the entirety of Yemeni territory. But, instead of protecting the Yemeni population, these attacks have created more chaos, despair and destruction.

The situation is especially bad in Aden, Yemen's main port, strategically located near Bab al-Mandab, the strait connecting the Indian Ocean to the Red Sea. Street fighting in Aden has intensified, mainly between the city's inhabitants, on one side, and the Houthis and army units loyal to 'Ali 'Abdallah Salih, Yemen's former president, on the other. There is no water available any longer, electricity is intermittent and food shortages are very serious. Life in Aden is unbearable without water and electricity, as the climate is very hot and humid. People are slowly starving. Those who can are trying to escape, but many do not have the opportunity.

In other parts of the country, the situation is deteriorating, too, with civilians being the main victims of this useless war. A camp of internally displaced people near the Saudi Arabian border was mistakenly bombed, killing many people. A dairy near the port town of Hudayda was targeted, killing dozens of workers inside, and recently another factory was hit. A family of seven people in Yemen's capital of Sana'a was killed in an air raid. And these are just a few of the stories. Many residents have fled to their ancestral villages or sought refuge elsewhere. Shops in the capital of Sana'a are closed, and water is running out. There are long queues at fuel stations, and diesel is no longer available. Those who have stayed behind describe the city as a ghost town.

On April 12, the International Organization for Migration (IOM) organized its first charter flight during the crisis, evacuating 141 "third-country nationals" from Sana'a. People with certain nationalities, such as Indian and Chinese, were flown to safety with the assistance of their governments. According to the IOM, 160,000 third-country nationals remain stranded in Yemen. The organization is also helping Yemenis who were on their way to Yemen when the airstrikes started and who are stuck at airports all over the world. Thousands of Yemenis are separated from their families, anxious to go home or desperate to leave the country. And yet, it seems to be easier to evacuate foreigners than to help Yemenis in their own country. It took days before the first airplane bearing humanitarian aid was able to land.

I am thinking of all the migrants who came to Yemen fleeing oppression, violence and destitution in the Horn of Africa. Most of them hoped to find work on the Arabian Peninsula, and used Yemen as a transit country. Since 2011 an increasing number of Ethiopians have crossed the Red Sea and the Gulf of Aden, outnumbering Somalis as new arrivals. One of the reasons was that brokers and smugglers were exploiting the weakened border controls and rule of law in Yemen. They convinced Ethiopians to migrate via Yemen, promoting it as an easy way to reach Saudi Arabia. Many were kidnapped upon arrival in Yemen, detained in "torture camps" and only released after having paid a ransom. I can only hope that the IOM will also repatriate the thousands of undocumented Ethiopians and Somalis in Yemen, but I fear for their fate. According to a new UN report, there were still Ethiopian migrants arriving in Yemen after the start of the airstrikes.

The current situation marks a grim new phase in Yemen's migration history. In the late nineteenth and early twentieth centuries, many Yemeni men migrated to the Horn of Africa, escaping the bad economic and political situation at home. They often returned to Yemen in the 1960s and 1970s, after the establishment of the Yemen Arab Republic in the north and the People's Democratic Republic of Yemen in the south. It is more than ironic that nowadays Yemenis have to flee to the Horn of Africa again.

Two Resolutions, a Draft Constitution (and Late Developments)

Sheila Carapico • *MERO*, Apr. 17, 2015

On April 14, three weeks into the Saudi-led air campaign called Operation Decisive Storm, the UN Security Council (UNSC) approved Resolution 2216. This legally binding resolution, put forward by Jordan, Council president for April, imposed an arms embargo on the Houthi rebels and former Yemeni president 'Ali 'Abdallah Salih and his son. There are also provisions freezing individual assets and banning their travel. Russia abstained. It seemed to fully endorse both the so-called Gulf Cooperation Council initiative, brokered by UN special envoy Jamal Benomar, and Operation Decisive Storm.

But then, within a day or two, Benomar resigned and Secretary-General Ban Ki-moon issued a much stronger plea for an immediate cessation of all hostilities.

As the purported legal basis for UNSC 2216, Jordan's proposal cited "a letter from the president of Yemen," who has fled his country for Riyadh, requesting from the GCC and the League of Arab States immediate "support, by all necessary means and measures, including military intervention, to protect Yemen and its people from the continuing aggression by the Houthis."

The April 14 resolution reads as if Saudi Arabia is an impartial arbitrator, rather than a party to an escalating conflict, and as if the GCC offers a "peaceful, inclusive, orderly and Yemeni-led political transition process that meets the legitimate demands and aspirations of the Yemeni people, including women." This is unmitigated nonsense. And it is contradicted by the testimony of rules-of-war monitors.

The Security Council expressed "grave alarm at the significant and rapid deterioration of the humanitarian situation." But it conspicuously neglected to demand a humanitarian ceasefire to halt the Saudi-led bombing campaign, even briefly, to allow essential medicines and food to reach Aden and other cities whose populations face death, destruction and devastation.

It is a particularly caustic omission. Only the day before, Ivan Simonovic, the UN's deputy secretary-general for human rights, said that the majority of the 600 people killed since the start of the Saudi assault are civilians. Both the Saudis and the Houthis are to blame, he explained. The UN High Commissioner for Human Rights' spokeswoman, Ravina Shamdasani, noted rules-of-war violations by both sides. The World Health Organization recorded 736 deaths and 2,719 wounded since the onset of Decisive Storm. As Human Rights Watch put it on April 13, "The [Saudi-led] coalition and the US should investigate alleged laws-of-war violations by coalition forces and facilitate the delivery of humanitarian aid to populations at risk."

By contrast, UNSC 2216 implies that only the Houthis are committing war crimes. Invoking Chapter VII of the UN charter as if circuitously and *ex post facto* to authorize Operation Decisive Storm, it demands that "all . Yemeni parties, in particular the Houthis, fully implement resolution 2201 (2015)," "refrain from further unilateral actions," and "unconditionally...end the use of violence." No mention of non-Yemeni parties.

Instead of condemning war crimes on both sides, or calling forcefully for a negotiated ceasefire, UNSC 2216 implicitly condones the Saudi-led, US-backed escalation. An indistinct nod toward diplomacy "welcomes" the GCC's restatement of a March 10 invitation to convene a "conference" in Riyadh. This proposal was disingenuous then, since the Saudis would hardly be neutral arbiters between a transitional regime they installed and a group they label "terrorists."

Praising the resolution, US Ambassador to the United Nations Samantha Power, known for her past advocacy of humanitarian intervention, declared that "a legitimate transition in Yemen can only be achieved through political negotiations and a consensus agreement among all political parties based on the GCC initiative and the outcomes of Yemen's National Dialogue Conference."

Meanwhile, in addition to providing intelligence and surveillance, Washington rushed advanced weapons to Saudi Arabia and Egypt to bolster the aerial offensive against Yemen.

The Jordanian-sponsored resolution gives the impression that these (unmentioned) actions support rather than defy international law. In nine separate paragraphs and clauses, UNSC 2216 lauds the GCC initiative, including its outcomes: the National Dialogue Conference and the resulting draft constitution for Yemen, also facilitated by Benomar. It reaffirms "the legitimacy of the president of Yemen, 'Abd Rabbu Mansour Hadi." Moreover it condemns "any actions that undermine the unity, sovereignty, independence and territorial integrity of Yemen."

UNSC 2216 and Power's remarks in mid-April follow up on a measure passed by the Security Council two months ago on February 15. Then, as the United States, other NATO powers and Gulf nations shut down their embassies in Sana'a and evacuated their diplomats, the world body unanimously voted for Resolution 2201, calling on the Houthis to surrender their military gains and on all Yemenis to get behind the GCC initiative and the draft constitution produced with the assistance of the special envoy, Benomar, in the name of the National Dialogue Conference.

This first resolution reflected Gulf and great power anxieties about minority guerrillas capturing the capital Sana'a, overthrowing the remnants of the central government, sowing chaos, and inadvertently leaving opportunities for Ansar al-Shar'ia (a local ally of al-Qaeda) to make even more mischief. Domestically, it appealed to some, especially in the governorates that made up independent South Yemen until unification in 1990, who prefer the interim government of Hadi to the Houthis, but who also aspire to independence rather than unity.

In February, as in April, the "international community" praised the GCC initiative and its outcomes as the only solution to Yemen's woes, with Hadi as the rightful leader and the draft constitution as a road map for the future. Actually, all three had already failed to deliver tranquility, social justice or a way forward.

[...]

In and of itself, the ensuing National Dialogue Conference was a sound idea, grounded in Yemeni precedents. It did help to tamp down tensions in 2012 and part of 2013. Some of its committees made real progress, thanks to some young and/or female intellectuals and technocrats. There were working groups on a range of issues—ranging from economic development to the Houthi and southern questions, respectively. But in the end the Conference did not produce the desired results. Most of the 565 delegates were aging politicians, veterans of past conflicts and corruption rackets. The dissident Houthis, the Southern Movement, and advocates of genuine change were underrepresented.

The National Dialogue, moreover, became a donor-dominated "transitology" project. Delegates earned generous per diems to meet in the five-star Mövenpick Hotel in Sana'a with foreign "experts" on subjects like federalism. This last item was not on the Conference agenda or part of its mission statement or committee structure—but nevertheless a federalism proposal was a major outcome of the Conference, and a central feature of the proposed constitution. Still, the federal map produced by the Conference was dismissed in popular responses as inadequate to address the real need for a regime change or to end the power struggle in Sana'a. It was, moreover, the imposition of the division into six regions that prompted the Houthis to deploy so as to stop that division. The Hirak also rejected this redesign.

The draft constitution overvalued in UNSC 2216 is premised on a "federal" solution to Yemen's problems. There's no doubt that the majority of Yemenis prefer decentralized local governance over one-man autocracy. Nor can anyone object to the numerous platitudes including promises to respect rights to asylum, health care and more. But the draft constitution, a product of the GCC initiative and foreign consultations, was not the answer to Yemen's problems it was made out to be. It seemed bizarrely derivative of the flawed American-backed constitution foisted on Iraq in 2005, or the similar failed arrangements introduced in Afghanistan.

The envisioned government structure is not fully federal if that term means regional autonomy and representation. The text specifies that the new House of Representatives shall consist of 260 members elected through a general, free, secret, direct and equal vote under the closed proportional list system. That is national constituency representation, whereby parliamentary representatives are elected from the whole country, not localities or provinces, as in the American or German federal systems. Yemen's draft constitution would marginalize regional forces, notably the Houthi movement (Ansar Allah), based in the Sa'dah governorate in the far north.

Moreover, oddly, the draft constitution stipulated that the south (the newly designated but ill-defined regions of Aden and Hadramawt) shall be represented in the House of Representatives based on "the land and population formula" at a share of 40 percent. This formula would give the south more seats than they had in the current (although legally defunct) 301-member legislature, or than they would earn based purely on population. It looked like a bid to win the support of southerners. At the same time, contrarily, the proposed national charter divided the south into two large regions in the "federal" system, a notion that is anathema to many Hirak activists, whose demands are for the restoration of independent southern sovereignty.

The draft constitution also created a new upper house of Parliament called the Federal Council, comprised of 84 members—12 from each of six newly created regions, six from the city of Sana'a and six from the city of Aden. This apportionment is cockeyed because the ostensible equality of representation from each of the six purportedly federal regions is skewed toward the former capitals of North and South Yemen, respectively. Other large metropolitan areas, notably Ta'iz, but also Hudayda—situated geographically, politically and metaphorically between Sana'a and Aden—were relatively underrepresented.

UN Security Council Resolution 2216, passed April 14, 2015, blocks
first aid to Yemeni victims. (April 16, 2015)
By Samer Mohammed al-Shameeri

Finally, the draft constitution specified that the president and vice president shall be elected together on a single ticket, provided that they are not from the same region. And yet the national constituency vote virtually guarantees a majority of conservative, status quo politicians from the more populous former North Yemen.

None of these provisions satisfied popular aspirations.

Under the leadership of the new Saudi king, Salman, the members of the GCC (except Oman) pulled together a war coalition including Egypt, Jordan and Morocco, backed by the United States and Great Britain. They rammed a flawed, legally questionable, unbalanced resolution through the Security Council that seemed to authorize a military operation that has closed all of Yemen's air and sea ports, caused a nationwide power outage, killed hundreds, wounded thousands, displaced tens of thousands, incapacitated emergency and medical facilities, halted food imports and terrorized millions.

[...]

Saudi Arabia attacking Iran but whacking Yemen. (April 6, 2015)
By Samer Mohammed al-Shameeri

The Moral Economy of Distance in the Yemeni Crisis
Jillian Schwedler and
Stacey Philbrick Yadav • *MERO*, May 6, 2015

In discussions of the ongoing war in Yemen, Yemeni activists, aid organizations and human rights groups are struggling to push the dire humanitarian situation and Yemen's increasing isolation to the fore. Yet most of the establishment in Washington and London continues to treat the spiraling conflict in southwest Arabia as a disembodied "thing"—a situation to be managed, a territory to be protected in a proxy war, a threat to be contained—rather than an acute crisis affecting close to 26 million people. When attention is directed toward the citizens of Yemen at all, these people are portrayed as another problem to be solved. How to address the susceptibility of Yemenis to Islamist extremism? How to quell their support for heavily armed tribes? How to limit the risk that a massive exodus from Yemen might pose to Europe and other locales, as "boatloads of desperate migrants" land on distant shores? The fact that oil prices surged after Saudi Arabia began bombing Yemen underlines the broad perception that what really matters is stability within Saudi Arabia and the maintenance of a key transit route and not what happens to Yemenis. The problem must be contained.

[...]

For Washington, the current concern, as with these previous examples, is to support a key ally, Saudi Arabia, and to crush AQAP. Yemen thus remains a problem to be dealt with, particularly the threats "it" poses to other nations: the threat of spreading Iranian power; the threat of the so-called Shi'i crescent; the threat of Sunni jihadis, whether ISIS or al-Qaeda, who threaten our moral vision. Yemen is a poor country, but few care about that as such. The lack of water, education and infrastructure only make the "problem" of the people worse. Yemen has no burgeoning neoliberal cityscape, no safe enclaves, no foreign direct investment, no Starbucks. Why? It is not safe. What makes a place unsafe? The people—backward, ignorant Yemenis. This view continues to be naturalized by Yemen's own leadership, beholden to Saudi Arabia. It is reflected in US material, tactical and, we would argue, moral support for the war.

This framing also encourages Americans to adopt an indifference toward Yemenis that is built on moral distance. It interpolates "us" by constructing our moral opposite, and even well-intentioned efforts to draw attention to the war advance this view. The beauties of Yemen—the romantic villages perched on mountain peaks, the gorgeous Old City of Sana'a with its gingerbread architecture, the mud-brick skyscrapers of the city of Shibam—these "historic" wonders worth saving are rendered inaccessible to us because the current-but-somehow-not-modern people, the Yemeni people, are too backward, too radical, too ignorant, for Western tourists to travel among them safely. The notion that Yemen's most valuable assets are its historic treasures rather than its people is reproduced by the viral circulation of images of Yemeni architecture and heritage sites, or perhaps a sympathetic image of Yemeni children. It is as though there is no innocent adult civilian—let alone "rights-bearing citizen"—to visualize.

Yemen Talks in Geneva

Gabriele vom Bruck • *MERO*, Jun. 14, 2015

On June 8, Yemen's (self-)exiled president, 'Abd Rabbu Mansour Hadi, conveyed his ideas about UN-sponsored talks in Geneva, due to start on June 15, and downplayed their scope. The conversations are to take place mainly between politicians handpicked by him and his Saudi hosts, on the one hand, and Ansar Allah (or the Houthi movement) and members of the formerly ruling General Party Congress (GPC) who do not support Hadi, on the other. These two sides roughly correspond to the alliances that have been fighting in Yemen since March.

On al-Arabiyya television, however, Hadi explained, "These are not talks. It is only a discussion about how to implement UN Security Council Resolution 2216 on the ground." UNSC 2216, passed in mid-April, endorsed Hadi as the "legitimate" elected leader of Yemen and invoked past resolutions backing the Gulf Cooperation Council initiative and the National Dialogue Conference it prescribed for ending Yemen's internal conflicts. The April resolution also imposed an arms embargo on the Houthis and their allies.

Hadi was adamant in his television appearance that the Geneva parleys are not aimed at reconciliation between the warring parties. In his keynote address at a conference sponsored by the German government in Berlin on June 11, former prime minister 'Abd al-Karim al-Iryani said, "We cannot [afford to] fail in Geneva." Al-Iryani thus stressed the urgency of an agreement requiring the good faith and sincerity of the negotiators. Hadi and his sponsors, however, seem intent on defining the terms of Ansar Allah's surrender rather than achieving a political settlement that leads to equal representation of all the country's factions in a future government.

Yemen's ambassador to the United Nations, Khalid al-Yamani, announced that the government-in-exile is sending seven representatives to Geneva, with two each for the anti-Hadi portion of the GPC and the Houthis, and three for the remaining parties, such as the Yemeni Socialist Party.

Hadi's choice of delegates offers clues as to the Saudi agenda in Yemen. At last supporting "revolutionary" change, the Saudis seem to favor two new political parties that are to be prominently represented at the meeting. Perhaps the most revealing representative is 'Abd al-Wahhab al-Humayqani, secretary-general of the *salafi* Rashad Union, founded in 2012 in the wake of the previous year's nationwide uprising against former president 'Ali 'Abdallah Salih. He is one of just two party leaders slated to participate in the talks. Neither man has played an important role in previous governments. The selection of al-Humayqani may indicate the Saudis' hope that Rashad can be propped up like the Egyptian al-Nour party to compete with the Muslim Brothers (now almost eliminated in Egypt and marginal in Yemen). Doubtless the founders of Rashad were inspired by al-Nour's stunning success in the Egyptian legislative elections in 2011–12, in which the *salafi* group garnered 25 percent of the vote. Al-Humayqani aspires to be a "clear Islamic voice." At the National Dialogue Conference, Rashad was represented by five members who stressed the party's commitment to peaceful negotiation.

*King Salman distributing money to Yemeni politicians in and beyond the
Hadi government. (May 4, 2015)
By Samer Mohammed al-Shameeri*

The Multiple Wars in Yemen

Susanne Dahlgren and
Anne-Linda Amira Augustin • *MERO*, Jun. 18, 2015

With UN-sponsored peace talks in Geneva involving the usual suspects
and only a few new faces, it is time to raise the question of Yemen's future
as a state.

The talks involve exiled president 'Abd Rabbu Mansour Hadi, the
Houthi movement Ansar Allah and minor figures from the long-time rul-
ing General People's Congress (GPC, now split into factions tied to Hadi
and former president 'Ali 'Abdallah Salih), the leading Sunni-identified
Islamist party Islah and its ally in Hadi's government-in-exile, the Yemeni
Socialist Party.

The only representatives outside the competing would-be regimes
of Hadi and the Houthis at the talks come from two recently established
parties, including the *salafi* Rashad Union, whose popularity in Yemen
remains to be seen. Hadi insists on implementing UN Security Council
Resolution 2216, which would compel the Houthis to withdraw from
major cities, including the capital of Sana'a, reinstate himself as head of
state and continue the transition toward a federal state, as agreed at the
GCC-brokered National Dialogue Conference last year. The Houthis

oppose the six-part federal plan but agree on key transition issues decided upon at the Conference. From their perspective, Hadi's regime has failed to execute the agreed-upon policies and, in any case, the situation became entirely different after Ansar Allah took over Sana'a last September. In the eyes of many Yemenis, whether they support the Houthis or not, they are right: Since the conclusion of the $24 million conference, very little has been done to address the demands put forward in the rallies gathering millions of Yemenis throughout the country in 2011.

The questions one has to ask at this stage: Is the National Dialogue Conference plan still viable as a road map for Yemen's future? And do the delegates at the talks have the authority in the first place to set the country on this path? Many factors point in another direction. Of the Geneva negotiators, only the Houthis seem to have a strong base of political support on the ground, at least in the areas where the movement hails from. Excluded from the talks are representatives of the South, who are battling Houthi aggression under the label Southern Resistance (al-muqawama al-janubiyya). As for Hadi, his term as transitional president ended in February 2014, and amid the current warfare, in the eyes of many Yemenis, he is a man who invited the Saudi-led coalition to kill civilians while kicking back in the luxury of a Riyadh palace. There is considerable reason to believe that he lacks the local support to return to power in Yemen.

Still, in the international media the war in Yemen is characterized as fighting "between forces loyal to the beleaguered president, 'Abd Rabbu Mansour Hadi, and those allied to Zaidi Shi'a rebels known as Houthis, who forced Mr. Hadi to flee the capital Sanaa in February." The expression "Hadi loyalists" misleads the world about what is happening in the shadow of the Saudi air strikes. This dubious category groups together forces as different as the eastern tribes, Popular Committees in various regions, the Southern Resistance and even al-Qaeda. Few of these forces actually engage in fighting for Hadi and his regime of failed promises. For some, Hadi's return to power is downright undesirable; for others, it is simply irrelevant. In central Yemen, such as in Ta'iz, the country's third-largest city, resistance to the Houthis springs from local motivations rather than support for Hadi. While the Southern Resistance supports the air strikes and receives military aid from the Saudi-led coalition, its ideas about postwar political solutions differ from the expressed Saudi aim of restoring Hadi. Basing the Geneva talks around the reinstatement of Hadi as leader of the country simply prolongs the suffering on the ground and generates a false sense of certainty about postwar stability.

The Houthi militias, assisted by units of the Yemeni army loyal to Salih and stationed throughout the country, are facing armed confrontation in eastern and central Yemen, and in the entirety of the South. The South is the territory that, prior to Yemeni unity in 1990, formed the independent state of the People's Democratic Republic of Yemen. In Marib, the province east of Sana'a, local tribes have united to stop the Houthis from taking over the oil fields, motivated by the tribal ethos of self-rule and alliance with similar-minded state leadership. Further to the southeast, the tribes in Shabwa have formed a coalition with the Southern Resistance.

As applied to the South, the expression "Hadi loyalists" stems from three misconceptions. First, the fact that Hadi is originally from the southern governorate of Abyan makes some believe he must have the fealty of his fellow southerners. The second error is to read too much into the fact that Hadi fled to Aden, of all places, in February and was initially welcomed there after the Houthis introduced their five-man Presidential Council. That body deposed him de facto, though he had already resigned. Once in Aden, Hadi withdrew his resignation.

The Southern Resistance, the militias fighting against the Houthi-Salih invasion of the South, consists of Popular Committees and groups of local vigilantes who pledge themselves to defend "the people of the South." The Resistance is part of the pro-independence Southern Movement that has grown steadily since 2007 with the mission of reclaiming the full independence of the South. Activists in this movement consider Hadi and his regime (which includes many southerners) responsible for the years-long marginalization of the South and the erstwhile state's violence against peaceful demonstrators there. That violence claimed hundreds of victims in the South while the world was focused on the dialogue in Sana'a. For many, the war in the southern governorates is a replay of the 1994 civil war that ended with President Salih conquering the South and sealing Yemeni unity by force. Southerners call it "occupation." While the Southern Resistance lacks a central command, it has unified the various territories of the South in an unprecedented way. This is a popular resistance movement that organizes locally, involves all sectors of society, men and women, and has fended off the much better equipped Yemeni army and Houthi militia for weeks. Victories in al-Dhali' governorate prove the steadfastness of the fighters, many of whom have no military training as a result of systematic discrimination against southerners in the army and security forces.

Saudi warplane feeding Yemen to al-Qa'ida terrorism. (June 26, 2015)
By Samer Mohammed al-Shameeri

Here is the third misconception that gives rise to the term "Hadi loyalists." Some assume that because the Popular Committees were initially set up by Hadi's government to take care of security in areas without an army or police presence, and remained on the state payroll, they must support Hadi's comeback. In central Yemen, Popular Committees fight for local concerns, too, allied with tribes and other social forces. The common denominator is resistance to Houthi-Salih aggression and protection of local territories—not an affinity for Hadi.

One of the dramatic consequences of the fighting on the ground, as opposed to the Saudi-led air strikes, is the division of the country. For the Southern Resistance, it is a war between North and South. There is no money or might in the world that would bring southerners back to "unity" under a regime in Sana'a, whether headed by the Houthis or by Hadi. Acknowledging that fact might bring the international community closer to lasting solutions to the Yemeni crisis.

The narrative of "Hadi loyalists" is propaganda aimed at lending legitimacy to the Saudis' project in Yemen. According to this rhetoric, sadly adopted by the Saudis' allies and the world media, the Saudis are simply "assisting" Yemenis who want to bring back the proper government. Saudi Arabia has been militarily and non-militarily involved in every single political crisis in Yemen over the past five decades, simply to ensure that a regime on its leash prevails. Yet its strategy of bombing has largely proved counterproductive as more and more civilians die and the blockade of aid convoys exacts a heavy humanitarian toll. What the Saudis could do is to sever the link between their former man in Sanaʿa, ʿAli ʿAbdallah Salih, and the Houthis. The war in Yemen has a lot to do with power struggles in the capital. But for Yemenis elsewhere in the country, the fighting is about protecting their neighborhoods from invasion by the troops of the Houthis and Salih and achieving a decent standard of living, something Hadi and his government were never able to deliver.

The GCC Needs a Successful Strategy for Yemen, Not Failed Tactics

James Spencer • *MERO*, Sept. 11, 2015

For the last 45 years, the Gulf Cooperation Council has tried to mitigate its Yemen problem through short-term tactics, rather than constructing and giving resources to a strategy for solving it. That policy has failed repeatedly. A bold and lasting transformation is needed, not the same ineffectual meddling.

Traditionally, the attitude of most GCC members toward Yemen has been fond but standoffish. The Gulf states have been fairly generous in funding projects and providing aid, but have held populous Yemen at arm's length, for reasons both demographic and ideological, the latter being fear of Marxism and republicanism.

Saudi Arabia has always regarded Yemen as a direct threat. King ʿAbd al-ʿAziz is reputed to have warned his sons that "the good or evil for us will come from Yemen," and so to keep it weak and divided. It is unclear exactly what the Saudi royal was wary of: Yemeni intentions of taking over the entirety of Saudi Arabia, efforts by Yemen's Hamid al-Din dynasty to defeat their al-Saud rivals, or merely attempts by Yemen to recover the three provinces of Asir, Jizan and Najran that ʿAbd al-ʿAziz had captured from

Saudi commander instructing fighter pilot to target civilian homes. (May 11, 2015)
By Samer Mohammed al-Shameeri

Imam Yahya in 1934. But the king's advice was taken to heart, and has been implemented ever since. "The Saudis want a moderate government in Sanaa—on a short leash," Michael Van Dusen, a long-time senior staffer for the House Foreign Affairs Committee, wrote in 1982, referring to hundreds of millions of dollars in annual disbursements to both the Yemeni government and Yemeni tribal leaders. Those payments now total several billion dollars per year, and go to individual officials and security men as well as the original recipients. Those on the Saudi payroll run the gamut of Yemeni politics. This policy "degrades the authority of the central government" in Sanaʿa, argues a descendant of Imam Yahya, ʿAbdallah Hamid al-Din. "In what other countries do citizens receive a salary from a foreign government?" In many ways, the Saudi approach in Yemen is reminiscent of Iranian policy in Iraq, which is castigated as interference by nationalist Shiʾi and Sunni Arabs in Iraq, and by the Saudis and their Western friends alike.

In addition, and as it has done in many Muslim countries, Saudi Arabia subsidized the export of puritanical Wahhabism into a nation that traditionally was Shafiʿi Sunni in the south, and Zaydi and Ismaʾili in the north. This state-sponsored evangelism was perceived as a threatening political encroachment on Zaydi space. It also grated on many Yemenis' national sensibilities, something the Wahhabis should have known, given the words of the Prophet: "The people of Yemen have come to you, most sensitive in their souls, softest of hearts! Belief is from Yemen, wisdom is from Yemen! Pride and arrogance are found among the camel owners; tranquility and dignity among the sheep owners."

The 2011 uprising in Yemen brought millions of people into the streets, protesting against precisely the elite corruption and autocracy that Saudi Arabia (with Western backing) had worked to entrench. Saudi policy toward Yemen since the popular revolt is almost certainly an attempt to maintain the status quo ante. Indeed, the GCC initiative that claimed to break the political impasse has been seen as an effort to achieve an apparent transition of power while ensuring, *sub rosa*, that the same coterie of Saudi clients remain in place. Certainly, the Saudi-led Operation Decisive Storm is an attempt to reinstate 'Abd Rabbu Mansour Hadi to the presidency. Yet Hadi was President 'Ali 'Abdallah Salih's long-term vice president, his clique shows traits similar to the deposed Salih's, and a terrorist-traced *salafi*, 'Abd al-Wahhab al-Humayqani, has reportedly been appointed as Hadi's "adviser." Many Yemenis will see al-Humayqani as a Saudi-placed *éminence grise*.

Not only is this policy expensive, but it also does not work to keep Yemen docile: "The Saudis have really gotten very little for their money," according to Barbara Bodine, a former US ambassador in Sana'a. One reason, as the scholar Maria Eleftheriadou notes, is that many of the tribal leaders on the Saudi dole "became 'city sheikhs' having moved to Sanaa," where they steadily lose "their moral authority, their power of persuasion, especially among the younger generation." All of these problems come at a time when Saudi state incomes are falling (and likely to remain low) while domestic costs are rising (and likely to keep going up).

The "kinetic" approach of Decisive Storm is equally ineffective. The Israelis, and to a lesser extent US administrations, have adopted the tactic of "mowing the grass"—periodic military operations to keep perceived security threats manageable. Sixty-five years have shown this policy to be not only financially and morally ruinous, but also actively counterproductive: It generates ill will among the population, and encourages the *salafi* jihadism it aims to remove.

The GCC states could continue doing the same thing but expect a different result—Einstein's definition of madness—or they could try a different way of achieving the desired end state of a non-threatening Yemen. The dying king 'Abd al-'Aziz's admonition has always been interpreted negatively. "Beware of Yemen; it is your Achilles' heel," as Van Dusen paraphrased it in 1982. Yet the king left equal the possibility of good coming from Yemen, too. So, how could that be achieved?

Europe spent much of the last thousand years wracked by war after bloody war, with various nations trying to subordinate, or at least weaken, neighbors and "allies," to no good effect. Only a decision to move to a strategy of mutual benefit finally achieved a peaceful Europe, and led to the prosperity (and gridlocked democracy) of the European Union. A prosperous, truly federal Yemen would be no military threat to the GCC as a whole or to Saudi Arabia individually. Indeed, were a federal Yemen admitted to the GCC, it could again supply cheap labor, but the remittances would also increase the consumer base for GCC goods and services. The only conflict would be for contracts.

The GCC fears that the Zaydi Houthis are a fifth column for Iran, and claims they receive a copious Iranian weapons supply. In fact, the Fiver Shi'a—with their founding doctrine of resistance to an unjust ruler—are an ideological threat to the Islamic Republic's theory of *velayat-e faqih* (rule of the jurisprudent), and were mostly armed by Salih. The Gulf states could regard the Zaydis as a cherished Arab ally against the Iranians, whose Safavid antecedents destroyed the first Zaydi state. Instead, GCC policy is driving Zaydis into Iranian arms.

This problem is not new or theoretical (nor are Persian hegemonic pretensions). As an Athenian politician advocated 2,500 years ago:

> When a free community, held in subjection by force, rises, as is only natural...we fancy ourselves obliged to punish it severely; although the right course with freemen is not to chastise them rigorously when they do rise, but rigorously to watch them before they rise, and to prevent their ever entertaining the idea.

The GCC tactic of divide, bribe and rule is a consistent failure. A new strategy is urgently needed, one based on the European model of building mutual advantage. It's time to change.

Conclusion

Another round of halfhearted UN-brokered peace talks—involving only representatives of the Hadi government and the Houthi movement with their Salih allies—folded in December 2015 after only a few days. The optimism of the "peaceful youth" and even the more modest expectations for the National Dialogue Conference were replaced by heartbreak and despair.

The most dramatic dimension of the crisis is the humanitarian catastrophe: thousands of civilian casualties; more than two million people displaced; whole neighborhoods reduced to rubble; ongoing electricity blackouts; acute shortages of medicine, water and fuel; an astounding 20 million persons food-deprived; a total collapse of the nation's health care system, according to the World Health Organization (WHO). It will take billions of dollars to rebuild essential infrastructure including hospitals, schools and bridges, not to mention houses, markets, agricultural terraces and factories. Some damage to World Heritage sites is irreparable at any cost. Ecological destruction has yet to be estimated.

Implicated in this tragedy are the Western nations and even the United Nations Security Council, which have overseen a scheme of high-tech coercion that is both sadistic and expensive. Apparently oblivious to war crimes, Paris, London and Washington persist in replenishing Saudi and UAE arsenals. UNSC Resolution 2216 ignored the aerial bombardment and naval blockade responsible for the most shattering annihilation and human suffering. During months of wanton, disproportionate belligerence, the so-called "international community" neglected to call for a

Houthis depriving Ta'iz of drinking water. (October 2015)
By Samer Mohammed al-Shameeri

ceasefire. GCC governments and their allies also quashed an October 2015 proposal put forward by the Netherlands for an impartial international inquiry into rules-of-war violations by all sides; the pleas of Oxfam, Doctors Without Borders, the International Committee of the Red Cross/Crescent, WHO and other agencies fell on deaf ears.

Additionally, rancor and recriminations between regions and communities, and the radicalization of some individuals and groups, could be even more difficult to mend than the physical infrastructure. Moreover, while Yemen—specifically the country's impoverished majority—bears most of the corporeal injuries, material damage and psychosocial trauma from kinetic warfare, the Saudi kingdom's sectarian bombast also targets domestic minorities and independent thinkers. There is a real risk of blowback from the war, including but not limited to greater menace from al-Qaeda and the so-called Islamic State. Stability seems illusive.

The dispatches reproduced here illustrate longstanding connections among events and circumstances in the Arabian Peninsula—how the societies, economies, politics and natural environments are intertwined—and also shed light on American involvement in this subregion of the Middle East. The Saudi-instigated military campaign in Yemen underscores the Kingdom's profound anxieties and antipathies towards its poor neighbor and intensifies its entanglement. Regardless of the denouement of this conflict, the interconnections are more penetrating than ever before.

•••••

The title of this volume is *Arabia Incognita*, meaning Unknown, Misunderstood, or Unrecognized Arabia. As the old order on the Peninsula collapses, some analysts and reporters have begun referring to a "forgotten war" in Yemen. Yemenis respond sardonically that it is impossible to forget what was never comprehended to begin with.

As this anthology goes to press, there's no good news for the war-torn peninsula. I do hope, however, that Arabia might be less incomprehensible in the future. Human rights activists and area specialists are calling more attention to the militarization of a contest for state power. Investigative journalists, counter-terrorism experts and think-tank analysts—until now unmindful of the subcontinent's internal convulsions and their global implications—are studying up. "Arabia Felix" may be a distant reality, but at least the Peninsula may not remain Incognita.

About the Editor

Sheila Carapico is widely recognized as a leading expert on Yemen. She is the author of *Civil Society in Yemen: The Political Economy of Activism in Modern Arabia* (Cambridge University Press, 1998, reissued 2007) and numerous other books, book chapters, and articles about Yemen, the Arabian Peninsula, and the region. Carapico acquired her reputation as a Yemen expert through her time as a Fulbright research scholar in the country and consultancy work she did there for organizations including Human Rights Watch, the Royal Netherlands Embassy, and the International Fund for Agricultural Development. During 2010 and the crucial spring of 2011, she was Visiting Chairperson of the Department of Political Science at the American University in Cairo. She teaches Political Science and coordinates the International Studies program at the University of Richmond and is a long serving member of the MERIP collective. Her most recent book is *Political Aid and Arab Activism: Democracy Promotion, Justice, and Representation* (Cambridge University Press, 2014)

About MERIP

The Middle East Research and Information Project (MERIP) is a progressive, independent non-profit based in Washington, DC. Since 1971 MERIP has provided critical analysis of the Middle East, focusing on political economy, popular struggles, and the implications of US and international policy for the region.